Sustainable Solar Housing

Volume 2 – Exemplary Buildings and Technologies

Edited by S. Robert Hastings and Maria Wall

London • Sterling, VA

First published by Earthscan in the UK and USA in 2007

Volume 1:   ISBN-13:   978-1-84407-325-2
Volume 2:   ISBN-13:   978-1-84407-326-9

Typeset by MapSet Ltd, Gateshead, UK
Printed and bound in the UK by Cromwell Press, Trowbridge
Cover design by Susanne Harris

Published by Earthscan on behalf of the International Energy Agency (IEA), Solar Heating & Cooling Programme (SHC) and Energy Conservation in Buildings and Community Systems Programme (ECBCS).

Disclaimer Notice: This publication has been compiled with reasonable skill and care. However, neither the Publisher nor the IEA, SHC or ECBCS make any representation as to the adequacy or accuracy of the information contained herein, or as to its suitability for any particular application, and accept no responsibility or liability arising out of the use of this publication. The information contained herein does not supersede the requirements given in any national codes, regulations or standards, and should not be regarded as a substitute for the need to obtain specific professional advice for any particular application.

Experts from the following countries contributed to the writing of this book: Austria, Belgium, Canada, Germany, Italy, the Netherlands, Norway, Sweden and Switzerland.

For a full list of Earthscan publications please contact:

Earthscan
8–12 Camden High Street
London, NW1 0JH, UK
Tel: +44 (0)20 7387 8558
Fax: +44 (0)20 7387 8998
Email: earthinfo@earthscan.co.uk
Web: **www.earthscan.co.uk**

22883 Quicksilver Drive, Sterling, VA 20166-2012, USA

Earthscan is an imprint of James and James (Science Publishers) Ltd and publishes in association with the International Institute for Environment and Development

A catalogue record for this book is available from the British Library

Library of Congress Cataloging-in-Publication Data has been applied for

The paper used for this book is FSC-certified and
totally chlorine-free. FSC (the Forest Stewardship Council)
is an international network to promote responsible
management of the world's forests.

Mixed Sources
Product group from well-managed
forests and other controlled sources
www.fsc.org Cert no. TT-TOC-2082
© 1996 Forest Stewardship Council

Contents

Part II TECHNOLOGIES

Foreword

Achieving housing that consumes four to ten times less end energy for space heating is an ambitious goal. A growing number of projects demonstrate that this is not only possible, but affordable, in a real market situation.

This volume of a two-volume set presents a selection of six exemplary housing projects representing single family, row and multi-family housing in climates ranging from Lindas, Sweden, to Zurich, Switzerland. The projects combine aesthetics and high performance with regard to very low energy demand and low environmental life-cycle impact.

The success of these projects is a result of good design and the rational use of technologies. This volume also provides information on these technologies, including building envelope systems, ventilation systems, heat delivery (often using the ventilation system), heat production, heat storage, electricity production and control systems.

As the demand for such high quality components increases and more planners have experience in the design of such structures, the costs can be expected to continue to decrease in a situation where energy prices are anticipated to continue to rise. The future for high-performance housing looks very positive!

Robert Hastings

S. Robert Hastings
AEU Architecture, Energy and Environment Ltd
Wallisellen, Switzerland

Maria Wall

Maria Wall
Energy and Building Design
Lund University
Lund, Sweden

List of Contributors

Andreas Bühring
Fraunhofer Institute for Solar
Energy Systems (ISE)
D-79110, Freiburg, Germany
buehring@ise.fhg.de
www.ise.fhg.de

Hans Eek
Arkitekt Hans Eek AB
Alingsås, Sweden
hans.eek@ivl.se

Daniela Enz
AEU Architecture, Energy
and Environment Ltd
Wallisellen, Switzerland
CH 8304
daniela.enz@aeu.ch

Hans Erhorn
Fraunhofer-Institut für Bauphysik
Stuttgart, Germany
DE-70569
erh@ibp.fhg.de

Gerhard Faninger
Faculty for Interdisciplinary Research
and Continuing Education (IFF)
University of Klagenfurt
A-9020 Klagenfurt, Germany
Gerhard.Faninger@uni-klu.ac.at

Wolfgang Feist
Passivhaus Institut
D-64283
Darmstadt, Germany
info@passiv.de
www.passivehouse.com

Anne Haas
EMPA 175
CH-8600 Dubendorf, Switzerland
anne.haas@empa.ch

S. Robert Hastings
AEU Architecture, Energy
and Environment Ltd
Wallisellen, Switzerland
CH 8304
robert.hastings@aeu.ch

Frank-Dietrich Heidt
Fachgebiet Bauphysik und Solarenergie
Universität Siegen
D-57068 Siegen, Germany
heidt@physik.uni-siegen
www.nesa1.uni-siegen.de

Björn Karlsson
Energy and Building Design
Lund University, Sweden
bjorn.karlsson@ebd.lth.se

Berthold Kaufmann
Passivhaus Institut
D-64283
Darmstadt, Germany
berthold.kaufmann@passiv.de
www.passivehouse.com

Joachim Morhenne
Morhenne Ingenieure GbR
DE-42277 Wuppertal, Germany
info@morhenne.com

Johan Nilsson
Energy and Building Design
Lund University, Sweden
johan.nilsson@ebd.lth.se

Bengt Perers
Energy and Building Design
Lund University, Sweden
bengt.perers@ebd.lth.se

Carsten Petersdorff
Ecofys GmbH
D-50933 Köln, Germany
c.petersdorff@ecofys.de

Werner Platzer
Fraunhofer Institute for Solar
Energy Systems (ISE)
D-79110, Freiburg, Germany
werner.platzer@ise.fraunhofer.de

Alex Primas
Basler und Hofmann
CH-8029 Zürich, Switzerland
aprimas@bhz.ch

Christian Reise
Fraunhofer Institute for Solar
Energy Systems (ISE)
D-79110 Freiburg, Germany
christian.reise@ise.fraunhofer.de

Johann Reiss
Fraunhofer Institut für Bauphysik
DE-70569 Stuttgart, Germany
johann.reiss@ibp.fhg.de

Helmut Schoeberl
Schoeberl und Poell OEG
A-1020 Wien, Austria
helmut.schoeberl@schoeberlpoell.at

Rüdiger Schuchardt
Universität Bochum
Ruhr-Universität Bochum
D- 44801 Bochum, Germany
schuchardt@lee.ruhr-uni-buchum.de
www.lee.ruhr-uni-bochum.de

Benoit Sicre
Fraunhofer Institute for Solar
Energy Systems (ISE)
D-79110 Freiburg, Germany
benoit.sicre@ise.fraunhofer.de
www.ise.fhg.de

Johan Smeds
Energy and Building Design
Lund University, Sweden
johan.smeds@ebd.lth.se

Karsten Voss
Bauphysik und Technische
Gebäudeausrüstung (BTGA)
D-42285 Wuppertal, Germany
kvoss@uni-wuppertal.de
www.btga.uni-wuppertal.de

Maria Wall
Energy and Building Design
Lund University,
Lund, Sweden
maria.wall@ebd.lth.se

List of Figures and Tables

Figures

Tables

List of Acronyms and Abbreviations

AC	alternating current
ach	air changes per hour
AFC	Potassium oxide fuel cell
AHU	air heating unit
AM	application module
AS	application software
AST	application interface
ATS	architecture towards sustainability
A/V	area to volume ratio
BAT	best available technology
BCI	Batibus Club International
BCU	bus coupling unit
BI	business intelligence
C	Celsius
C_3H_8	propane
CED	cumulative energy demand
CERT	Committee on Energy Research and Technology
CH_4	methane
CHP	combined heat and power
CI	competitive intelligence
cm	centimetre
CO	carbon monoxide
CO_2	carbon dioxide
CO_2eq	carbon dioxide equivalent
COP	coefficient of performance
CPC	compound parabolic concentrator
dB	decibel
DC	direct current
DHW	domestic hot water
DOE	US Department of Energy
ECBCS	Energy Conservation in Buildings and Community Systems
EHS	European Home System
EHSA	European Home Systems Association
EHX	earth-to-air heat exchanger
EIB	European Installation Bus
EIBA	European Installation Bus Association
EnBW	Energie Baden-Württemberg
EPS	expanded polystyrene insulation
ERDA	US Energy and Research Administration
eta-hx	earth-to-air heat exchanger
ETS	EIB tool software
EU	European Union

g	gram
GW	gigawatt
GWP	global warming potential
h	hour
H	hydrogen
H_2S	hydrogen sulphide
H_2SO_3	sulphurous acid
HE	heat exchanger
HR	heat recovery
HV	heating and ventilation
HVAC	heating, ventilating and air conditioning
Hz	hertz
IEA	International Energy Agency
ISO	International Organization for Standardization
J	joule
K	Kelvin
Kd	Kelvin degree days
kg	kilogram
KI	carcinogenicity index
km	kilometre
KNX	Konnex Association
kW	kilowatt
kWp	kilowatt peak
l	litre
LC	line coupler
LCA	life-cycle analysis
LCI	life-cycle inventory
LCIA	life-cycle impact assessment
LHV	lower heating value
LON	local operating network
μm	micrometre
m	metre
MCDM	multi-criteria decision-making
MCFC	Molten carbonate fuel cell
MHz	mega hertz
MJ	megajoule
mm	millimetre
MW	megawatt
N	nitrogen
NCS	net cost savings
NES	net energy savings
NO_x	nitrogen oxide
O	oxygen
ODP	ozone depleting potential
OECD	Organisation for Economic Co-operation and Development
OSB	oriented strand board
Pa	Pascal
PAFC	phosphoric acid fuel cell
PC	personal computer
PCM	phase-change material
PE	primary energy

PEF	primary energy factor
PEM	polymer electrolyte membrane
PEM-FC	polymer electrolyte membrane fuel cell
PEST	political, economics, social and technological
PLC	power line carrier
PP	plastic pipe
ppm	parts per million
PUR	polyurethane
PV	photovoltaic(s)
PV/T	photovoltaic thermal
rh	relative humidity
s	second
S	sulphur
SF	solar fraction
SFP	specific fan power
SHC	Solar Heating and Cooling Programme
SO_2	sulphur dioxide
SO-FC	solid oxide fuel cell
SPF	seasonal performance factor
SV	voltage supply system
SWH	solar wall heating
SWOT	strengths, weaknesses, opportunities and threats
TI	transparent insulation
TIM	transparent insulation materials
TP	twisted pair
TQA	total quality assessment
UCTE	Union for the Coordination of Transmission of Electricity
UK	United Kingdom
US	United States
VAT	value-added tax
VIP	vacuum insulation panel
VOC	volatile organic compound
W	watt

INTRODUCTION

S. Robert Hastings

I.1 Realities

Houses being built or renovated today should be designed considering two simple realities:

1   Within the building's lifetime, oil and natural gas will cease to be an inexpensive and reliable energy source.
2   Renewable energy, which must replace these fossil fuels, will be more expensive.

Accordingly, it only makes sense that housing design should aim for very low energy consumption. This is almost embarrassingly easy to achieve, in theory. The simple steps needed are to:

* minimize energy demand by:
    – reducing heat and air transport through the envelope;
    – recover heat from exhaust air to temper entering fresh air;
    – specifying high-efficiency technical systems; and
* use renewable energy from:
    – window solar gains and occupancy;
    – active solar thermal systems and biomass;
    – photovoltaic (PV) systems.

It is not just simple in theory; over 4000 such housing projects in Europe have been built. These high-performance buildings require only 15 kWh/m^{2}a end energy or less for space heating. Their total primary energy use for space and water heating and electricity for technical systems does not exceed 45 kWh/m^{2}a. Such housing, to date, tends to cost up to 10 per cent more than conventionally built housing. This, however, can be considered the investment needed to build housing ready for the future.

The investment also brings returns in improved comfort in several important ways:

* better air quality as a result of automated controlled ventilation;
* better thermal comfort since walls and, in particular, windows, are no longer cold surfaces; and
* better natural lighting through conscious design to maximize daylighting effectiveness.

This book examines six high-performance housing projects that demonstrate high energy performance and superior comfort. The projects are located in climates ranging from cold (Sweden) to temperate (Germany, Switzerland and Austria). They represent diverse housing types, (single family, row housing and apartment blocks) in both light frame and masonry construction.

The book then presents a choice of technologies that can be applied to build high-performance housing, addressing envelope construction, ventilation, heat distribution (often using the ventilation system), heat production, heat storage, and electricity production and appliances.

Source: Karin Kroiss, UWE Kroiss Energiesysteme, AT 4062 Kirchberg-Thening, www.energiesysteme.at

Figure I.1 *Single family house in Thening*

I.2 Exemplary buildings

Each of the exemplary projects was selected for a special feature.

The Lindas row houses in Sweden are impressive because they achieve high-performance in a cold northern climate with long winter nights. Equally notable is the courage of the client and architect to build not just one prototype house, but a whole housing tract of row houses. It is also interesting to see solar hot water production given the very short and often overcast days during half of the year in Sweden. This is offset, however, by the other half of the year, with long days and an equal demand for domestic hot water (DHW).

The row houses in Gelsenkirchen, Germany, provided an ideal field laboratory to examine how effective different constructions and design are in achieving high performance. Of interest here was not just the energy consumed over the operational life of the buildings, but also energy consumption over the whole life cycle, from construction through 50 anticipated years of service to demolition at the end. It was also interesting to see what proportion the infrastructure (streets and utilities) make of the total energy picture of a community. The project also served as a demonstration project, promising the transition from a coal and heavy industry economy and fossil fuel dependency to a new era based on solar energy. This was one of the first of an ambitious state programme to build 50 solar communities.

Sunny Woods in Zurich shows that engineering housing to require very little energy can also lead to prize-winning architectural design. Integration of vacuum tube solar thermal collectors in the balcony balustrades, large windows for passive solar and daylight gains, and a full surface photovoltaic roof for electricity production are aesthetic qualities belonging to this project. The project also demonstrates that very low energy housing can also fulfil the high expectations of buyers on the high end of the real estate market.

Figure I.2 *Installation of a vacuum-insulated roof panel*

The Wechsel apartments in Stans, Switzerland, by contrast, are for the middle of the market buyers. Photovoltaic and thermal solar collectors, as well as mechanical ventilation with heat recovery, were also possible within the building budget.

Most challenging was to build high-performance housing as social housing, given the budget constraints of the state. Ingenuity was called for because techniques to solve problems such as thermal bridges and fire breaks had to be developed in order to save costs without compromising performance.

Lastly, the single family detached house in Thening, Austria, as a house form, achieved the same level of performance as with larger structures. 'Small' also means a very high area to volume (A/V) ratio of envelope surface area losing heat to the heated volume.

These projects demonstrate that there are many approaches which can achieve high-performance, very low energy housing. Part I of this book examines a selection of technologies to achieve this performance.

I.3 The technologies

As mentioned at the beginning of this chapter, the first objective is to ensure that the heat inside remains inside during the heating season, and that the heat outside stays outside during summer. This is the job of the envelope. For comfort and energy reasons, the envelope must be air tight, so the next job is to guarantee a supply of fresh air – hence, a ventilation system is needed. The third job is to produce and distribute the small amounts of heat still required for space and water heating. The final job is to supply the electricity. As with building heating, the first objective is to minimize the need for electricity. According to the budget of the client, electricity can then be produced from solar energy.

I.3.1 The envelope

The dilemma in the design of the envelope is how to achieve a high degree of insulation with a minimal wall thickness and to avoid thermal bridges. Here, physics proves to be an unkind restraint.

Most insulating materials hinder heat flow by means of entrapped still air, which, compared to most solids, is a poor conductor. Examples include mineral wool, fibre glass, polystyrene, polyurethane and also natural insulation materials, such as cellulose, straw, sheep wool and cork. Unfortunately, achieving high insulation quality requires numerous still air cells – hence, thick walls and roofs. This thickness takes away from habitable space.

An alternative is to hinder heat transport via radiation and convection. The best imaginable example is the vacuum insulation panel (VIP). Several firms now market such panels. Whole houses have been insulated with VIP as demonstration projects; but the costs are still high for wider market penetration. Currently, special applications are attractive, such as roof terraces. Windows, the weakest elements of the envelope, also use this technology to achieve better U-values. Selective coatings of the cavity face of the glass inhibit heat radiation from the room side to the exterior. To further reduce heat losses, air in the cavity is replaced by Argon or Krypton.

Regardless of the insulation system, the construction must be detailed to minimize short circuits (for example, structural bearing elements penetrating the insulation) and be air tight. It is also, of course, desirable to protect the expensive investment in the envelope from moisture damage.

Finally, it should be emphatically stated that when housing is very well insulated, it is not inherently more prone to overheating in summer. Indeed, the insulation keeps out the heat, which builds up on the opaque envelope surface. The windows are critical. However, closed windows, whether they are single glazed ($U = 6.0$ W/m²K) or super glazed ($U = 0.5$ W/m²K), will trap too much heat in summer. Therefore, the obvious conclusion is that sun shading is essential – ideally, outside the window to keep the heat on the outside.

I.3.2 Ventilation

Whereas physics imposes an unfortunate constraint on insulation systems, human limitations pose two constraints on achieving good room air quality. First, occupants (as well as materials) generate humidity, carbon dioxide (CO_2) and odour. Second, occupants in a room are insensitive to the quality of the air. A constantly open window wastes energy and intermittent opening requires someone to get up throughout the night. For these reasons, mechanical ventilation of tightly constructed, low energy housing is essential. To be consistent with the low energy goal, heat from the room air should be recovered before it is exhausted. Whereas mechanical ventilation has long been accepted in commercial and institutional buildings, not to mention air craft, occupants are more critical of their home environment. So, at a low budget, home ventilation must provide superior service – for example, to avoid heat stratification, drafts, noise, sound transport and dust propagation. To add a further complication, the ventilation system may also be expected to transport the heat: the subject of the following section.

I.3.3 Heat delivery and recovery

When the envelope is super insulated, very little heat must be delivered to the room to keep it warm – indeed, so little that it no longer makes sense to invest heavily in the heat delivery system. Therefore, a simple, low capital cost solution must be found. In many high-performance housing projects, this is done by heating the ventilation air up to a maximum of 50°C.

Under coldest weather conditions, the challenge is then to ensure that the required volume of air at this maximum temperature supplies the needed heating power. However, there is a second challenge: to ensure that bringing in and heating cold, dry outside air does not decrease the room humidity below acceptable levels.

A third challenge is to make certain that the electricity (considering its high primary energy value) consumed by the fan motors does not defeat the low energy goal. A further energy 'overhead' is defrosting. Condensation from warm, humid room air passing across the surface and separating it from sub-zero incoming ambient air can freeze and block the air passage. A more expensive solution is preheating the ambient air in an earth tube. Another system, recently available for residential applications, is the rotating heat exchanger. It offers the further benefit of moisture recovery from exhaust air to humidify the supply air.

The first generations of residential ventilation and heat delivery systems had problems. Today, proven and optimized-from-experience systems are available on the market. The conclusion is not to reinvent the wheel.

I.3.4 Heat production

Even 'net zero energy houses' and, even more extreme, 'energy plus houses' still need heat production. Both concepts typically achieve zero or a plus by producing enough solar electricity from photovoltaic panels to equal or exceed their total yearly energy consumption – calculated on the basis of primary energy. This is by no means to say that these houses do not need energy input. Given the weak solar radiation during the short winter days, the energy production is minimal in winter, when heating demand occurs. So, heat

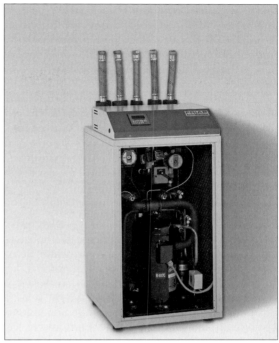

Source: FRIAP AG, CH-3063 Ittigen BE, friap@friap.ch, www.friap.ch

Figure I.3 *A compact heating system*

must be produced. Indeed, if electric heating is used, this must be penalized with the same primary energy factor for electricity that made the net zero or positive energy title possible. The challenge is, then, to produce a very small amount of heat with low capital and ecological costs. Several good solutions are available.

The most prevalent solution is a heat pump, using as its heat source the exhaust room air directly or, in temperate climates, a ventilation heat exchanger. Its limitation is that in very cold weather, it must switch to resistance heating. However, during most of the heating system it can deliver from 1 kW of electricity up to 3 kW of heat. If it is coupled to a ground heat exchanger (an anti-freeze solution circulated through a buried pipe circuit), an even higher output is possible.

Wood pellet stoves offer the advantages of using wood as a fuel (CO_2 neutral), being highly automated and operating with a high efficiency due to controlled combustion.

For apartment buildings or as a central plant for a row of houses, a condensing gas boiler may be a solution. Nominal efficiencies exceeding 100 per cent are possible. A drawback is that, given the relatively small absolute amount of heat needed, the fixed costs, maintenance and investment costs are high. These can be tolerated better if shared among multiple housing units.

Given the small energy magnitude for space heating, domestic water heating takes on new importance. This end use may even exceed the space heating. Unlike space heating where the target temperature is 20°C to 22°C, domestic water needs to be heated to 50°C and, possibly, periodically to 60°C. This higher 'exergy' requirement (ability of energy to do work) places a higher demand on the heating production system.

For ecological reasons, an obvious solution is a solar thermal system. With only 1 m² to 2 m² of collector per person, this proven technology can cover half the water heating demand. While, economically, it can be argued that if the heat production is by a heat pump or wood pellet stove, these systems should also heat DHW. By year-round operation, their high capital costs are more quickly amortized. It can also be argued, however, that psychologically it is appealing to shut off these technical systems for half of the year or more and simply use sunshine to make hot water.

Some clients think this through further and decide to increase the collector area – for example, from 6 m² to 20 m² or more – and also increase the storage tank from 500 litres to 2000 litres, as well as to supply some of the needed space heating. The expectations, nevertheless, must take into account the shortened heating season of high-performance housing.

I.3.5 Heat storage

Solar radiation striking the envelope of a house could easily cover the entire need for space and water heating for the year. The problem is to store it, with minimal losses and at an affordable price. On a less ambitious scale, storage can store heat from sunny periods when heat production exceeds demand in order to make it available for overcast periods. Solar water tank technology is very highly optimized, with various solutions, including how to preserve the stratification in the tank, minimize tank heat losses and programme the control strategy to maximize the overall storage collector total system efficiency.

For space heating, the most direct form of storage is the building mass itself. Wooden frame housing, growing in popularity in Europe and long dominant in North America, lacks the heat storage capacity of masonry and concrete construction. Such massive construction increases the usability of passive solar gains by being able to store daytime window solar gains and then releasing the heat at night. An interesting means of increasing the heat storage capacity in light-frame construction is to incorporate a phase change material. An example is the addition of micro-encapsulated paraffin in gypsum board, dramatically increasing its thermal capacity.

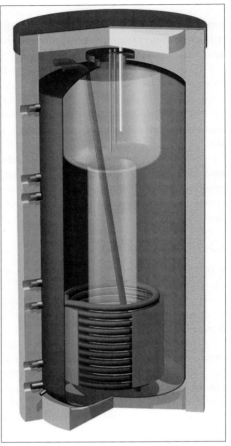

Source: Wagner & Co, Coelbe, www.wagner-solar.com

Figure I.4 *A solar water storage 'tank in tank'*

I.3.6 Electricity

This is the most expensive energy form and it also consumes the most primary energy to produce. Accordingly, it is highly desirable to generate it from the solar radiation striking the building envelope. Photovoltaic conversion of light to electricity is a proven technology, has no moving parts, produces no noise and no emissions, and is reliable over decades. The only limitation is its cost. The investment needed to produce a photovoltaic kWh must be compared to the investment needed to save a kWh through insulation, air tightness, high quality windows and ventilation with heat recovery – even considering the primary energy factors.

To increase the amount of energy that can be won by a photovoltaic system and to improve its economics), one approach is to capture some of the 'waste' heat generated by the panels. Given that a photovoltaic panel at best converts up to 15 per cent of the solar resource to electricity, 85 per cent is lost by either reflection or as heat. The goal of hybrid PV systems is to capture and transport some of

this waste heat – for example, to temper ventilation air. The solutions must compete
economically with other heat sources (such as
heat recovery from a heat exchanger).

Finally, the most economical and environmental kWh of electricity is that which did
not need to be produced. It therefore makes
sense to select electrical appliances (and the
technical systems for the heating, ventilation
and water heating equipment) that need as
little electricity as possible. An investment in
a more efficient washing machine can save
more energy than the marginal investment in
another conservation technology. However,
the lifetime of the component must also be
considered. Investing in a highly insulated
façade provides energy savings for the
lifetime of the structure. Once built, it is difficult and likely uneconomical to make later
improvements.

1.4 Conclusions

Achieving high-performance, very low energy
housing is theoretically simple: keep expenses
low (energy losses) and maximize the income
('free' internal and solar gains, and heat recovery). That this is possible, in practice, has
been demonstrated by over 4000 housing
projects in Europe alone. Their success has
involved a learning process by the building
designers, but also by equipment manufacturers. Today, there is much known to help new
designers 'get it right' and there is a diversity
of high-quality, proven components and
systems to achieve such performance. It is the
purpose of this publication (in its two
volumes) to share this experience with you:
the planners of the next generation of high-
performance housing.

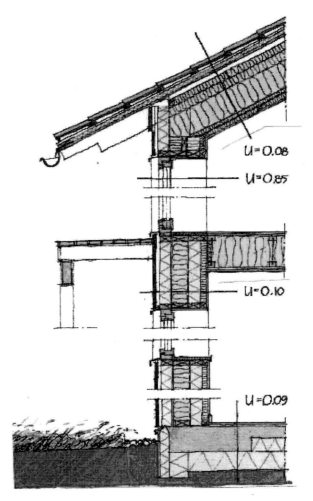

Source: Hans Eek, Arkitekt Hans Eek AB, Alingsås, Sweden,
hans.eek@ivl.se

Figure I.5 *Wall section of the row
houses in Lindas*

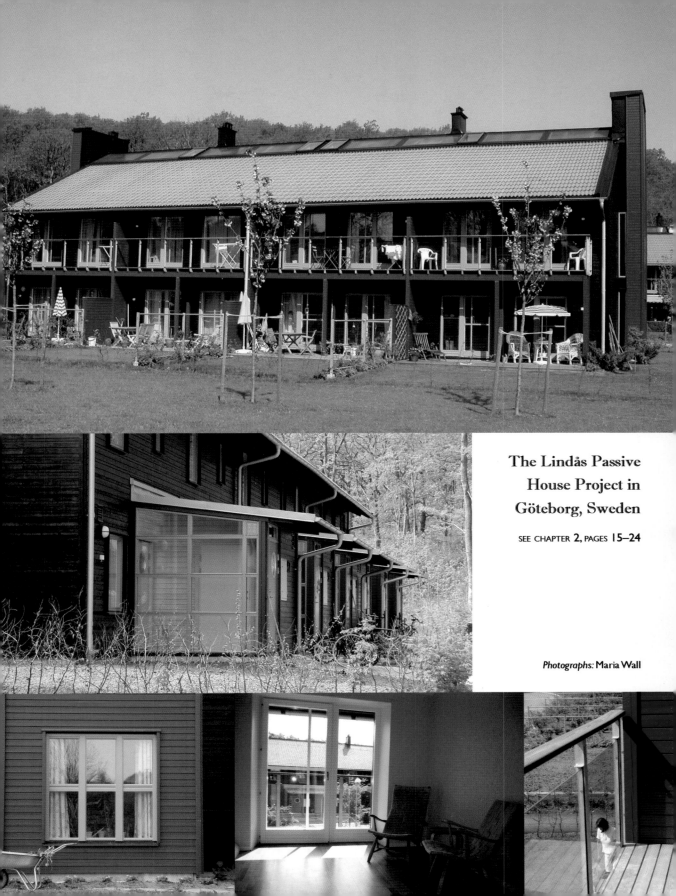

The Lindås Passive
House Project in
Göteborg, Sweden

SEE CHAPTER 2, PAGES 15–24

Photographs: Maria Wall

The Lindås Passive House Project in Göteborg, Sweden

SEE CHAPTER 2, PAGES 15–24

Photographs: Hans Eek

Gelsenkirchen Solar Housing Estate, Germany

SEE CHAPTER **3**, PAGES **25–36**

Photographs: Carsten Petersdorff

Sunny Woods
Apartment Building,
Zurich, Switzerland

SEE CHAPTER **4**, PAGES **37–52**

Photographs: Beat Kämpfen

Wechsel
Apartment
Building,
Stans,
Switzerland

SEE CHAPTER **5**,
PAGES **53–68**

Photographs:
Beda Bossard

THIS PAGE AND OPPOSITE:

Vienna Utendorfgasse Passivhaus
Apartment Building

SEE CHAPTER **6**, PAGES **69–76**

Photographs: Helmut Schoeberl

Plus Energy House,
Thening, Austria

SEE CHAPTER **7**, PAGES **77–86**

Photographs: UWE Kroiss
Energiesysteme

Part I

EXEMPLARY BUILDINGS

1

Overview

Daniela Enz and S. Robert Hastings

1.1 The diversity of the projects

It is interesting to observe how the different strategies and technologies presented in this book have been applied by designers in exemplary housing projects, and with what degree of success. Six projects from Sweden, Germany, Austria and Switzerland are documented in this chapter. Three building types are represented: single family detached housing, row housing and apartment blocks. This overview shows what absolute values are achieved, as well as the ranges. Except for the housing in Gelsenkirchen, the projects all achieve extremely low primary energy use for space and water heating, including electricity for technical systems (see Figure 1.1.1). It is also interesting to observe that the energy consumed to heat DHW is more or less equal to that required for space heating.

Each project has its own distinct features. While one architect focused mainly on finding and demonstrating an economical solution on how to construct a Passivhaus building, the others strived to develop sophisticated energy concepts, optimizing ecological aspects or integrating solar technologies within the building design.

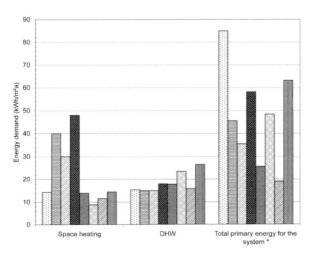

□ 1. Lindas (SE)
▨ 2a. Gelsenkirchen (DE)
▨ 2b. Gelsenkirchen (DE)
■ 2c. Gelsenkirchen (DE)
▨ 3. Thening (AT)
□ 4. Sunny Woods (CH)
▨ 5. Stans (CH)
▨ 6. Vienna (AT)

Note: The total primary energy demand for the system includes heating, domestic hot water, pumps and fans. Household electricity is not included.
Source: AEU Ltd, Wallisellen

Figure 1.1.1 *Energy demand*

1.2 Building envelope and construction

All six projects are located either in a cold or temperate climate, where a compact building form with a well-insulated and air-tight building envelope with minimized thermal bridges is essential to reduce heat losses through transmission or air leakage. The high quality of the building envelopes is shown in Figure 1.2.1. Except for the low energy project, Gelsenkirchen, the U-values for walls, roof and floor range from 0.10 to 0.15 W/m²K.

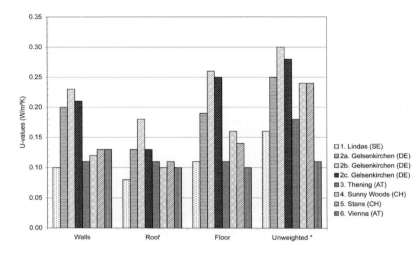

Note: The mean U-value weighted for the building envelope includes walls, roof, floor, windows and doors. It is the weighted average U-value for the entire envelope in m² of surface.

Source: AEU Ltd, Wallisellen

Figure 1.2.1 *U-values of the building envelope components*

High quality windows are equally important. The U-values for the windows, including the frame and glazing, range from to 0.64 to 0.9 W/m²K, except for the low energy buildings in Gelsenkirchen. The two projects, Sunny Woods and Stans, both have good U-values for the walls, roof and floor; but the overall average U-values for the whole envelope are not among the best. This is because these projects have large window areas. To be fair, the passive solar gains must be considered relative to the worsening of the overall envelope U-values for these projects. As can be seen in Figure 1.2.2, all projects have high quality windows.

A preference for prefabricated, lightweight constructions or mixed constructions can be observed in our documented projects. A method called cumulative energy demand (CED) was applied to compare these two constructions. It quantifies energy use over the whole life cycle of a house, from manufacturing of materials through construction, operation and, finally, demolition. This total picture can be very revealing, as seen in Chapter 3 on the solar energy housing estate Gelsenkirchen, with its 71 houses.

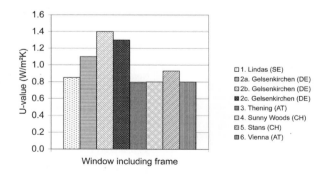

Source: AEU Ltd, Wallisellen

Figure 1.2.2 *Window U-values*

1.3 Technical systems

Almost all of the analysed buildings have a solar thermal system. Flat-plate collectors or vacuum collectors are integrated either in the façade or placed on the roof. The very low remaining space heating demand of these buildings makes the energy needed for domestic water heating an important end use. A solar DHW or combined DHW and space heating system further reduce the consumption of non-renewable energy.

Four of the six projects have a grid-connected photovoltaic (PV) installation on the roof. The power supplied by the systems ranges from 1 kWp (kilowatt peak) up to over 16 kWp. Different PV technologies as thin film, poly-crystalline or mono-crystalline solar cells were used. In low energy buildings, electricity represents a considerable part of the energy balance, especially if this is considered in units of primary energy.

All projects have a mechanical ventilation system with heat recovery. The efficiency of the systems range from 80 per cent to 95 per cent. Three projects have earth pipes to preheat the supply of fresh air. This prevents the heat exchanger from freezing during very low temperatures.

To produce the needed remaining heat, a full range of technologies has been used, including heat pumps, biomass, gas or electric-resistance elements. The latter is used in the Lindas row house project, which accounts for the very high primary energy demand seen in Figure 1.1.1. The range of technologies used in the houses is summarized in Table 1.3.1.

Table 1.3.1 *Technical systems*

	Direct gain	Water collector	PV	Earth pipe	Mechanical ventilation	Heat recovery	Heat pump	Biomass	Gas	Electric resistance
1 Lindas	•	•			•	•				•
2 Gelsenkirchen	•	•	•		•	•				
3 Thening	•	•	•	•	•	•	•			
4 Sunny Woods	•	•	•	•	•	•	•			
5 Stans	•	•	•	•	•	•		•		
6 Vienna	•				•	•			•	

2

The Lindås Passive House Project in Göteborg, Sweden

Hans Eek and Maria Wall

2.1 Project description

In an environment of great natural beauty at Lindås, Sweden, 20 km south of Göteborg, the city-owned company Egnahemsbolaget built 20 terrace houses. The goal was to demonstrate that it is possible to build houses at normal costs with such a low heating demand that even in a Scandinavian climate no conventional heating system is required. The terrace houses were designed by EFEM Arkitektkontor as the result of a research project in cooperation with Chalmers University of

Source: Hans Eek

Figure 2.1.1 *Twenty terrace houses in four rows; solar collectors on the roof*

Technology, Energy and Building Design at Lund University, the Swedish National Testing and Research Institute and the Swedish Research Council for Environment, Agricultural Sciences and Spatial Planning (Formas).

2.1.1 Architectural concept

The buildings were designed to provide a pleasant indoor environment with minimum energy use. The courtyard façade towards the south has large windows to make full use of solar heat. Balconies and roof overhang provide protection against excessive solar radiation during the summer. Because of the common walls of the 11 m deep row houses, there is only a minimal external wall surface and this is highly insulated and air tight. The roof window above the staircase allows daylight to penetrate into the middle of the house and also provides a strong stack effect for effective ventilation in summer.

Source: EFEM Arkitektkontor

Figure 2.1.2 *Site plan*

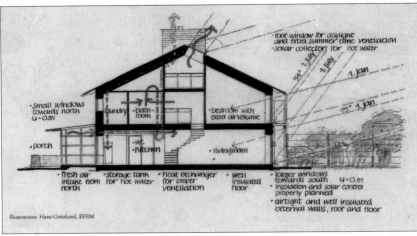

Source: EFEM Arkitektkontor

Figure 2.1.3 *Section*

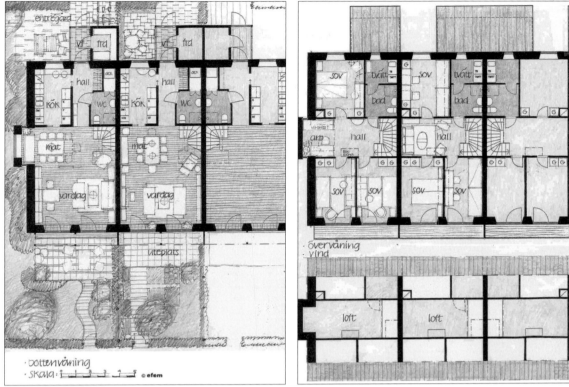

Source: EFEM Arkitektkontor

Figure 2.1.4 *Floor plans: (left) ground floor; (right) first floor and attic*

Source: Hans Eek

Figure 2.1.5 *View from the south*

2.2 Energy

2.2.1 Energy concept

The goal of building housing that requires no conventional heating system in this climate was achieved by the following means:

- a highly insulated, air-tight building envelope with:
  - a mean U-value of the building envelope = 0.16 W/m²K;
  - an air tightness measured to be 0.3 l/sm² at 50 Pa;
- minimized thermal bridges:
- energy-efficient windows with a mean U-value = 0.85 W/m²K;
- efficient ventilation with heat recovery (circa 80 per cent); and
- 5 m² of solar collectors for DHW per housing unit.

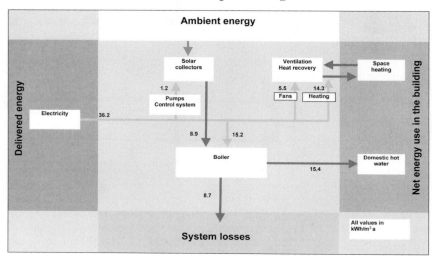

Source: Maria Wall, diagram format by AEU (Robert Hastings)

Figure 2.2.1 *Energy supply for domestic hot water (DHW), space heating and ventilation. The values are the average energy supply and use for the 20 units, based on monitoring*

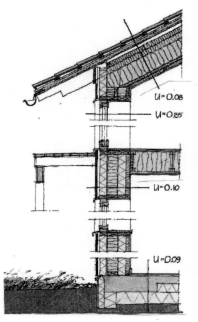

Source: EFEM Arkitektkontor

Figure 2.2.2 *Section*

2.2.2 Building envelope

The opaque building envelope is in lightweight construction and highly insulated (see Table 2.2.1).

Table 2.2.1 *Constructions*

Roof (roof tiles of clay)	
Counter and tiling batten	6.0 cm
Expanded polystyrene	3.0 cm
Underlay felt	
Timber	2.2 cm
Ventilated air space/rafters	5.0 cm
Masonite rafters and mineral wool	45.0 cm
Double polyethylene sheets	
Rafters and mineral wool	4.5 cm
Gypsum board	1.3 cm
Total	**67.0 cm**
Exterior walls (from inside to outside)	
Gypsum board	1.3 cm
Studs and mineral wool	4.5 cm
Expanded polystyrene	12.0 cm
Polyethylene sheet	
Studs with mineral wool	17.0 cm
Gypsum board	0.9 cm
Expanded polystyrene	10.0 cm
Battens/ventilated air space	3.4 cm
Wood panel	2.2 cm
Total	**51.3 cm**
Floor (from inside)	
Parquet	2.5 cm
Foamed polyethylene	0.5 cm
Concrete	10.0 cm
Expanded polystyrene	10.0 cm
Polyethylene sheet	
Expanded polystyrene	15.0 cm
Drainage layer macadam	30.0 cm
Total	**68.0 cm**

2.2.3 Windows

There are two types of three-pane windows. One type is operable. It is glazed with two low-emissivity coatings. One of the gaps between the panes is filled with argon, the other with air. The other window type is fixed. It is glazed with two low-emissivity coatings. Both gaps are filled with krypton gas. The energy transmittance is circa 50 per cent and the visual transmittance is 64 per cent for the operable window and 68 per cent for the fixed. The mean U-value of the windows for a house unit is 0.85 W/m^{2}K.

Source: Maria Wall

Figure 2.2.3 *Windows in the end wall*

2.2.4 External door

The door is a Swedish standard type.

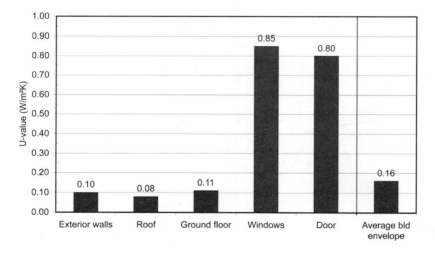

Source: Maria Wall, diagram format by AEU (Robert Hastings)

Figure 2.2.4 *U-values of the building envelope parts*

2.2.5 Ventilation

The exhaust air in a counter-flow heat exchanger heats supply air. It provides approximately 80 per cent heat recovery. During the summer, the heat exchanger can be turned off (automatic bypass) and the house may be ventilated without preheating of the supply air and by opening windows.

Living in these houses requires no more effort or knowledge than to live in conventional housing. If it is cold outside, the occupants do not open the windows. If it is warm and sunny, they do. If it is too warm, they open windows on both sides of the house and the roof to create a through draft, and lower the blinds or the awnings outside the south-facing windows.

2.2.6 Heat production and distribution

Part of the space heating demand is covered by usable heat gains from the occupants (circa 1200 kWh/year) and by energy efficient appliances and lighting (2900 kWh/year). The remaining space heating demand is covered by electric resistance heating (900 W) in the supply air.

The houses have been designed for normal Scandinavian climatic conditions. Very low outdoor temperatures over extended periods are rare and are regarded as extreme. In such cases, the indoor temperature may drop by a degree or two.

2.2.7 Hot water supply

Five m^2 of solar collectors per unit cover approximately 40 per cent of the hot water demand. The 500 litre storage tank is equipped with an electric immersion heater to cover the rest of the demand.

Source: Hans Eek

Figure 2.2.5 *Solar collectors and roof windows*

2.2.8 Planning

The computer program DEROB–LTH was used during the design stage (conducted by Maria Wall) to study the energy performance, passive solar energy use and indoor climate.

2.2.9 Energy performance

More energy is actually needed than was planned. This is partially explained by occupants heating the houses to higher indoor temperatures and having more electric appliances than was assumed during the planning stage. The variation in energy use among the households is large, varying between 45 and 97 kWh/m^{2}a. There is no strong correlation between total energy use and number of occupants per household, nor whether the house is an end or middle unit. Nevertheless, these houses, on average, consume 50 per cent to 75 per cent less energy than equivalent houses built according to the national building code.

Table 2.2.2 *Monitored average energy use in kWh/m²a for the 20 units*

Heating of space and ventilation air (electricity)	14.3
Domestic hot water (electricity)	15.2
Fans and pumps	6.7
Lighting and household appliances	31.8
Delivered energy demand	68.0
Domestic hot water (solar energy)	8.9
Total monitored energy demand	**76.9**

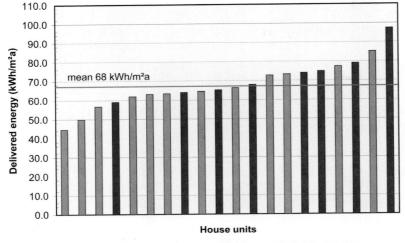

Source: Maria Wall, based on data from Ruud and Lundin (2004)

Figure 2.2.6 *Monitored delivered energy per house unit during a year: DHW heating, space heating, electricity for mechanical systems and household electricity; the dark bars are end units*

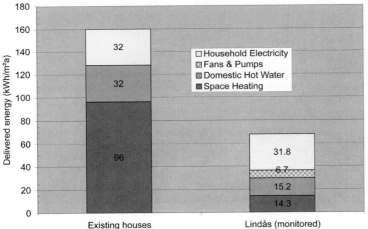

Source: Maria Wall, based on data from the Swedish Energy Agency (www.stem.se) and Ruud and Lundin (2004)

Figure 2.2.7 *Delivered energy in the Swedish existing building stock (average single family houses, according to the Swedish Energy Agency) compared with the terrace houses in Lindås*

2.3 Economy

Building costs are estimated to be normal. The higher costs resulting from insulation, achieving greater air tightness, and optimizing 'passive solar heating' and heat recovery from ventilation air are offset by the much lower costs of the heating system and the savings in operating costs due to the extremely low energy costs.

The project was financed by Formas and the European Union (through the CEPHEUS project) during the planning and evaluation phase. Investment costs were carried by Egnahemsbolaget, Göteborg.

2.4 Innovative products

Swedish standard products have been used.

2.5 Conclusions

Interviews with the occupants show that they are, in general, very satisfied. They especially appreciate the indoor air quality and the good ventilation. The technical systems are very easy to understand and manage (Boström et al, 2003; Ruud and Lundin, 2004).

The occupants have decided to keep their houses warmer than is common in traditionally heated houses at approximately 23°C during wintertime. The reason for this is not clear. In the case of the end units, some extra heating may be needed since the heat recovery of the ventilation was less than expected and the windows have a higher U-value than planned. Extra heating may be required if a higher indoor temperature is preferred and only a small household is living in the end unit.

The ventilation heat exchanger should be improved. The control system has not performed as expected during the monitoring period. The function of the defrosting system could also be enhanced.

The efficiency of the solar DHW system was only 37 per cent, instead of the expected 50 per cent. This is partially explained by the higher than planned heat losses from the storage tank. The tank was poorly insulated and larger than needed for the installed DHW system.

More household electricity is used than was expected. The occupants have more electrical appliances than assumed and these are less energy efficient than was anticipated.

The building costs are somewhat higher than the costs for a conventional house; but the payback time is very short. When these houses are mass produced, the costs will be the same or even lower than for conventional houses because they do not need a traditional heating system.

The design process was carried out in collaboration with the client, builder, architect, consultants and researchers. A series of seminars with different themes (for example, on windows, construction, ventilation systems and summer comfort) was attended by all of the parties involved. In this way, different alternatives were discussed and everyone was informed about final decisions and the reasoning behind them. During the construction phase, the architect Hans Eek visited the building site several times to explain the importance of air tightness and how to ensure correct construction. The houses have proved to be a good way of demonstrating that it is possible to plan affordable housing which requires very little energy and provides high comfort. They have inspired further developments of new high-performance housing in Sweden.

Acknowledgements

We thank the owner, the Swedish National Testing and Research Institute and the architectural firm EFEM for providing information, plans and photos of this project.

References

Boström, T., Glad, W., Isaksson, C., Karlsson, F., Persson, M.L. and Werner, A. (2003) *Tvärvetenskaplig analys av lågenergihusen i Lindås Park, Göteborg*. Arbetsnotat no 25, Energy Systems Program, Linköping University, Linköping, Sweden

Hoffmann, C. (2004) 'Reihenhäuser in Göteborg', in C. Hoffmann et al (eds), *Wohnbauten mit geringem Energieverbrauch. 12 Gebäude: Planung, Umsetzung, Realität*, C.F. Müller Verlag, Heidelberg, pp211–222

Ruud, S. and Lundin, L. (2004) *Bostadshus utan traditionellt uppvärmningssystem – resultat från två års mätningar*, SP Report 2004:31, SP Energiteknik, Borås, Sweden

Wall, M. (2005) 'Terrace houses in Gothenburg – the first passive houses in Sweden', in *9th Internationale Passivhaustagung*, Ludwigshafen, Germany, pp561–566

Wall, M. (2006) 'Energy-efficient terrace houses in Sweden: Simulations and measurements', *Energy and Buildings*, vol 38, pp627–634

3

Gelsenkirchen Solar Housing Estate, Germany

Carsten Petersdorff

3.1 Project description

3.1.1 Portrait and context

Gelsenkirchen is part of the Ruhr region in Germany, which had a steel and coal economy. Due to the sharp decline of these industries, the city is undergoing a major transition. The 'city of 1000 fires' is changing to the 'city of 1000 suns'. A housing estate was built on a former coal mine site as one of the first of 50 planned 'solar settlements' in North Rhine-Westphalia. The campaign was launched in 1997 by three ministries (economic affairs, housing and construction, and science and research) and the North Rhine-Westphalia State Initiative on Future Energies.

Source: Carsten Petersdorff

Figure 3.1.1 *The solar housing estate in Gelsenkirchen*

The aim of the campaign is to greatly reduce the energy requirement through appropriate construction methods, while also covering much of the remaining energy needs with solar energy.

To analyse the actual energy performance of this pilot project, AG-Solar, acting for the government of North Rhine-Westphalia, commissioned the evaluation. The houses were monitored and were based on measured energy.

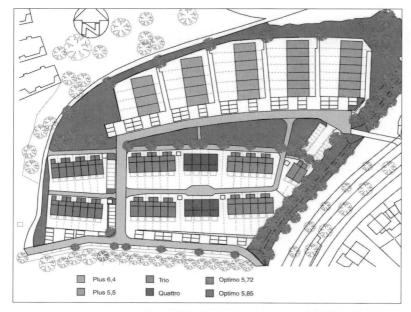

Plus 6,4	Trio	Optimo 5,72
Plus 5,5	Quattro	Optimo 5,85

Source: Carsten Petersdorff

Figure 3.1.2 *Site plan*

Source: Carsten Petersdorff

Figure 3.1.3 *Wooden frame houses, southern tract*

The building site of 38,000 m² is located centrally in Gelsenkirchen. Two different project developers built special house types. In the southern part of the site, 22 houses in light construction and 16 massive construction houses were built. The northern part of the site consists of 33 massive houses with gable roofs.

Source: Carsten Petersdorff

Figure 3.1.4 *Massive houses, southern tract*

Source: Carsten Petersdorff

Figure 3.1.5 *Massive houses, northern tract*

3.1.2 Architectural concept and construction

Wood structure houses in the southern tract

These 22 wooden frame houses have 5 to 6 rooms in 3 storeys. Two thirds of these houses have no basement; the others have unheated basements. All windows of the main rooms are orientated to the south. The shed roof slopes at an angle of 8° to the north and is covered with vegetation.

Massive houses – southern tract

These 16 massive houses correspond architecturally to the wooden frame houses, with the difference that all houses have an unheated basement.

Massive houses – northern tract

The 34 massive houses of the northern tract each have 5 to 6 rooms over 2 storeys and gable roofs that are orientated to the south.

3.2 Energy

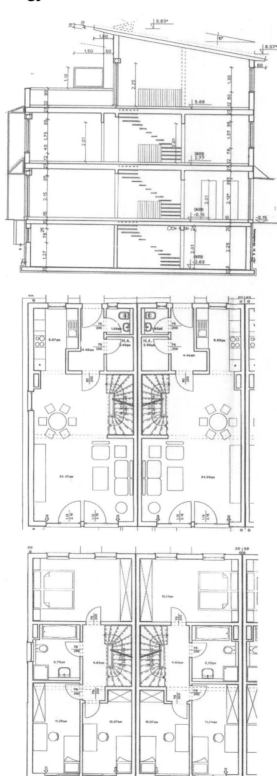

Source: Carsten Petersdorff

Figure 3.2.1 *Section*

Source: Carsten Petersdorff

Figure 3.2.2 *Ground floor plan*

Source: Carsten Petersdorff

Figure 3.2.3 *First floor plan*

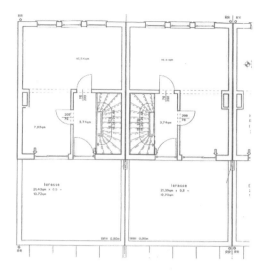

Source: Carsten Petersdorff

Figure 3.2.4 *Top floor plan*

3.2.1 Energy concept

All houses were built to have a maximum heating demand of about 40 kWh/m²a, achieved with passive and active solar energy use.

3.2.2 Building envelope

Windows

- g-value = 0.6;
- U-value (glass) = 1.1 W/m²K; and
- U-value (frame) = 1.4 W/m²K.

External walls

- gyp-board = 1.25 cm;
- plywood = 1.3 cm;
- mineral fibre batts/framing = 14.0 cm;
- plywood = 1.3 cm;
- wood strapping/air gap = 3.0 cm;
- counter-wood strapping = 3.0 cm;
- board siding = 2.5 cm; and
- total = 26.35 cm.

Floor slab on grade

- levelling cement with PE-foil = 8 cm;
- sound deadening insulation = 9 cm;
- concrete floor slab = 20 cm;
- insulation (XPS) = 8 cm;
- gravel = 7 cm;
- clean fill = 5 cm; and
- total = 57 cm.

Roof

- gyp-board/PE-foil = 1.3 cm;
- mineral fibre insulation/rafters = 24 cm;
- wood fibre panels = 2 cm;
- separation foil (PE);
- roof weather barrier (PVC);
- protection layer = 1 cm;
- substrate for planting = 5 cm; and
- total = 33.3 cm.

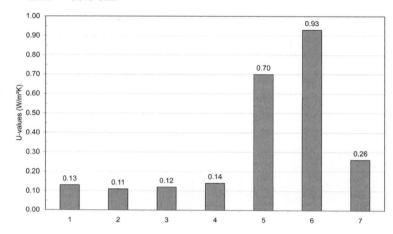

Source: Carsten Petersdorff

Figure 3.2.5 *U-values*

3.2.3 Ventilation

Mechanical ventilation

The wood frame houses have central ventilation systems with very efficient fans (12 W) for the extraction of used air. Fresh air is admitted through de-central special openings in the façade.

Mechanical ventilation with heat recovery

The 16 massive houses in the southern part of the area are equipped with a de-central (room) ventilation system with heat recovery. As room air is exhausted, the system warms a small heat storage mass. After a time interval, the fan reverses and draws outside air in over the mass, thus tempering it. The units are coupled in pairs: while one ventilator extracts, the other draws in fresh air. Each house has a total of six fan/storage systems.

3.2.4 Heat production and distribution

The heating systems of the northern and southern tracts differ. The 29 single family houses in the northern tract each have their own solar-assisted gas-fired condensing boiler for space heating and hot water. Solar collectors cover up to 65 per cent of the energy demand for DHW production.

The 48 single family houses in the southern tract have a micro-district heating system per house row. Solar heat and electricity produced on the house roof tops are also centrally collected and distributed. Solar energy also covers 65 per cent of the DHW need. These central units are managed by the local utility.

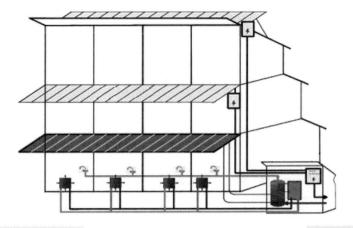

Source: Carsten Petersdorff

Figure 3.2.6 *Heat distribution, south housing tract*

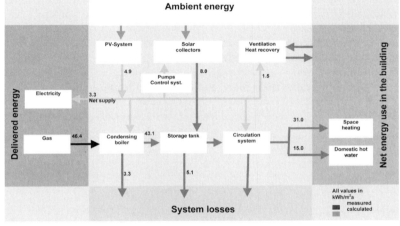

Source: Carsten Petersdorff

Figure 3.2.7 *Energy flow diagram*

3.2.5 Electricity

All houses have a grid-connected photovoltaic (PV) system. In the northern tract, the 1.5 kWp systems are installed on the roofs, oriented to the south. In the southern part, the 1 kWp systems are used as sunshades for the south-facing windows of the first floor.

Source: Carsten Petersdorff

Figure 3.2.8 *Roof-mounted photovoltaic system*

3.3 Life-cycle analysis

3.3.1 Approach

To assess the whole life cycle, the cumulative energy demand (CED) methodology was used. Such an investigation was of particular interest in this project because:

- many houses were built in a limited number of construction variations, making it possible to draw conclusions on such factors as the influence of massive houses versus light construction, or having a cellar or slab on grade;
- the houses are well insulated and incorporate solar thermal and PV systems; and
- individual house systems and central (row house) systems could be compared.

As a first step, an inventory was made of all construction materials used. This was very time consuming because of the complexity of constructions. For example, pipes for drinking water consist of plastic, aluminium, a plastic surface layer and insulation. The masses of the materials were multiplied by specific CED values to calculate the primary energy input for the production of the housing.

Three different house types were investigated:

1   massive houses in the northern part of the settlement (Plus);
2   wooden frame houses (Trio and Quattro); and
3   massive houses (Optimo), with nearly the same floor plans as the wooden frame houses.

3.3.2 Results

The buildings represent the main part (78 per cent of the CED); but the infrastructure contributes a significant 22 per cent, as shown in Figure 3.3.1.

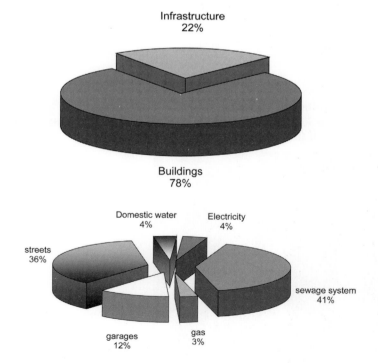

Source: Carsten Petersdorff

Figure 3.3.1 *Cumulative energy demand (CED) contribution from buildings (light grey) and infrastructure (dark grey)*

Source: Carsten Petersdorff

Figure 3.3.2 *Infrastructure*

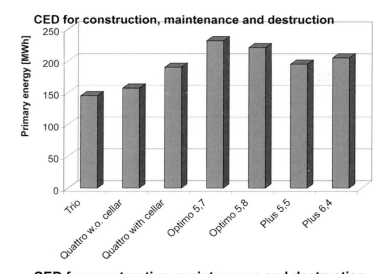

Source: Carsten Petersdorff

Figure 3.3.3 *Comparison of building types*

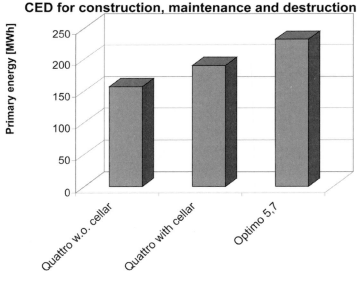

Source: Carsten Petersdorff

Figure 3.3.4 *Comparison of constructions*

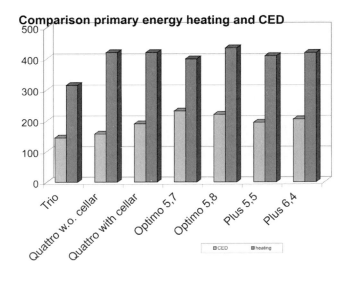

Source: Carsten Petersdorff

Figure 3.3.5 *Annual primary energy for heating and construction per house*

The infrastructure

The infrastructure of the settlement includes roads, sidewalks, park surfaces and garages, as well as wires for electricity and communication, and pipes for gas, water and wastewater. The CED breakdown is presented in Figure 3.3.2. It is surprising that the construction of the sewage system represents higher energy expenditure than the much larger traffic surface. This is caused by the comparatively low CED value for road surfacing, since bitumen is a petrochemical by-product. The large mass of energy-intensive materials (for example, cement) for paving, concrete curbs and park surfaces are the main sources of the CED for the traffic infrastructure.

The buildings

Figure 3.3.3 compares the CED of the different house types. The building envelope accounts for approximately 90 per cent of the CED! Interior fittings and services (gas, water, heating and electricity installation) represent 7 per cent of the CED. The solar systems make up the remaining 3 per cent, of which the greatest cause is the photovoltaic system.

The wooden frame houses (Quattro) and massive houses with similar structure (Optimo) allow a comparison of the two constructions. Results are separately illustrated in Figure 3.3.4.

The direct comparison shows that wood frame construction has a 20 per cent lower CED than the massive construction. This is partially explained because the internal energy of the wood is rated as neutral. The strong influence of concrete becomes clear by comparing the houses in light construction with and without cellars. Adding a cellar increases the CED by approximately 22 per cent.

Comparison of CED and energy for heating and electricity

In addition to the energy input for construction, maintenance and decommissioning, energy is, of course, consumed during its operational lifetime. This includes energy used for household electrical appliances, hot water and space heating.

Energy used during the operational life time accounts for an overwhelming 85 per cent of the primary energy used. While electricity and hot water demand primarily depend on user behaviour, the space heating demand is strongly correlated with the insulation quality and ventilation system of the building. Over 50 years, the primary energy demand for heating alone amounts to approximately 22 GWh per house and is therefore in the range of the primary energy use for construction, maintenance and decommissioning (see Figure 3.3.5).

3.3.3 Life-cycle analysis conclusions

The main results of the study are as follows:

- The massive houses (Optimo) cause a CED that is 20 per cent higher than the similar houses in lightweight construction (Quattro houses).
- The construction of light frame houses causes less CED than masonry houses. Comparing the Quattro houses with and without basements, the strong influence of reinforced concrete is especially evident, increasing the CED by 22 per cent.
- When the CED of the whole site development is considered, the construction of the houses themselves account for 77 per cent (15 GWh) over their 50-year life expectancy; the infrastructure (roads, pipes, etc.) results in 23 per cent of the CED on a per house basis.
- Over this period of 50 years, the primary energy demand for heating amounts to approximately 22 GWh and is therefore in the range of the primary energy use for construction, maintenance and decommissioning.
- The CED from additional insulation and solar technologies is easily justified by the resulting energy savings.

Building costs:

including value-added tax and planning costs and the land

Table 3.4.1
The building costs

	(€)
from	180,000
to	235,000

Costs for mounting, PV and solar collectors:

including value-added tax and planning

The central plant	(€)
Average cost	40,819
Land cost for the central plant	2362

Photovoltaic and solar thermal	
Photovoltaic	8175
Structure	1151
Solar thermal	3670
Engineering	716
Coordination and administration	1023
Blower-door test	511
Total	**15,245**

3.4 Economy

The objective of the project was to build houses that are affordable for young families. Therefore, the houses were targeted to cost between 180,000 and 235,000 Euros (including VAT and the building site). The ministries in North Rhine-Westphalia coordinated their subsidy programmes for solar energy housing estates. As a result, photovoltaic and solar thermal systems were subsidized. The local energy utility also supported the solar systems.

The additional costs for the energy-related measures can be assumed to be less than 5 per cent more than conventional house construction.

References

Wagner, H. J. et al (2002) *Endbericht Ökologische Bewertung im Gebäudebereich, Förderungsprojekt des Landes Nordrhein Westfalen*, Universität GH Essen und Ecofys, Essen, Germany
Wiesner, W. (2001) *Zwischenbericht für das Jahr 2001 – Koordination und Durchführung der Evaluierung der Solarsiedlung Gelsenkirchen Bismarck im Rahmen des Programms 50 Solarsiedlungen NRW*, TÜV Emissionsschutz und Energiesysteme GmbH, Köln, Germany

Websites

50 Solarsiedlungen www.50solarsiedlungen-tuv.de
Projektträger ETN www.ag-solar.de/
Information about the campaign 50 Solar Housing Estate North Rhine-Westphalia: www.50-solarsiedlungen.de
Information about the Solar City Gelsenkirchen: www.solarstadt.gelsenkirchen.de/

4

Sunny Woods Apartment Building, Zurich

Daniela Enz and Alex Primas

4.1 Project description

4.1.1 Portrait and context

The Passivhaus Sunny Woods was built in 2000/2001 by the Swiss architect, Beat Kämpfen. Its name explains its concept. The six-family dwelling is located on a south-facing hill close to the woods in a residential area of Zurich. Solar energy and wooden construction were the themes of the design.

Source: Beat Kämpfen, Zürich, www.kaempfen.com

Figure 4.1.1 *South façade*

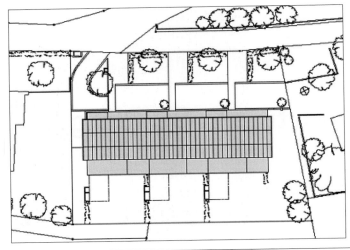

Source: Beat Kämpfen, Zürich,
www.kaempfen.com

Figure 4.1.2 *Site plan*

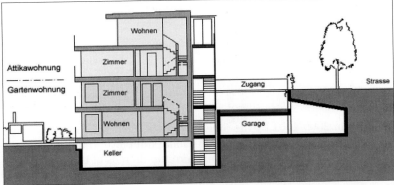

Source: Beat Kämpfen, Zürich,
www.kaempfen.com

Figure 4.1.3 *Cross-section*

Source: Beat Kämpfen,
Zürich, www.kaempfen.com

Figure 4.1.4 *Attic*

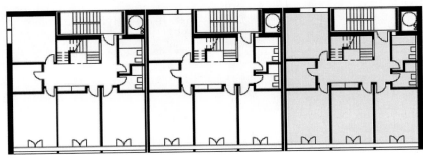

Source: Beat Kämpfen,
Zürich, www.kaempfen.com

Figure 4.1.5 *Second
floor*

4.1.2 Architectural concept

The building consists of six spacious legally and technically almost autonomous maisonette units, with an
elevated standard and price. The lower units have a
small garden; the upper units have a large roof terrace.
Each dwelling has the character of a single family house
and is directly accessible from the street, with a level
difference of half a storey up or down.

The bedrooms are situated on the entrance level and
adjoin the neighbouring apartments, which is acousti-
cally advantageous (see Figure 4.1.3).

The generously glazed main rooms are oriented to
the south. The bathrooms, staircase and the technical
room are situated in the northern-oriented part of the
apartment. The north, east and west façades have only
small windows.

Parking is available in the underground garage.

Source: Beat Kämpfen, Zürich, www.kaempfen.com

Figure 4.1.6 *Timber construction*

4.1.3 Construction

Sunny Woods is one of the first multi-family houses in Switzerland with four floors in timber construction. It is built with large prefabricated wooden panels. Concrete is used only for the cellar, the
staircase for exterior access and the underground parking. All other floors are wooden frame construction with a 7 cm cement cover and acoustic insulation mats. The wooden frame roof is covered with
aluminium roofing panels on which photovoltaic panels are mounted.

4.2 Energy

4.2.1 Energy concept

Sunny Woods won both the Swiss and European solar prizes. It is the first apartment building in
Switzerland designed to achieve a net annual zero-energy balance. The project is based on passive-
solar design principles. The exactly south-oriented windows open almost the entire south façade. In
order to make use of the solar gains in this timber construction building, a levelling cement grout of 7
cm and black slate paving tiles of 1.5 cm were added to the floor.

The passive-solar design combines the following technical features:

- highly insulated air-tight building envelope: U-value(average): 0.24 W/m²K; pressurization test
  (50Pa): 0.6 h⁻¹;
- minimized thermal bridges;
- energy efficient windows: U-value(including frame): 0.8 W/m²K;
- efficient ventilation with heat recovery (90 per cent efficiency) and ground preheating;
- photovoltaic (PV) roof, grid connected thin film solar cells: 16.2 kWp;
- vacuum collectors for DHW and heating: 6 m² per living unit; and
- efficient appliances.

4.2.2 Building envelope

Attention was given to details in order to avoid thermal bridges. The back-vented exterior walls are
46 cm thick. The wooden panel construction allowed less thick walls to this high insulation standard
than would have been possible with masonry construction.

Source: Naef Energietechnik, Ingenieur- und
Planungsbüro, Zürich, www.igjzh.com/naef/

Figure 4.2.1 *Fan*

Source: Naef Energietechnik, Ingenieur- und Planungsbüro, Zürich,
www.igjzh.com/naef/

Figure 4.2.2 *Air heater*

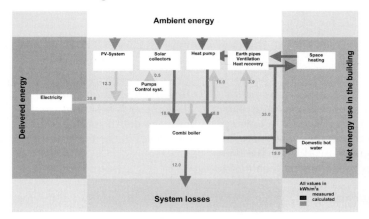

Source: Naef Energietechnik, Ingenieur- und
Planungsbüro, Zürich, www.igjzh.com/naef/

Figure 4.2.3 *Energy supply; the
values refer to the entire building*

The parts of the façade that are difficult to insulate – the roof deck of the attic, the ceiling fronts and
window frames of the south façade, and the front doors – were additionally covered with a vacuum
insulation 2 cm thick.

The windows are triple-glazed solar glass with krypton gas filling.

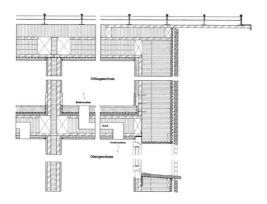

Source: Beat Kämpfen, Zürich, www.kaempfen.com

Figure 4.2.4 *Detail section of north façade*

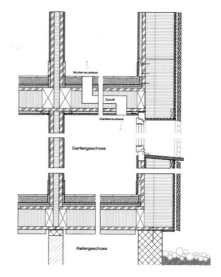

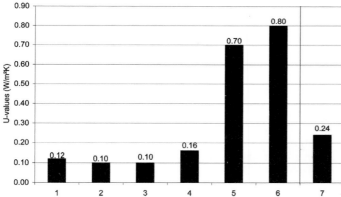

Notes: U-values (W/m²K):
1: exterior walls;
2: roof;
3: terrace;
4: floor to cellar;
5: window (glass);
6: window (including frame), mean value;
7: average U-value building envelope.
Source: Beat Kämpfen, Zürich,
www.kaempfen.com

Figure 4.2.5 *U-values*

Source: Naef Energietechnik, Ingenieur- und
Planungsbüro, Zürich, www.igjzh.com/naef/

Figure 4.2.6 *Ground pipe*

Source: Beat Kämpfen, Zürich,
www.kaempfen.com

Figure 4.2.7 *Vacuum collectors as balcony railing*

Source: Beat Kämpfen, Zürich,
www.kaempfen.com

Figure 4.2.8 *Thin film solar cells on the roof*

4.2.3 Roof (from outside to inside)

- PV panels with an air gap beneath;
- aluminium sheet metal roof = 6.0 cm;
- water barrier;
- sloped mineral wool = 6.0–30.0 cm;
- three-layer slab = 3.0 cm;
- box-section slab/mineral wool = 18.0 cm;
- battens/mineral wool = 3.0 cm;
- moisture barrier;
- gypsum board = 1.5 cm;
- total = 40.5–64.5 cm; and
- U-value = 0.10 W/m²K.

4.2.4 Ceiling

- Natural stone paving tiles = 1.5 cm;
- levelling cement grout = 7.0 cm;
- polyethylene foil;
- acoustical insulation = 3.5 cm;

- glued wooden block panels = 3.0 cm;
- box-section slab/mineral wool = 18.0 cm;
- glued wooden block panels = 3.0 cm;
- mineral wool = 3.0 cm;
- gypsum board = 1.5 cm;
- sound deadening foil = 0.5 cm;
- gypsum board = 0.9 cm; and
- total = 41.9 cm.

4.2.5 Ventilation

The supply air is preheated in polyethylene pipes buried in the ground. The pipes, with a diameter of 150 mm and a length of 30 m, are buried at a depth of 3.5 m. Each apartment is supplied with fresh air preheated in two of those pipes.

The air is further tempered by heat recovered from the exhaust air via a cross counter-flow heat exchanger. The ground preheating prevents the heat exchanger from freezing during the winter.

4.2.6 Heat production and distribution

The heat is distributed by the fresh air supply. Each apartment has the ventilating pipes in its own ceiling with outlets on the floor for the upper floor and outlets on the ceiling for the lower floor (see Figure 4.2.6). Radiators in the bathrooms provide additional comfort.

The ventilation air is heated with a water–air heat pump supplied by the solar collectors. The solar thermal system provides heat for both DHW and space heating. Each living unit has 6 m² of vacuum collectors that also serve as the balcony railing. The storage tank stores 1400 litres of water.

The two-storey high plant rooms are next to the bathrooms on the north side in the insulated entrance area. This de-central solution allows for short pipes.

4.2.7 Electricity

The entire roof is covered with 202 m² (generator area) grid-connected thin-film solar cells with a capacity of 16.2 kWp, which is equivalent to the electricity consumption for ventilation and heating (with heat pump) in this building. According to the project specifications, the house is energy self-sufficient (excluding energy for household appliances).

To comply with local codes, the roof is only sloped 3°. This reduces the yearly electricity gains. The cells have an efficiency of 8 to 10 per cent.

4.3 Life-cycle analysis

4.3.1 Approach

Within the system boundaries, energy consumed for the production, renewal and disposal of materials were considered. The underground parking was excluded from the system boundaries. In the calculation of primary energy for electricity used by the technical systems of the house, the mix of Swiss electricity production were assumed. Household appliance electricity was excluded.

Table 4.3.1 shows selected basic parameters of the house. The data on the amount and type of materials used in the building was collected from construction plans and submission documents.

For the amorphous silicone photovoltaic panels (Unisolar, triple thin-film cells), the inventory material properties are only roughly estimated. In order to give an impression of the influence of this uncertainty in the inventory, the calculations were also carried out for a PV system with crystalline PV panels of similar peak power according to data from Frischknecht et al (1996).

Source: Beat Kämpfen, Zürich,
www.kaempfen.com

Figure 4.3.1 *North entrance*

Table 4.3.1 *Basic parameters*

Parameter	Description	Unit	Value
Building volume	4900 m³ heated; 2800 m3 unheated	m³	7700
Floor area	Net heated floor area	m²	1233
Solar collector	36 m² vacuum tube collector, DHW and space heating	KWh/a	17,340
PV system	Amorphous triple-cell modules (16.2 kWp)	KWh/a	15,000
Space heat demand	Covered to 60 per cent through environmental + solar heat	kWh/a	10,790
Heat for domestic hot water (DHW)	Covered to 82 per cent through environmental + solar heat	kWh/a	28,900
Electricity, heat pump	Air–water heat pump for space heating and DHW	kWh/a	9420
Electricity, other	Electricity used for ventilation and pumps	kWh/a	5580

Note: Data refer to the design values of the entire apartment building.

4.3.2 Results

All results refer to the m² net heated 'carpet area' and year (building life span: 80 years). For comparison, a reference building is considered: a two-storey row house without a cellar made of brick walls with polystyrene insulation. The six units each have 120 m² net carpet area. The heat demand of 65 kWh/m²a (DHW: 25 kWh/m²a) is met with a conventional gas furnace.

4.3.3 Life cycles of the building assessed with Eco-indicator 99

In Figure 4.3.3, the impact of construction, renewal, disposal, transportation and operation on the total cycle is shown. The weighting method Eco-indicator 99 (hierarchist) was used.

The most important conclusions derived from Figure 4.3.3 are the following:

•   The total impact over the life cycle for Sunny Woods is only 37 per cent (design value) or 44 per cent (measured value) that of the reference building.

- Different types of PV systems influence the total impact by about 10 per cent.
- The impact of the material used for renewal over the building's lifetime is similar to the impact of the initial building construction.
- The disposal of construction materials is driven by the concrete used. The disposal of the materials during periodical building renovations is less important.
- If no PV system were built, the electricity mix used for the building operation would amount to about 20 per cent of the total impact of the house. The impact of the electricity need by the heat pump with the Swiss electricity mix (high amount of hydro energy and low share of fossil fuels) is nearly offset by the output of the PV system. For the European electricity mix (Union for the Coordination of Transmission of Electricity, or UCTE), the house with a PV system clearly has an advantage and reduces the total impact by 25 per cent. In this case, the impact payback time for the amorphous PV cells would be four years.

Source: Beat Kämpfen, Zürich,
www.kaempfen.com

Figure 4.3.2 *Bird's eye view*

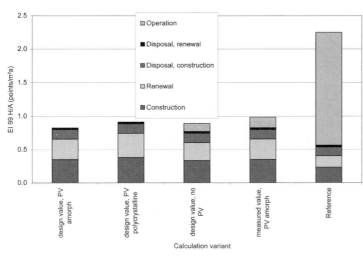

Source: Beat Kämpfen, Zürich,
www.kaempfen.com

Figure 4.3.3 *Life-cycle phases, Eco-indicator 99 H/A*

4.3.4 Building components assessed with Eco-indicator 99

In Figure 4.3.4, the impact of the different material groups over the life cycle was analysed using the Eco-indicator 99 method (hierarchist).

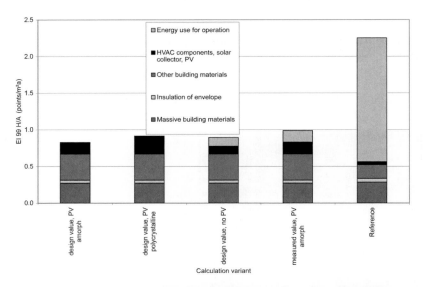

Source: Beat Kämpfen, Zürich, www.kaempfen.com

Figure 4.3.4 *Building components, Eco-indicator 99 H/A*

Source: Beat Kämpfen, Zürich, www.kaempfen.com

Figure 4.3.5 *Living room, middle attic apartment*

The following can be observed from Sunny Woods (see Figure 4.3.4):

- The insulating materials constitute only 5 per cent of the total impact of the building.
- The massive building materials amount to 33 per cent of the total impact of the building. This impact is primarily caused by the cellar and the cement cover of the floors.
- The heating and ventilation system makes up only 5 per cent of the total impact of the building (construction and renewal, excluding the solar and PV system).

- The thermal solar collector amounts to about 6 per cent of the total impact of the building (construction and renewal, including pipes, heat exchanger and storage tank).
- The amorphous-cell PV system leads to about 6 per cent of the total impact of the building (construction and renewal, including parts for roof mounting). Using the inventory of the crystalline-cell PV system as a 'worst' case scenario, this impact share rises to 16 per cent.

Within the other building materials (47 per cent of the total impact), an important share (19 per cent of the total impact) is caused by the windows, which have a higher impact due to the triple glazing with krypton filling.

4.3.5 Influence of the building components: Assessment with cumulative energy demand (CED)

Larger differences appear in the cumulative energy demand (CED) of non-renewable energy, as shown in Figure 4.3.6.

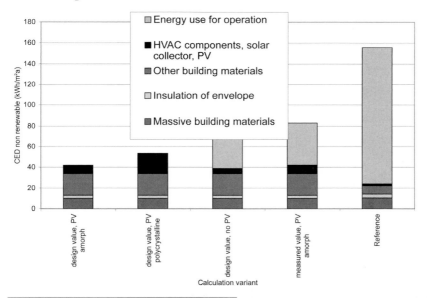

Source: Beat Kämpfen, Zürich, www.kaempfen.com

Figure 4.3.6 *Non-renewable cumulative energy demand of building components*

Source: Beat Kämpfen, Zürich, www.kaempfen.com

Figure 4.3.7 *Living room, west attic apartment*

The cumulative energy demand on non-renewable energy over the life cycle of Sunny Woods ranges from 27 per cent (design value) to 53 per cent (using measured energy data) of the CED of the reference building. The installation of the PV system is favourable because it minimizes the amount of non-renewable energy. The sensitivity of the inventory data used for the PV system is higher than in the calculation with Eco indicator 99 (>20 per cent of total impact). The polycrystalline PV cells data of Frankl (2002) result in a CED that is 68 per cent lower than the CED using the data in the calculations. The high difference between the design value and measured value is caused by a much higher heating demand, mainly due to an inadequate functioning of the shading devices.

The results are similar to the results from Eco-indicator 99 for the impact share of the different building components. Here, the insulation share is 7 per cent and the massive building materials 23 per cent of the total impact. The PV system amounts to 8 per cent, the solar system to 5 per cent and the other heating, ventilating and air conditioning (HVAC) components to 6 per cent of the total non-renewable CED of the building.

In addition to the non-renewable energy, the following renewable energy is used over the life cycle of the building with amorphous PV cells (design values):

- hydro power for electricity: 2.1 kWh/(m²a); and
- biomass (mainly wood): 20.8 kWh/(m²a).

In total, the share of renewable energy makes up 35 per cent of the total energy. The main part of the energy in biomass is used for construction.

4.3.6 Life-cycle analysis conclusions

The construction, renewal and disposal of the Passivhaus Sunny Woods have a very low impact over the life cycle of the building compared to a reference building in the same climate. To a large extent, this is a result of the low energy level needed for the operation of the building. The thick insulation results in a 5 per cent to 7 per cent negative impact for embodied energy compared to the resulting large energy savings.

The output of the large PV roof offsets the energy for heating and DHW. Due to the uncertainty within the inventories for the PV cells, a clear conclusion here is, however, difficult. The impact

Source: Beat Kämpfen, Zürich, www.kaempfen.com

Figure 4.3.8 *Technical room*

reduction (18 per cent to 49 per cent) compared to an operation of the building is clear if the UCTE electricity mix is used in the calculations. If the electricity mix contains a high amount of hydro power (40 per cent for the Swiss mix), the result depends on the cell type (embodied energy; quality of the inventory) and the assessment method used. Using CED for the assessment, the building with a PV system shows, in all cases, the best result (24 per cent to 40 per cent lower than without the PV system).

Sunny Woods demonstrates the low life cycle of a building's minimized losses and high solar gains. Ecological optimization of such buildings is difficult and may negatively affect fire safety, acoustics or the space concept.

The excellent energy performance could still be improved. Heating hot water uses three times more primary energy than does space heating. If the building is seen in a wider context, the impact of the inhabitants' mobility is important since the total annual impact of the building equals only about 5800 km driven with a passenger car per apartment (Eco-indicator 99 H/A).

4.4 Economy

The initiative for the project came from the architect, Beat Kämpfen, who bought the property as a total contractor. He planned the building and sold the apartments 'turnkey', ready for a fixed price before construction started. Since all homebuyers came from the surrounding neighbourhood, direct advertising by an onsite billboard had much more effect than advertisements in newspapers. The selling process was, however, difficult due to the new kind of building that Sunny Woods represented. There were concerns about the timber construction (fire security and durability) and unease regarding the Passivhaus concept. Ecological aspects were secondary for the homebuyers. The favourable location and the high floor-plan quality had a higher significance.

4.4.1 Building costs

Table 4.4.1 *Account classification: All costs, including planning honorarium and 7.6 per cent value-added tax*

	(€/m³)	(€/m²)	Total, €
Mean costs	427	1400	3,289,761
Living area (standard finishings)	511	1703	2,554,630
Garage, cellar	272	865	735,599

Source: Beat Kämpfen, Zürich, www.kaempfen.com

Table 4.4.2 *Account classification: All costs, including 7.6 per cent value-added tax, excluding planning honorarium*

Costs for technical system	(€/m³)	(€/m²)
Electric installations (without luminaire)		102,167
PV installation		183,900
Heating/ventilation		326,933
Ground piping	13,622	
Installations in the plant room	190,711	
Ventilation system	54,489	
Solar thermal collectors	68,111	
Sanitary installations (without kitchen)		108,978

Source: Beat Kämpfen, Zürich, www.kaempfen.com

Source: Beat Kämpfen, Zürich, www.kaempfen.com

Figure 4.4.1 *Shading south façade*

4.4.2 Costs for energy measures

A big part of the additional costs in the Sunny Woods project compared to other buildings was caused by the photovoltaic system. The heating system increased costs by around 30 per cent to 40 per cent and the autonomy of each apartment (with their own systems) also increased costs.

Altogether, the pure construction costs exceeded the costs of a conventional building by around 5 per cent.

4.4.3 Innovative components

- Building envelope:
    - walls: wooden block panels (Pius Schuler AG, www.pius-schuler.ch).
- Space heating and DHW:
    - vacuum collectors (B. Schweizer Energie AG, Chnübrächi 36, CH-8197 Rafz, Switzerland).
- Electricity:
    - Unisolar-Baekert standard photovoltaic panels at 32 Wp (amorphous silicone triple thin-film cells) (Fabrisolar AG, www.fabrisolar.ch and www.flumroc.ch/photovoltaik).

Acknowledgements

We thank the architect and energy planner for providing information, plans and photos of this project.

References

Frankl, P. (2002) 'Life Cycle Assessment (LCA) of PV Systems – Overview and Future Outlook', conference (PV in Europe – From PV Technology to Energy Solutions), Rome, Italy

Frischknecht, R., Bollens, U., Bosshart, S. and Ciot, L. M. (1996) *Ökoinventare von Energiesystemen: Grundlagen für den ökologischen Vergleich von Energiesystemen*, Institut für Energietechnik, ETH Eidgenössische Technische Hochschule, Zürich

Hoffmann, C., Hastings, R. and Voss, K. (2003) 'Mehrfamilienhaus in Stans', in *Wohnbauten mit geringem Energieverbrauch. 12 Gebäude: Planung, Umsetzung, Realität*, C.F. Müller Verlag, Heidelberg, pp211–222

Kämpfen, B. (2002) 'Mehrfamilienhaus Sunny Woods', in *Tagungsband zur 6. Europäischen passivhaustagung, Basel, January 2002*, Fuldaer Verlagsagentur, Fulda, pp87–96

Schmidt, F. (2002) 'Das Passivhaus wird schick', in *Schweizer Energiefachbuch*, KünzlerBachmann Verlag, St Gallen, Switzerland, pp65–69

5

Wechsel Apartment Building, Stans, Switzerland

Daniela Enz and Alex Primas

5.1 Project description

Source: Beda Bossard, BARBOS Büro für Baubiologie Bauökologie and Energie

Figure 5.1.1 *South façade*

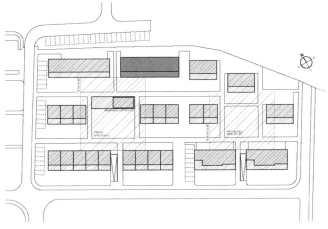

Source: Beda Bossard, BARBOS Büro für Baubiologie Bauökologie and Energie

Figure 5.1.2 *Site plan*

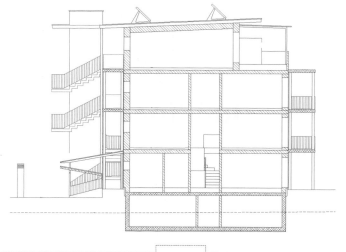

Source: Beda Bossard, BARBOS Büro für Baubiologie Bauökologie and Energie

Figure 5.1.3 *Cross-section*

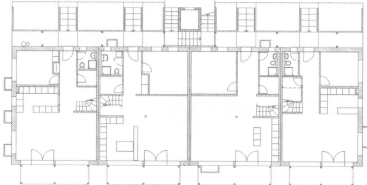

Source: Beda Bossard, BARBOS Büro für Baubiologie Bauökologie and Energie

Figure 5.1.4 *Ground plan*

Source: Beda Bossard, BARBOS Büro für Baubiologie Bauökologie and Energie

Figure 5.1.5 *Prefabricated timber construction*

5.1.1 Portrait and context

Since August 2001, eight families have lived in the apartment building Wechsel in Stans, a village in central Switzerland. Wechsel is the first multi-family Passivhaus in Switzerland. The building is part of a housing estate with 12 apartment buildings planned by BARBOS Bauteam GmbH.

The builder aimed for an energy efficient building using passive and active solar gains that is ecological and cost effective. The remaining heat energy demand was to be provided by renewable energies. After discussing the heating production and distribution, the solution was deemed to be a Passivhaus construction.

5.1.2 Architectural concept

The four-storey building consists of eight apartments, of which six are maisonettes. The top floor has a 4m offset, used as a terrace. The compact cube is oriented to the south (30° west). The main rooms are generously glazed and face south. The floor plan of each apartment differs slightly, reflecting the occupants' individual preferences.

The technical room, utility room and private cellars are situated in the basement. Parking is available in the underground garage.

5.1.3 Construction

The building is in timber construction. The prefabricated wooden elements for the interior and exterior walls are selectively reinforced with steel beams and steel pillars, and were mounted within a few days. The ceilings are combined timber/concrete structures.

The unheated basement is constructed with masonry and concrete. The balconies and the staircase for the exterior access at the north façade, as well as the balconies to the south, are constructed with steel and reinforced concrete, respectively. They are statically and thermally completely separated from the well-insulated cube.

5.2 Energy

5.2.1 Energy concept

The south façade has a big window ratio of 50 per cent. Spacious rooms to the south let solar gains enter deep into the building. The other façades have only small windows.

The building has the following technical features:

- highly insulated air-tight building envelope: U-value(average): 0.26 W/m²K; pressuration test (50 Pa): 0.6 h⁻¹;
- minimized thermal bridges;
- energy efficient windows: U-value (including frame): 0.9–1.07 W/m²K;
- efficient ventilation with heat recovery (80 per cent efficiency) and ground preheating;
- solar collectors for DHW and heating: 40.5 m²;
- wood pellet heating system: 9–25kW, 70 per cent coverage;
- photovoltaics (PV) on the roof, grid-connected single crystal silicon solar cells: 1.44 kWp; and
- efficient appliances.

The specific space heating demand is 11.6 kWh/m²a. Demand for DHW amounts to 15.9 kWh/m²a. The primary energy demand for the system is 19.1 kWh/m²a. These values refer to the heated net living area.

Figure 5.2.1 *Ventilation*

Figure 5.2.2 *Control system*

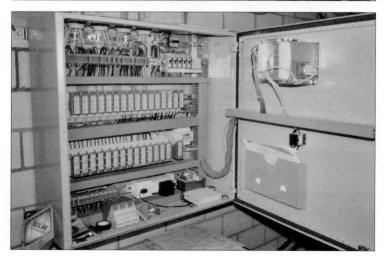

Figure 5.2.3 *Energy supply*

Source: P. Wälchli, ETH Student, Zürich

Figure 5.2.4 *Fibre cement slabs and wooden slats*

5.2.2 Building envelope

Due to the compact building volume and the strict structural and thermal separation of heated and unheated zones, the insulation layer could be applied continuously, thus minimizing thermal bridges.

The prefabricated back-vented exterior walls achieve an excellent U-value of 0.13 W/m^{2}K, with a construction thickness of less than 40 cm.

For fire safety, the northern façade is covered with fibre-cement panels. The other façades are faced with vertical white-stained wooden siding.

The windows with a Heat Mirror TC 88 inner film are filled with krypton. The U-value of the glass is 0.7 W/m^{2}K, the g-value is 0.5. Depending on the window size, the U-value of the entire window with a wooden frame varies between 0.9–1.07 W/m^{2}K.

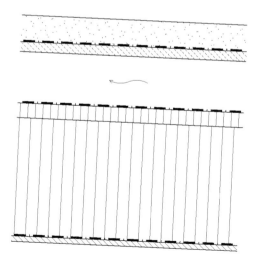

Source: Beda Bossard, BARBOS Büro für Baubiologie Bauökologie and Energie

Figure 5.2.5 *Roof*

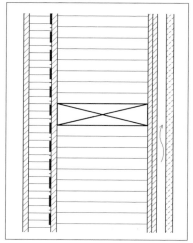

Source: Beda Bossard, BARBOS Büro für Baubiologie Bauökologie and Energie

Figure 5.2.6 *Wall*

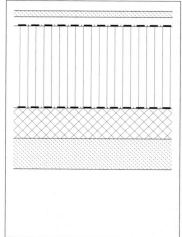

Source: Beda Bossard, BARBOS Büro für Baubiologie Bauökologie and Energie

Figure 5.2.7 *Terrace*

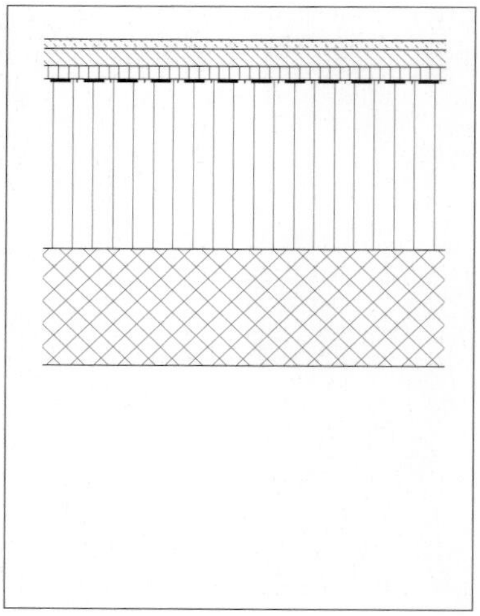

Source: Beda Bossard, BARBOS Büro für Baubiologie Bauökologie and Energie

Figure 5.2.8 *Floor to cellar*

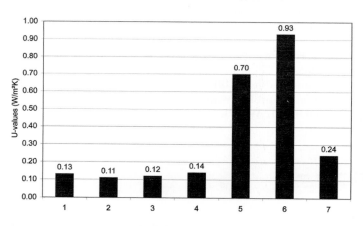

Notes: U-values (W/m^{2}K):
1: exterior walls;
2: roof;
3: terrace;
4: floor to cellar;
5: window (glass);
6: window (including frame), mean value;
7: average U-value building envelope.

Source: Beda Bossard, BARBOS Büro für Baubiologie Bauökologie and Energie

Figure 5.2.9 *U-values*

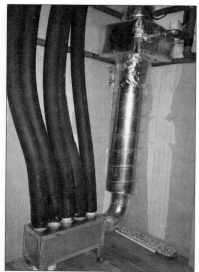

Source: Beda Bossard, BARBOS Büro für Baubiologie Bauökologie and Energie

Figure 5.2.10 *Supply air with heater coils* (top right) *and absorbing ducts* (middle right)

Source: Beda Bossard, BARBOS Büro für Baubiologie Bauökologie and Energie

Figure 5.2.11 *Solar collectors and PV installation on the roof*

5.2.3 Roof (from outside to inside)

- Humus substrate (extensive planting);
- protective and drainage felt;
- water barrier;
- wood casing = 2.7 cm;
- air gap = 14.0 cm;
- roofing membrane;
- wood fibreboard = 4.0 cm;
- wood rafter/mineral wool = 32.0 cm;
- moisture and wind barrier;
- gypsum board = 1.5 cm;
- total (without green roof) = 54.2 cm; and
- U-value = 0.11 W/m^{2}K.

5.2.4 Exterior walls (from inside to outside)

- Gypsum board = 1.5 cm;
- battens with mineral wool = 6.0 cm;
- moisture and wind barrier;
- gypsum board = 1.5 cm;
- wooden straps/mineral wool = 24.0 cm;
- gypsum board = 1.25 cm;
- gypsum board = 1.25 cm;
- air gap = 2.4 cm;
- wood casing = 1.9 cm;
- total = 39.8 cm; and
- U-value = 0.12 W/m2K.

5.2.5 Terrace

- Wooden slats = 2.4 cm;
- protective layer = 4.0 cm;
- water barrier;
- wood rafter/mineral wool = 32.0 cm;
- moisture and wind barrier;

- timber/concrete structure = 12.0 cm;
- wooden block panels = 12.0 cm;
- total = 62.4 cm; and
- U-value = 0.13 W/m^{2}K.

5.2.6 Floor to cellar

- Parquet flooring = 1.5 cm;
- gypsum board = 2.5 cm;
- acoustical insulation = 2.0 cm;
- moisture and wind barrier;
- cork insulation = 26.0 cm;
- reinforced concrete = 18.0 cm;
- total = 50.0 cm; and
- U-value = 0.14 W/m^{2}K.

5.2.7 Ventilation

The supply air is preheated in polyethylene pipes buried in the ground. The pipes, with a diameter of 200 mm and a length of 4 m × 25 m, are buried at a depth of 1.8 m. The ground preheating prevents the heat exchanger from freezing during the winter.

The air is further tempered by heat recovered from the return air via a cross counter-flow heat exchanger with an efficiency of 80 per cent. The air is then transported to the apartments via shafts in the party walls. Each apartment has a separate supply air and return air trunk.

The supply air is further tempered to a maximum of 46°C by heater coils and supplied through the floor and the wall outlets. The return air is exhausted in the kitchen and bathrooms, and is led outdoors via the heat recovery system.

During the summer, the heat recovery system can be left out by using a bypass.

5.2.8 Heat production and distribution

The heating energy for the Wechsel apartment building is produced by a wood pellet heating system and by solar collectors.

The wood pellets heating power can be varied between 9 kW and 25 kW. The annual heat production from the wood pellets amounts to 25.5 kWh/m^{2}a. This comes up to 70 per cent of the entire heating energy demand of 36.5 kWh/m^{2}a. This is the sum of 14.5 kWh/m^{2}a for space heating and 22 kWh/m^{2}a for DHW heating.

The 18 solar collectors on the roof are arranged in two arrays and have a tilt angle of 45°. The total absorber area amounts to 40.5 m^2. The solar fraction is 30 per cent.

The solar collectors and wood pellet heating system both supply a combi-boiler, whereas the collectors have priority. The wood pellet heating system only turns on when the collectors cannot supply the demand.

The hot water in the boiler provides the apartments' DHW and is used to heat up the supply air to a maximum of 46°C through a water/air heat exchanger.

The heat is distributed by the fresh air supply. Radiators in the bathrooms provide additional comfort.

5.2.9 Electricity

The Wechsel apartment building uses 15.7 kWh/m^{2}a for household electricity and 3.1 kWh/m^{2}a for electricity for technical systems (pumps, lift and control system).

The 12 m^2 roof-mounted PV system is grid connected. It uses single crystal silicon solar cells. The total nominal output is 1.44 kWp. The eight series-connected modules are oriented directly to the south and have a tilt angle of 30°. During the first year, the installations yielded 1694 kWh. The PV electricity is used to dehumidify the unheated cellar.

5.3 Life-cycle analysis

5.3.1 Approach

Within the system boundaries, the production, renewal and disposal of all materials that have an influence on the total energy demand of the house were considered. The two underground parking areas were excluded from the system boundaries. The Swiss electricity mix was used for the electricity demand of the ventilation system and the pumps. In addition, in some results the electricity demand of the household appliances was included.

Source: Beda Bossard, BARBOS Büro für Baubiologie Bauökologie and Energie

Figure 5.3.1 *View from the north*

Table 5.3.1 shows some basic parameters for the Wechsel house. The data on the amount and type of materials used in the building were collected from construction plans, building documentation and technical reports.

Table 5.3.1 *Basic parameters for the Wechsel house*

Parameter	Description	Unit	Value
Building volume	Total according to SIA 116	m³	5209
Floor area	Net heated floor area	m²	998
Solar collector	40.5 m² flat collector, DHW and space heating	KWh/a	11,000
PV system	Mono-crystalline cell modules (12 m², 1.44 kWp)	KWh/a	1200
Space heat demand	Covered to 30 per cent through solar heat, 70 per cent with biomass	kWh/a	14,500
Heat for domestic hot water (DHW)	Covered to 30 per cent through solar heat, 70 per cent with biomass	kWh/a	22,000
Biomass demand	Pellets demand for space heating and DHW	kWh/a	26,500
Electricity, other	Electricity used for ventilation and pumps	kWh/a	3100

Note: Data refers to the design values of the entire multi-family house consisting of eight flats.

Source: Beda Bossard, BARBOS Büro für Baubiologie Bauökologie and Energie

Figure 5.3.2 *Balconies to the south*

5.3.2 Results

All results refer to the impact per m² net heated area and year (building life span: 80 years). For comparative purposes, a reference building is always shown. This two-storey row house without a cellar, made of brick walls with polystyrene insulation, consists of six units with 120 m² net carpet area and covers its heat demand of 65 kWh/m²a (DHW: 25 kWh/m²a) with non-condensing gas heating.

5.3.3 Life cycles of the building assessed with Eco-indicator 99

In Figure 5.3.4, the share of construction, renewal, disposal, transportation and operation on the total impact over the entire life cycle is shown. The analysis was carried out with the weighting method Eco-indicator 99 (hierarchist).

The most important conclusions to be derived from Figure 5.3.4 are as follows:

- The total impact over the whole life cycle for the Wechsel house is only 42 per cent (design value) to 45 per cent (measured value) of the reference building.
- The operation of the building (without household electricity) has a share of 13 per cent (design value) to 19 per cent (measured value) of the total impact of the building.
- Nearly half of the total impact is caused by the floors, cellar and foundation, which consist, to a large extent, of cement-based materials (such as concrete).

Source: Beda Bossard, BARBOS Büro für Baubiologie Bauökologie and Energie

Figure 5.3.3 *Kitchen*

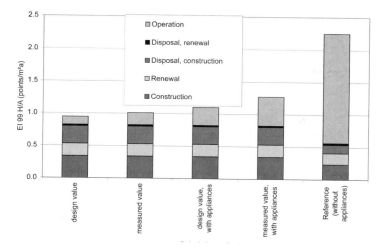

Source: Eco-indicator 99 H/A, www.esu-services.ch

Figure 5.3.4 *Life-cycle phases, Eco-indicator 99 H/A*

- The influence of the electricity used for household appliances is relatively low, with 14 per cent to 20 per cent of the total impact. The reason for this is the high share of renewable energy in the Swiss electricity mix (40 per cent hydropower) and the low energy demand for the household appliances (12.6 kWh/m^2a design value; 21.4 kWh/m^2a measured value).

5.3.4 Building components assessed with Eco-indicator 99

Figure 5.3.5 shows the impact of the different material groups over the entire life cycle, analysed with the Eco-indicator 99 method (hierarchist).

The most important factors regarding the Wechsel building are as follows (see Figure 5.3.4):

- The impact of the insulating materials makes up only 7 per cent of the total impact of the building. Over 50 per cent of this impact results from the floor insulation, which is made of cork.
- The massive building materials amount to 32 per cent of the total impact of the building. This impact is caused primarily by the cellar, the foundation and the cement cover of the floors.
- The impact of the heating and ventilation system makes up only 6 per cent of the total impact of the building (construction and renewal, excluding solar and PV systems).

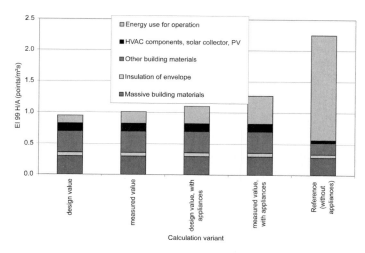

Source: Eco-indicator 99 H/A, www.esu-services.ch

Figure 5.3.5 *Building components, Eco-indicator 99 H/A*

- The thermal solar collector and the PV system comprise approximately 7 per cent of the total impact of the building (construction and renewal, including pipes, heat exchanger and storage tank).

The Wechsel apartment building shows similar results to the Sunny Woods apartment building in Zurich (see Chapter 4), with the difference of a lower impact for the heating, ventilating and air conditioning (HVAC) components due to the small PV system used here.

5.3.5 Influence of the building components: Assessment with cumulative energy demand (CED)

When assessing the CED, substantial differences in the non-renewable energy are shown (see Figure 5.3.6).

The CED of non-renewable energy over the whole life cycle of the Wechsel apartment building comprises 27 per cent (design value) to 53 per cent (measured value) of the CED of the reference building. Due to the use of renewable energy for space heating and DHW, the share of the use of non-renewable energy for the building operation is, with 2 per cent to 3 per cent of the total impact of the building, very small. A larger impact, as shown in the assessment with Eco-indicator 99, is the influence of electricity use for household appliances. Due to the low efficiency of nuclear power generation, household electricity has a share of 40 per cent to 50 per cent of the total impact of the building.

Similar results as for Eco-indicator 99 show the CED share of the different building components. Here the insulation has a share of 9 per cent and the massive building materials 23 per cent of the total impact. Within the HVAC components, the solar system and the PV system amount to 6 per cent and the other HVAC components to 5 per cent of the total non-renewable CED of the building.

In addition to the non-renewable energy demand, the following renewable energy is used over the whole life cycle for the building without household electricity (design values):

- hydropower for electricity: 5.5 kWh/m²a (over 50 per cent of the electricity is used for operating the building); and
- biomass (mainly wood): 50 kWh/m²a (58 per cent, or 28.9 kWh/m²a, of the wood is used within the pellet boiler).

The main part of the energy in biomass within the construction of the building is used as cork for insulation and as wood used within the floor covering.

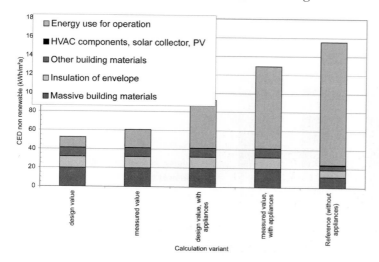

Source: Alex Primas, Basler and Hofmann Ingenieure und Planer, Zürich

Figure 5.3.6 *Building components – cumulative energy demand (non-renewable)*

5.3.6 Life-cycle analysis conclusions

Source: P. Wälchli, ETH Student, Zürich

Figure 5.3.7 *Access from the north*

The impacts of the construction, renewal and disposal of the Wechsel Passivhaus in Stans, compared to a reference house, show very good results with regard to the efficient use of non-renewable resources. As for the Wechsel building itself, the impact of massive building elements, such as the floors, the cellar and the foundations, is very important. The insulation materials have only a very small influence on the total impact of the building construction, but a high impact on the operational energy demand of the building.

The share of the operating energy on the total impact of the building is small due to the energy concept of the building, which is based on renewable energy. The difference between the measured values and the design values is mainly caused by the use of too optimistic design values (for example, the electricity requirements for the ventilation).

The electricity used for household appliances shows a large and important difference between the design value and the measured value. The main reason for this difference is the poor efficiency of the lighting systems used by the inhabitants. This result shows that in high efficiency buildings, the resourceful use of household electricity is significant. If design values were reached, the total impact

Source: P. Wälchli, ETH Student, Zürich

Figure 5.3.8 *Housing estate: View from the south*

of the building would be approximately 25 per cent lower. This leads to the conclusion that efficient household appliances (such as lighting, refrigerators, etc) are very important in a low energy house.

The most significant potential for optimization besides the electricity for the household appliances lies within the construction of the floors. A construction with smaller quantities of concrete and cement would bring an ecological improvement. On the other hand, acoustic problems may arise with a lighter floor construction, which must be avoided in a multi-family house.

5.4 Economy

The initiative for the project came from four families working together. The four remaining apartments were sold during the planning phase. Due to the attractive project and the favoured rural living area of Stans, selling the apartments was very easy.

The investment costs for the building (standard finishing) amounted to €2.58 million. The additional costs in the Wechsel project compared to a conventionally built house amounted to an extra 14.5 per cent.

Table 5.4.1 *Account classification: All costs, including planning honorarium and 7.6 per cent value-added tax*

Relative building costs	€/m³	€/m²	Total €
Building costs (standard finishings)	395	1645	2,058,000
Total investment costs (including building land)			3,100,000
Costs for technical systems			
PV installation			12,300
Annual operating costs			
Heating and general maintenance for the entire apartment building	Wood pellets heating system		1971
	Ventilation system		3005
	total		4976

Note: The project was supported by the Swiss Federal Office of Energy with a contribution of €61,300. An additional €20,400 was provided by the Swiss government for a post-occupancy evaluation of the project.

5.5 Lessons

Planning the heating and ventilation system at an early stage was necessary in order to optimize the arrangement of the pipes. On the one hand, room air conditioning could be improved; on the other hand, costs were reduced. Prefabricated wooden elements for the interior walls were advantageous regarding the installation of the piping.

Concerning indoor temperatures in winter, all apartments reached impressive values except for one apartment at the top floor where the ventilation system did not have enough power to heat the apartment. As a result, an electric arc furnace was used. Since the heating energy demand is very low and the use of the furnace only short term, this solution is acceptable. A possible solution to avoid such problems could be a hydraulic floor heating system, which means separating the heating and ventilation systems. One of the advantages would be the lower operating temperature of the floor heating system compared to the heater coils that heat up the ventilation air.

Visually, the Wechsel Passivhaus apartment building hardly differs from the other apartments of the housing estate, which are built to a conventional standard. Energy measures had a significant influence on the entire planning of the building; but optimized living comfort, as well as considera-

Source: P. Wälchli, ETH Student, Zürich

Figure 5.5.1 *Entrance ground floor*

tion of the occupants' preferences, were also important. The radiators in the bathrooms, for example, proved to be of value and provided additional comfort.

To conclude, the support of the occupants is crucial in the functioning of a Passivhaus building.

Acknowledgements

We thank the architect and energy planner for providing information, plans and photos of this project.

References

Betschart, W. and Rieder, U. (eds) (2000) 'Projektvorstellung: Überbauung Passiv-Acht-Familienhaus, Wechsel, 6370 Stans', in W. Betschart and U. Rieder (eds) *Fachtagung Energieeffizienz dank Passivhaus, Luzern, January 2001*, HTA Luzern, Luzern, pp95–115
Hoffmann, C. (2003) 'Mehrfamilienhaus in Stans', in C. Hoffmann et al (eds) *Wohnbauten mit geringem Energieverbrauch. 12 Gebäude: Planung, Umsetzung, Realität*, C.F. Müller Verlag, Heidelberg, pp171–182
Humm, O. (2002) 'Ein Passivhaus nach Schweizer Art', *Gebäudetechnik*, vol 1, pp14–19

6

Vienna Utendorfgasse Passivhaus Apartment Building

Helmut Schoeberl

6.1 Project description

Source: Schoeberl and Poell OEG, Vienna, www.schoeberlpoell.at

Figure 6.1.1 *The Vienna Utendorfgasse Passivhaus Apartment Building*

6.1.1 Portrait and context

During the planning and construction of the Utendorfgasse Passivhaus apartment building in Vienna, many fundamental questions regarding the planning of social housing according to the Passivhaus standard were addressed. The challenge was to meet this standard while keeping costs within the limited budget allowed for social housing. Schöberl und Pöll OEG succeeded in completing the first such project to this very high standard.

Key aspects of the project are as follows:

- high cost efficiency: extra costs for the Passivhaus standard; $\leq €75/m^2$ effective living area;
- low energy consumption – Passivhaus standard: space heating energy demand $\leq 15 \text{ kWh/m}^2\text{a}$; heat load $\leq 10 \text{ W/m}^2$; air tightness n50 ≤ 0.6 ach; primary energy demand $\leq 120 \text{ kWh/m}^2\text{a}$; and
- high comfort standards: controlled ventilation, acoustics, hygiene and user acceptance.

6.1.2 Architectural concept

The building site, Utendorfgasse 7 in Vienna, is 2600 m². An existing building is on the west side. Two of the three new buildings are attached to the existing fire walls of this neighbouring building. Each building, approximately 19 m long and 15 m deep, has a ground floor, three upper floors and an attic. The floors are reached via stair towers on the north side of each housing block. The footprint of the buildings is approximately 850 m², providing a living area of approximately 3000 m². Each living unit is approximately 75 m² in extent. All dwellings have south-facing windows, loggias, balconies or terraces. The 39 obligatory parking spaces are in an underground garage.

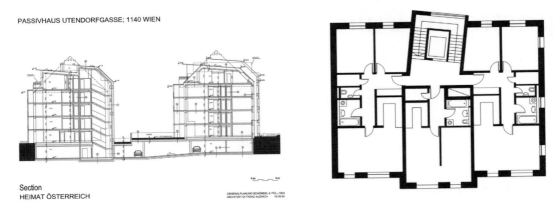

PASSIVHAUS UTENDORFGASSE; 1140 WIEN

Section
HEIMAT ÖSTERREICH

Source: Franz Kuzmich, Vienna

Figure 6.1.2 *Sketch of the section* (left) *and standard floor* (right) *of one of the three buildings*

6.1.3 Construction

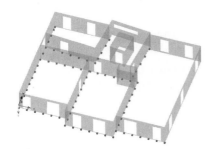

The thermal uncoupling of the bearing walls from the foundation was solved with a special thermal break consisting of a band of aerated concrete. This is then faced with brick masonry. The conventional solution of using a high bearing strength insulation, such as 'Purenit' was too expensive.

Source: Werkraum ZT OEG, Vienna, www.werkraumwien.at

Figure 6.1.3 *Static system of the thermal decoupling*

6.2 Energy

6.2.1 Passivhaus concept

Due to the high thermal quality of the building envelope, the heat load is only 9.4 W/m². The mean calculated space heating energy demand is 14.7 kWh/m²a, assuming a room temperature of 20°C.

The primary energy characteristic value for DHW, heating, ventilation and household electricity falls below the 120 kWh/m²a maximum of the Passivhaus standard. This is achieved by using energy efficient household appliances. The calculated primary energy demand for DHW, heating and ventilation is 46 kWh/m²a.

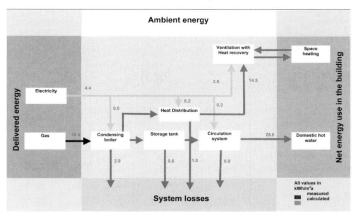

Source: Schoeberl and Poell OEG, Vienna, www.schoeberlpoell.at, and AEU GmbH

Figure 6.2.1 *Energy supply*

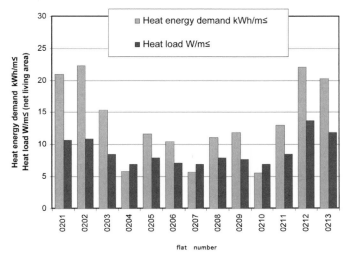

Source: TU-Vienna Zentrum für Bauphysik und Bauakustik, Vienna, www.bph.tuwien.ac.at

Figure 6.2.2 *Distribution of the heat load and the heat requirement of the units in Building 2*

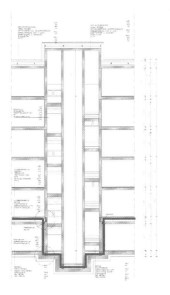

Source: Schoeberl and Poell OEG, Vienna, www.schoeberlpoell.at, and Franz Kuzmich, Vienna

Figure 6.2.3 *Insulation boundary for stair towers in section* (left) *and plan* (right)

6.2.2 Building envelope

A wall construction with 27 cm insulation was selected.

6.2.3 Exterior wall

- Thermal insulation with expanded polystyrene (EPS-F with ≤ 0.035 W/m²K or ≤ 0.040 W/m²K) = 27.0 cm;
- reinforced concrete = 18.0 cm;
- total = 45.0 cm; and
- U-value: = 0.125 or 0.143 W/m²K.

6.2.4 Roof

- Domitech roof (www.domico.at);
- mineral fibre insulation = 44.0 cm;
- vapour barrier = 0.4 cm;
- reinforced concrete = 20.0 cm;
- total = 64.4 cm; and
- U-value = 0.096 W/m²K.

6.2.5 Ceiling

- Reinforced concrete = 20.0 cm;
- adjustment ballast = 3.0 cm;
- subsonic noise insulation = 3.0 cm;
- separation situation = 0.02 cm;
- floating floor screed = 5.0 cm;
- floor covering = 1.5 cm;
- total = 32.5 cm; and
- U-value: 0.847 W/m²K.

6.2.6 Lowest floor ceiling

- Reinforced concrete = 30.0 cm;
- balance pouring = 3.0 cm;
- thermal insulation from expanded polystyrene (EPS) = 35.0 cm;
- foot fall sound insulation = 4.0 cm;
- vapour barrier = 0.2 cm;
- screed = 5.0 cm;
- floor covering = 1.5 cm;
- total = 78.7 cm; and
- U-value: 0.095 W/m²K.

The stair tower is included in the insulated building envelope and runs down to the underground parking. This has the following advantages:

- The temperature in the stair tower is approximately 17°C in January, instead of 4°C were it uninsulated.
- The continuity of the exterior envelope insulation is not interrupted and there are no subsequent thermal bridges.
- Complex connections between the dwellings and the staircase are avoided.
- The dwellings' entrance doors need not be highly insulating and expensive.

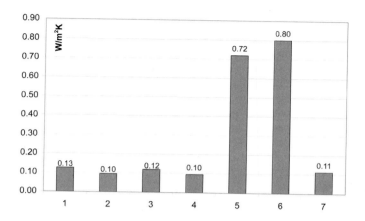

Notes: U-values (W/m²K):
1: exterior walls;
2: roof;
3: terrace;
4: floor to cellar;
5: window (glass);
6: window (including frame), mean value;
7: average U-value building envelope.
Source: Schoeberl and Poell OEG, Vienna,
www.schoeberlpoell.at, and AEU GmbH

Figure 6.2.4 *U-values*

The windows of the Utendorfgasse apartment building are of good quality:

- $U_{(overall)}$ = 0.92;
- $U_{(frame)}$ = 0.96;
- $U_{(glass)}$ = 0.81; and
- g-value = 0.48.

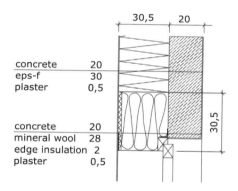

Source: Schoeberl and Poell OEG, Vienna,
www.schoeberlpoell.at, and Franz Kuzmich,
Vienna

Figure 6.2.5 *Fire protection of window from façade fire propagation*

6.2.7 Fire protection insulation perimeter

Because of the thick insulation used on the façade, special fire protection measures around the windows were necessary. To achieve this, a special detail was developed using mineral wool batts with an EPS cover.

6.2.8 Shading

The ground, first, second and third floors are sufficiently shaded by the loggias to protect them from solar overheating. In the top floor apartments, outside and inside sun shading is provided. Skylights have both internal and external shading.

6.2.9 Ventilation system

The ventilation system consists of:

- a roof-level central plant at each stair tower, with heat recovery, air filtering, a circulation fan and electrical preheating register as a freeze protection measure; and
- decentralized supply air heating for each housing unit, jet nozzles and speed-adjusted ventilators with four-step regulation by the occupants.

6.2.10 Heat production and heat distribution

A central heat production plant serves the whole complex of buildings with heat for space and water heating. It consists of a gas-fired boiler (80 kW) with a custom hot water tank. A circular pipe line supplies hot water to each apartment air register for space heating and a separate circuit provides DHW. The hot water is circulated by a pump (<200 W) controlled by a timer. The circulation runs from 4.00 am to 10.00 pm, but is freely adjustable to adapt to the life style of the occupants.

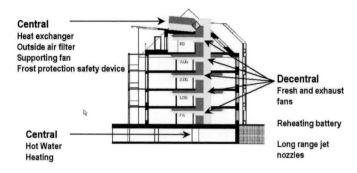

Central
Heat exchanger
Outside air filter
Supporting fan
Frost protection safety device

Decentral
Fresh and exhaust fans

Reheating battery

Central
Hot Water
Heating

Long range jet nozzles

Source: Schoeberl and Poell OEG, Vienna, www.schoeberlpoell.at

Figure 6.2.6 *Technical concept*

6.3 Economy

6.3.1 Extra costs for the Passivhaus standard

Achieving the Passivhaus standard versus merely meeting the low energy standards of Vienna for social housing cost, approximately, an additional €73/m² of living area. This amounts to about 7 per cent in extra costs above the budget for social housing. The main sources of this higher cost were the improved quality of the building envelope and the high-efficiency ventilation with heat recovery. Figure 6.3.1 shows the savings and additional costs.

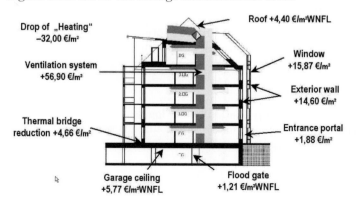

Drop of „Heating"
−32,00 €/m²

Ventilation system
+56,90 €/m²

Thermal bridge
reduction +4,66 €/m²

Roof +4,40 €/m²WNFL

Window
+15,87 €/m²

Exterior wall
+14,60 €/m²

Entrance portal
+1,88 €/m²

Garage ceiling
+5,77 €/m²WNFL

Flood gate
+1,21 €/m²WNFL

Source: Schoeberl and Poell OEG, Vienna, www.schoeberlpoell.at

Figure 6.3.1 *Constructional extra costs for the Passivhaus standard in the social housing per square metre of living area, excluding sales tax (2003)*

6.3.2 Passivhaus operational costs

Electricity accounts for 60 per cent of the operating cost. The second largest cost is the production of hot water. Space heating accounts for only about 15 per cent of the total operating costs.

References

Schöberl, H., Bednar, T. et al (2004a) *Anwendung der Passivhaustechnologie im sozialen Wohnbau (Applying Passive Technologies in Social Housing)*, Final report of the research and demonstration project, Federal Ministry for Transport, Innovation and Technology, Federal Ministry for Economic Affairs and Labour, Vienna

Schöberl, H., Hutter, S., Bednar, T., Jachan, C., Deseyve, C., Steininger, C., Sammer, G., Kuzmich, F., Münch, M. and Bauer, P. (2004b) *Anwendung der Passivhaustechnologie im sozialen Wohnbau (Applying Passive Technologies in Social Housing)*, vol 68, Fraunhofer IRB Verlag, Bauforschung für die Praxis, Stuttgart

Schöberl, H., Bednar, T. et al (2004c) *Applying Passive Technologies in Social Housing*, Summary, www.schoeberlpoell.at, Vienna

7

Plus Energy House, Thening, Austria

Daniela Enz

7.1 Project description

The Plus Energy House of the Kroiss family in Austria is an ecological passive house. It is located in Thening, about 15 km west of Linz. It was constructed using prefabricated timber elements. The architect, Andreas Karlsreiter, was able to surpass the ambition of the Kroiss family to erect a net-zero energy house: the house produces more primary energy than it consumes.

Source: UWE Kroiss Energiesysteme, Kirchberg-Thening, www.energiesysteme.at

Figure 7.1.1 *Plus Energy House, Thening, Austria: View south*

7.1.1 Architectural concept

The building is compact and oriented to the south. The northern façade has only one small window. A flexible interior was important and the solution was an ingenuously shaped ground floor plan which opens to the garden. More private areas are situated on the first floor.

Behind horizontal board siding made of spruce are high quality insulation, DHW panels, cellulose insulation and oriented strand board (OSB) panels.

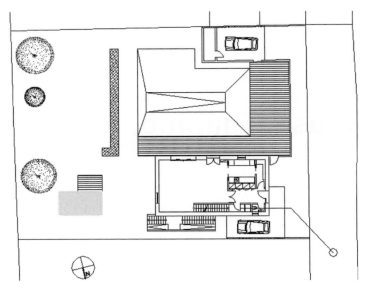

Figure 7.1.2 *Site plan*

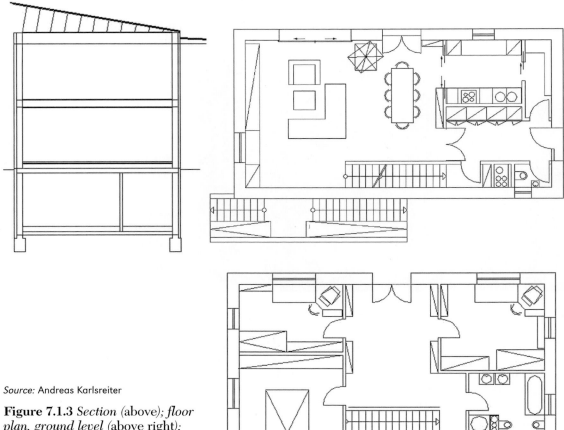

Figure 7.1.3 *Section* (above)*; floor plan, ground level* (above right)*; floor plan, first floor* (right)

7.2 Energy

7.2.1 Energy concept

The Passivhaus standard and a sustainable ecological design were achieved with the following energy concepts:

- timber construction with a high degree of insulation;
- 17 m² façade collector;
- ventilation system with 85 per cent heat recovery for heating and cooling;
- 6000 litre filter cistern for rainwater storage; and
- 10350 Wp grid connected photovoltaic system on the roof.

As a result of the high level of insulation and heat recovery, the normal requirement of having a flue for emergency heating was waived, resulting in significant cost savings.

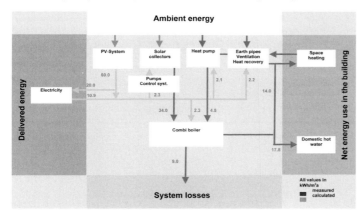

Source: UWE Kroiss Energiesysteme, Kirchberg-Thening, www.energiesysteme.at

Figure 7.2.1 *Energy supply concept*

The roof is sloped 10° to the south, allowing the photovoltaic (PV) panels to be architecturally integrated. The 86 m² PV modules were made by Solarfabrik using a carbon dioxide (CO_2) neutral production process. The one third more electricity produced than consumed is fed into the utility grid.

7.2.2 Data

- Living area = 150 m²;
- heated gross volume = 668 m²;
- area of envelope = 481 m²; and
- gross floor area = 206 m².

The constructions of the single components are as follows.

Cellar

- Floor covering tiles = 1.0 cm;
- Screed = 6.0 cm;
- PAE screen;
- 45/42 TSDP;
- polystyrenel = 10.0 cm;
- concrete = 10.0 cm;

- gravel = 30.0 cm;
- total = 57.0 cm; and
- U-value = 0.11 W/m²K.

Exterior walls

- Plaster fibre board (Fermacell) = 1.5 cm;
- installation layer with flax insulation = 6.0 cm;
- ecological vapour barrier;
- OSB panel = 1.5 cm;
- TJI beam/Isocell cellulose = 30.0 cm;
- DWD panel = 1.6 cm;
- total = 40.6 cm; and
- U-value: 0.11 W/m²K.

Ceiling

- Derived timber panel = 2.2 cm;
- gluelam = 32.0 cm;
- mineral fibre insulation = 10.0 cm;
- PAE screen as vapour barrier;
- timber board clamping = 2.4 cm;
- plaster board = 1.5 cm;
- total = 48.1 cm; and
- U-value: 0.11 W/m²K.

Roof

- Rubber screen;
- Rheinzink sheet metal;
- screen for condensation down spout;
- timber board clamping;
- ventilation area;
- screen against humidity = 2.4 cm;
- insulation element with closed pores screen = 11.0 cm;
- derived timber panel = 1.6 cm;

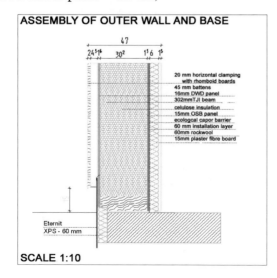

Source: Berchtold Holzbau GmbH, Wolfurt, www.berchtoldholzbau.com

Figure 7.2.2 *Exterior wall construction and foundation detail*

- gluelam, mineral fibre insulation = 10.0 cm;
- PAE screen as vapour barrier;
- timber board clamping = 2.4 cm;
- GKF = 1.5 cm;
- total = 28.9 cm; and
- U-value: 0.11 W/m²K.

Windows

The windows are Sigg Passivhaus windows with triple glazing.

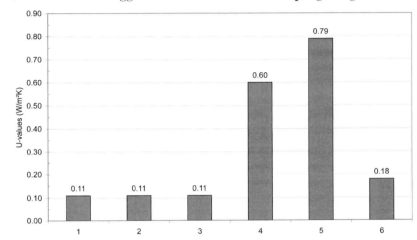

Notes: U-values (W/m²K):
1: exterior walls;
2: roof;
3: floor to cellar;
4: window (glass);
5: window (including frame), mean value;
6: average U-value building envelope.
Source: UWE Kroiss Energiesysteme, Kirchberg-Thening, www.energiesysteme.at

Figure 7.2.3 *U-values*

Building performance

- Total heating demand = 2800 kWh;
- heating demand per floor area = 14 kWh/m²a;
- heating load = 3.3 kW;
- area-related heating load = 16.2 W/m²; and
- envelope air tightness = 0.9 ach.

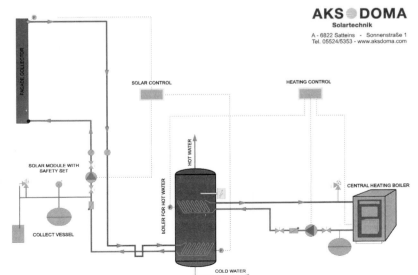

Source: AKS Doma Solar, www.aksdoma.com

Figure 7.2.4 *Solar collectors for warm water supply*

Source: AKS Doma Solar, www.aksdoma.com

Figure 7.2.5 *Façade solar collector absorber*

Source: UWE Kroiss Energiesysteme, Kirchberg-Thening, www.energiesysteme.at

Figure 7.2.6 *Mounting of the photovoltaic modules*

Source: UWE Kroiss Energiesysteme, Kirchberg-Thening, www.energiesysteme.at

Figure 7.2.7 *Living room*

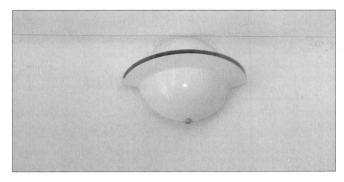

Source: UWE Kroiss Energiesysteme, Kirchberg-Thening, www.energiesysteme.at

Figure 7.2.8 *Room air supply ventilation jet*

Source: UWE Kroiss Energiesysteme, Kirchberg-Thening, www.energiesysteme.at

Figure 7.2.9 *Ventilation ambient air inlet*

Source: UWE Kroiss Energiesysteme, Kirchberg-Thening, www.energiesysteme.at

Figure 7.2.10 *Ground pipes*

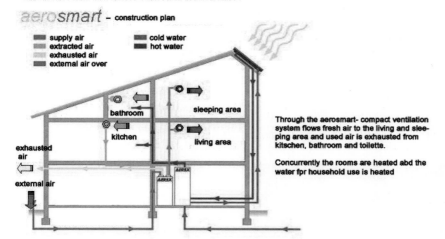

drexel und weiss energieeffiziente haustechniksysteme gmbh.

aerosmart – construction plan

- supply air
- extracted air
- exhausted air
- external air over
- cold water
- hot water

bathroom

sleeping area

kitchen

living area

exhausted air

external air

Through the aerosmart- compact ventilation system flows fresh air to the living and sleeping area and used air is exhausted from kitschen, bathroom and toilette.

Concurrently the rooms are heated abd the water fpr household use is heated

Source: UWE Kroiss Energiesysteme, Kirchberg-Thening, www.energiesysteme.at

Figure 7.2.11
Scheme of domestic engineering

The ventilation system serving the two-storey building has 85 per cent heat recovery. Through ground heat-exchanger pipes, 12°C warm air enters the system, is cleaned through two filters and is delivered to the living rooms at 300 mm/sec. The air is exhausted from the kitchen, bathroom and toilet. The air-to-air heat exchanger raises the incoming air temperature at least 4 K. The electric heat pump supplies the remaining heat needed to ensure that air delivered to the living spaces is between 16°C and 20°C at a rate of one air change per hour. In summer, the ground-cooled ventilation air helps to keep the house comfortable. Energy saving lamps of 460 W are used in the house.

7.3 Economy

7.3.1 Building costs

Table 7.3.1 *Building costs*

Relative building costs (turnkey ready, including bath, kitchen, lighting, carport and garage, excluding PV system)	(€/m³)	(€/m²)	Total €
Costs	403	1795	269,150
Costs of technical components			Euros
PV system			87,200
Electrical installation			5100
Heating/ventilation			18,200
Solar system			5830
Rainwater supply			3640

Note: The purchase of the photovoltaic system was assisted by grants from Upper Austria.

7.3.2 Innovative components

- Public support: OÖ Energiesparverband (regional energy agency; www.energiesparverband.at);
- architect: Andreas Karlsreiter (www.energiesysteme.at/prod02htm);
- timber house: Berchtold Holzbau (www.berchtoldholzbau.com);
- windows: Tischlerei Sigg (www.sigg.at);
- ventilation: Drexel und Weiß (www.drexel-weiss.at);

- calculation: E-plus (www.e-plus.at);
- photovoltaic: Stromaufwärts (www.stromaufwaerts.at);
- Solar system: AKS Doma Solar (www.aksdoma.com);
- Rainwater: GEP Umwelttechnik (www.gep-umwelttechnik.com); and
- Energy concept: Uwe Kroiss Energiesysteme (www.energiesysteme.at).

7.3.3 Awards

The Kroiss family received the Upper Austrian Award for Environment and Nature (*Oberösterreichischen Landespreis für Umwelt und Natur*) 2001 and the Austrian Solar Award (*Österreichischen Solarpreis*) 2002. The environmental academy of Upper Austria (Umweltakademie des Landes Oberösterreich) accepted the Kroiss family in the Pioneer of Climate (*Klimapionier*) programme.

Acknowledgements

We thank the owner, architect and energy planners for providing information, plans and photos of this project.

Part II

TECHNOLOGIES

8

Introduction

S. Robert Hastings

The success of the exemplary buildings presented in the previous section is the result of good design, but also of the capabilities of high-performance systems and components selected to work effectively together as a whole building/system complex. This section examines the systems which together make a high-performance housing project possible.

It begins with the building envelope, since providing a highly insulating and air-tight shell for the building is the first priority. When the envelope is very air tight, a ventilation system is essential to assure good air quality and to avoid excessive humidity problems and potential mould growth in winter. The next logical step is to incorporate a heat recovery system between the exhaust and supply air flows. In a highly insulated building, heating ventilation air requires a proportionally very large amount of energy. Modern heat recovery systems can recover 80 per cent or more of the heat otherwise lost in the exhaust air, minimizing this energy demand.

Once the heat demand is drastically reduced, the next challenge is to produce and deliver the heat efficiently, economically and with maximum comfort. The ventilation system can deliver heat as well as fresh air to each room. This is a standard solution in American homes, but new territory in many other countries. Housing with a very small heating demand is an ideal condition for air heating. Because so little heating power is needed, the volume of air needed for hygiene reasons is sufficient to deliver the needed heat at temperatures below 55°C. This minimizes the noise of the air flow and the smell of burned dust which occurs at higher temperatures. Last, but hardly least, the double use of the ventilation system and elimination of the need for another system saves construction and operating costs.

The next logical issue is the origin of the heat. The most ecological source is the sun. Solar water and air collector systems are mature, reliable solutions. Both offer the advantage of being able to supply heat for space heating and domestic water heating. The latter represents a large fraction of the total energy demand of very low energy housing. But solar thermal systems must be considered 'back-up systems'; a primary system is still needed. Indirect solar use in the form of biomass (primarily wood or wood pellets) is a good primary supply system. Another indirect source is an earth-to-air heat exchanger which in winter draws on the solar energy naturally accumulated in the ground over the summer. District heating where the heat is produced from burning refuse can also be termed a renewable energy source, given the inevitability of humans producing refuse. Other heat production systems are also examined, including less ecological or sustainable solutions, to allow a more comprehensive comparison for selecting a system. Many of the heat production systems could be operated more efficiently if there were an effective means to store heat, be it for a few days or a season. Two types of heat storage are reviewed, sensible and latent heat storage.

Given its very high primary energy values, electricity is a key topic. Accordingly, adding photo-voltaic electric generation can dramatically reduce the total primary energy balance of such housing. Similarly, selecting appliances with low energy consumption is only sensible. A saved kWh of electricity is magnified by the primary energy factor, in this book 2.35 for the non-renewable part of electricity generation. Hence, a high efficiency refrigerator, dish washer, washing machine and range; as well as efficient fans, pumps and controllers for the technical systems of the house result in a major reduction in the total primary energy balance.

This section ends with a technology looking to the future but available today, building information systems. Such systems can not only offer optimized control and performance of the technical systems of a house, but also convenience, comfort and security for the occupants.

Indeed, very low energy housing is building looking to the future. Not only does it help slow the rate of depletion of non-renewable resources, it offers better comfort. The key, as mentioned in the opening, is to select highly efficient systems which work well together and as part of a whole, sustainable building concept.

9

Building Envelope

9.1 Opaque building envelope

Hans Erhorn and Johann Reiss

9.1.1 Concept

Typically, 50 per cent to 75 per cent of the heat losses of conventional buildings results from transmission losses through the building envelope. These losses can be drastically reduced – for example, in Germany a 50 per cent reduction has been achieved since 1970.

This reduction has been halved again by high-performance houses. The transmission losses of a typical house (with 1.5 to 2.0 m² of building envelope per m² heated floor area) can be expected to be less than 0.3 W/K per m² floor area. Air leakage and natural ventilation losses can amount to 0.4 W/m²K. These can be reduced to as low as 0.1 W/m²K by making the envelope air tight and adding an energy efficient ventilation system. The resulting total losses due to transmission and ventilation can then be as low as 0.3 and 0.5 W/K per m² of heated floor area, as can be seen in Figure 9.1.1.

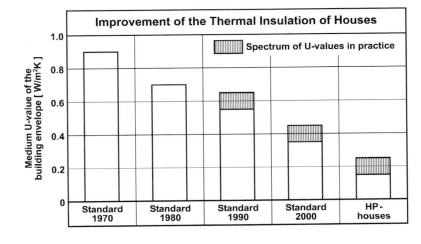

Source: Fraunhofer-Institut Bauphysik

Figure 9.1.1 *Development of the mean U-values of building envelopes (including windows) of buildings in Germany over the last 35 years*

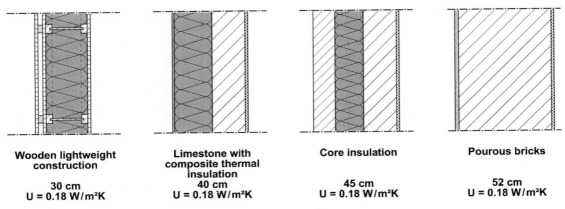

Source: Fraunhofer Institut für Bauphysik, Stuttgart, www.ibp.fraunhofer.de

Figure 9.1.2 *Comparison of different wall construction types achieving the same U-value by means of varying materials and dimensions: (a) wooden lightweight construction (30 cm; U = 0.18 W/m²K); (b) limestone with composite thermal insulation (40 cm; U = 0.18 W/m²K); (c) core insulation (45 cm; U = 0.18 W/m²K); porous bricks (52 cm; U = 0.18 W/m²K)*

Also important is how much heating power is needed. The heating peak load of such high-performance houses range from 6 W/m² in mild climates (design temperature 0°C) to 15 W/m² in cold climates (design temperature –30°C). This amounts to only one third to one fourth of the heating power required by conventional new housing.

Numerous building envelope constructions achieve this impressive performance.

Roofs radiate house heat to the cold winter sky, which can be up to 50 K colder than the ambient temperature. In the summer, they receive the strongest solar heating due to the high sun angles. This is why roofs are usually the most highly insulated envelope component.

External walls

Different wall constructions can achieve the same insulation value, but result in greatly varying thicknesses. Figure 9.1.2 shows constructions ranging from 33 cm to 52 cm.

Figure 9.1.3 shows an innovative, advanced development of the wooden lightweight construction (Kluttig et al, 1997). I-studs or I-joists (TJI) are used to reduce the wood ratio of the construction to

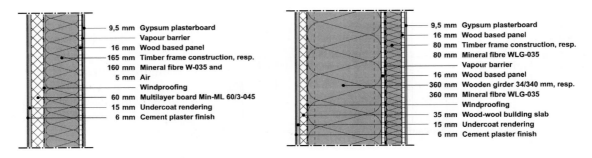

Source: Kluttig et al (1997)

Figure 9.1.3 *Improved lightweight constructions: (a) energy-optimized construction of the external wall of a low energy house; (b) vertical section through the external wall of a high-performance house*

improve the U-value still further. U-values of less than 0.1 W/m²K can be realized with such constructions.

Cellar ceilings/slabs

Over the year, the temperature difference between unheated cellars or the ground and heated space is only about 30 per cent to 80 per cent of the difference to the ambient air. This heat loss source can, however, reduce the effectiveness of the insulation of other parts of the building envelope with regard to heating energy demand.

A double-layered arrangement of the insulation has turned out to be an effective solution. The floor's acoustic insulation can be increased. Under-floor suspended plumbing and ducts can be insulated in this manner. A second insulation layer below the basement ceiling or slab on grade reduces the main transmission losses and thermal bridges from connecting walls or the foundation. Because of these thermal bridges, the U-values of the cellar or slab should not exceed 0.2 W/m²K.

The complete building envelope

Figure 9.1.4 presents the floor area-related heat loss of the different external building parts of a typical high-performance house. The losses are covered by the gains represented in the first column. Windows and ventilation cause more than 60 per cent of the losses (though windows also deliver passive solar gains). Once the opaque surfaces are well insulated, they lose little heat by comparison.

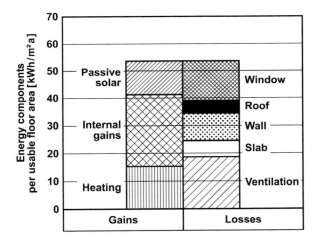

Source: Fraunhofer Institut für Bauphysik, Stuttgart, www.ibp.fraunhofer.de

Figure 9.1.4 *Presentation of the heat losses of different building parts of a high-performance house related to the floor area in moderate climates (Germany)*

Investment costs for the different parts of the building envelope relative to insulation qualities are presented in Figure 9.1.5 (Erhorn et al, 2000). Achieving good insulation of the opaque envelope costs much less than is the case, for example, with windows. Generally, the roof has the lowest investment costs, followed by the cellar ceiling and the external wall. The rate of increase in costs relative to the improved insulation levels is very moderate. Increasing the insulation levels from conventional to high-performance may cost only €30 to €50/m². Furthermore, some of these added costs can be offset because the heating plant and distribution system can be smaller.

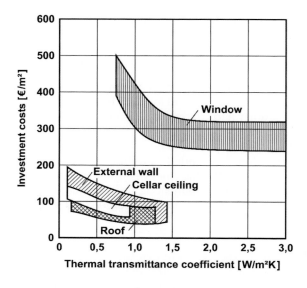

Source: Fraunhofer Institut für Bauphysik, Stuttgart, www.ibp.fraunhofer.de

Figure 9.1.5 *Comparison of investment costs and thermal insulation quality of the different parts of the building envelope in Germany (cost basis 2002)*

Solution development into detail is important

The benefit of increased insulation can be reduced by as much as 25 per cent by thermal bridges. In the case of a 150 m² single family house, the increase in heating energy demand can be up to 2000 kWh/a for a moderate climate.

Avoiding thermal bridges may save more energy at less cost than investments in a more expensive heating plant, added insulation or a solar system!

9.1.2 Variations of material

Thermal insulation materials insulate because they entrap still air. Indeed, the thermal conductivity of the insulation materials is close to that of a non-ventilated air space ($\lambda = 0.024$ W/mK). Numerous insulation materials are available: mineral wool and fibreglass insulation are mineral materials; bulk insulation is mostly of volcanic origin. Polystyrene and polyurethane are synthetic materials produced by the chemical industry. Natural insulation materials include cork, wood, hemp fibres, cellulose, cotton and sheep wool. An overview of the properties and characteristics of different insulation materials is provided in Table 9.1.1 (Energiesparen im Altbau, 2000).

The thermal conductivity of an insulating material can be reduced in various ways. For example, an inert gas can be entrapped in the cellular structure of insulation. Another approach is to embed an infrared efficient substance, such as graphite, to reduce the radiation exchange across voids in the material structure. Extremely effective is the evacuation of the cell voids of a material. The conductivity of high-performance insulation materials can thus be reduced to less than 0.01 W/mK.

9.1.3 Example insulation systems

Graphite-embedded EPS (Neopor)

The thermal conductivity of insulation material is influenced by the skeleton structure of the foam; the lighter the foam, the higher the thermal conductivity (because of the higher air–gap ratio). Embedding graphite in expanded polystyrene (EPS) achieves a comparable insulation effect at a very low density. The radiant heat transfer across the cell pores is hindered, resulting in to up to a 20 per cent reduction in the conductivity, as shown in Figure 9.1.6. Compared to conventional EPS, less than half of the raw material is needed to achieve the same resulting insulation effect (see www.basf.de).

Table 9.1.1 *Properties of insulation materials*

Insulation material	Thermal conductivity	Ingredients	Long-term performance	Recycling capability	Health aspects	Remarks
Cork	0.045	Bitumen	With wetness fungal decay	Yes	Possibly carcinogenic (Benzoapyrene)	Permanent elastic; use only tar-less products
Coco	0.0445	Ammonium sulphate (fire protection)	–	Yes	–	
Wood-fibre boards	0.045	Soft wood	Like massive wood	Yes, biodegradable	–	
Cellulose	0.040	Borax; boric acid	No mould; pest resistant	Yes	Possibly containing PCB (printing ink); fine dust in high concentration critical	Pay attention to dust-poor installation
Foam glass	0.040–0.055	Quarry sand; recycling glass	Ageing resistant; pest resistant	Reusable; not recyclable	–	
Rock wool	0.035–0.04		Un-decayable; pest resistant	Rarely reusable or transferable	Insulation material with KI > 40 or without harmlessness certificate should not be used;	Incorrectly mounted status harmless
Fibreglass	0.035–0.04		Un-decayable; pest resistant	Rarely reusable or transferable	Insulation material with KI > 40 or without harmlessness certificate should not be used	Incorrectly mounted status harmless
Extruded polystyrene	0.03–0.04		Durable; pest resistant	Reusability unknown	If burning toxic gases	–
Expanded polystyrene	0.035–0.04		Not UV-resistant; moisture resistant; un-decayable	Partly recyclable	If burning toxic gases	–
Polyurethane boards	0.025–0.035		2	Durable	Non-recyclable	–
Perlite	0.055–0.07	–		Possibly increased radio activity	–	

Source: Energiesparen im Altbau (2000)

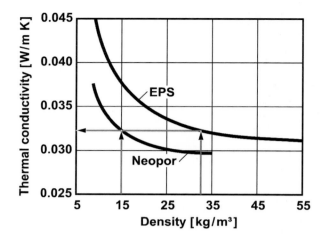

Source: www.basf.de

Figure 9.1.6 *Comparison of the thermal conductivity of standard expanded polystyrene (EPS) and graphite embedded material*

High-performance brick constructions

The brick industry has developed new bricks specifically for high-performance houses. One strategy is to optimize the hole configurations and reduce the conducting bridges in cross-section. Figure 9.1.7 shows two such constructions with conductivities below 0.09 W/mK.

Another strategy is to produce the brick in an extrusion process. This leads to a new foam material with conductivity below 0.04 W/mK. A monolithic brick in this construction can have a U-value below 0.1 W/m²K (www.wienerberger.de).

Source: Fraunhofer Institut für Bauphysik

Figure 9.1.7 *(a) Optimized hole configurations; and (b) reduced brick piers in high-performance brick stones*

High-performance plaster systems

The plaster industry has also improved the properties of plaster layers to be suitable for high-performance houses. One strategy is to integrate glass bubbles within the plaster mix. This application is known from the transparent insulation industry; but the advantages of the transparent plaster alone on high-efficiency brick constructions had not been studied. Figure 9.1.8 shows an application on brick stones. Absorption of solar radiation and convective heat transfer to the outside air no longer occur at the same layer. This improves the gains from both direct and diffuse solar radiation. The measured heat losses from such a wall are 15 per cent to 25 per cent lower than a conventional plaster system (www.sto.de).

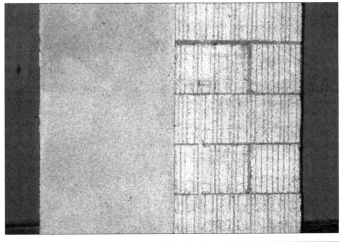

Source: Fraunhofer Institut für Bauphysik

Figure 9.1.8 *Application of glass-bubble plaster compared to conventional plaster on brick*

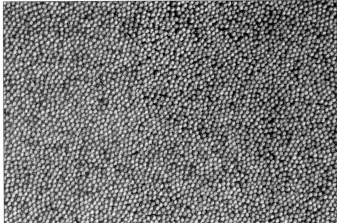

Source: Fraunhofer Institut für Bauphysik

Figure 9.1.9 *Application of an infrared-coated plaster system with lotus effects*

For plaster on the interior face of walls, phase-change materials (PCMs) can be integrated within the structure. In one example, micro-encapsulated wax droplets are mixed into the plaster, as shown in Figure 9.1.10. As a result, the thermal capacity of the wall is increased. This reduces temperature peaks, decreasing the risk of overheating in summer. It can also increase the usability of passive solar gains in winter. This technology is still under development (see www.ise.fhg.de/english/press/pi_2001/pi05_2001.html).

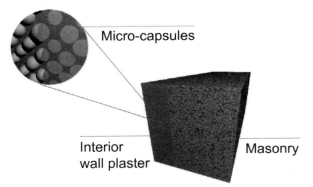

Micro-capsules

Interior wall plaster

Masonry

Source: www.ise.fhg.de/english/press/pi_2001/pi05_2001.html

Figure 9.1.10 *Principle scheme of micro-encapsulated phase-change material (PCM) in plasters*

Polyurethane (PU) insulation systems

Polyurethane (PU) is a hard-covered plastic foam cell structure derived by using an expanding agent. The thermal conductivity varies between 0.025 and 0.035 W/mK. The material is heat resistant up to 90°C. Typical applications are roofs, ceilings or interior walls (see www.ivpu.de).

Table 9.1.2 *Typical applications of polyurethane insulation systems*

Fields of application	Step roof, above rafters	Step roof, below rafters	Flat roof	Terrace/ parking deck	Gradient roof	Ceilings/ walls	Attic	Floor	Internal insulation	Inner ceilings	Industrial buildings
PU products with different coatings											
Special paper WLG 035	□	□	■	■	■	□	□	■	□	□	□
Mineral fleece WLG 030	■	□	■	■	■	■	■	■	■	■	■
Aluminium lamination WLG 025	■	■	■	■	□	■	■	■	■	■	■
Composite film WLG 025	■	■	■	■	□	■	■	■	□	■	■
Composite film WLG 030	■	■	■	■	□	■	■	■	□	■	■
Non-laminated boards WLG 030	□	□	■	■	■	□	□	□	□	■	□
Composite elements WLG 030	■	■	□	□	□	■	■	■	■	■	■
Formed components	□	□	■	□	□	□	□	□	□	□	■
In-situ foam	□	□	■	□	□	■	□	□	□	□	■

Vacuum insulation systems

Evacuated building elements enclosing a vacuum are now on the market. As a result, the thermal conductivity is reduced by more than factor 11 compared to conventional materials, as illustrated in

Source: www.vip-bau.ch

Figure 9.1.11 *Vacuum insulation material panel compared to mineral wool panel of the same thermal resistance*

Figure 9.1.11. This allows much slimmer constructions for high-performance houses. One construction uses an evacuated silica gel covered by a high-performance aluminium foil. The gas pressure in the construction is approximately 1 mbar; the leakage rate is predicted to be below 2 mbar per year. For protection during transport and at the building site, the units are glued into a polystyrene panel. A disadvantage of such a construction is the limitation of sizes available and the fact that the panels can not be cut to fit at the building site. Another factor limitation, to date, has been the fact that such panels cost ten times more than conventional insulation. Within the framework of International Energy Agency (IEA) Energy Conservation in Buildings and Community Systems (ECBCS) Annex 39, the quality of vacuum insulation panels (VIPs) and possible applications were investigated (see www.ecbcs.org).

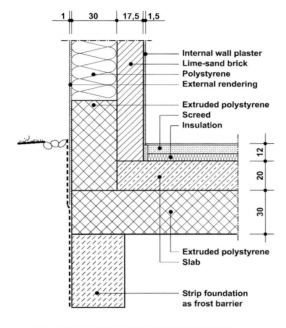

Source: Fraunhofer Institut für Bauphysik

Figure 9.1.12 *Exemplary wall-ceiling joint with minimized thermal bridge effect and optimized air tightness*

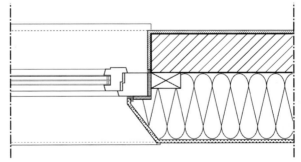

Source: www.marmorit.de

Figure 9.1.13 *Daylight wedges in insulation systems allowing a better use of daylight:* (left) *window in a wall with 'light-wedges';* (above) *horizontal section of the window in the wall*

9.1.4 Design insights

References

Kluttig, H., Erhorn, H. and Hellwig, R. (1997) *Weber 2001 – Energiekonzepte und Realisierungsphase [Energy Concepts and Their Stages of Realisation]*, Report WB 92/1997, Fraunhofer Institute for Building Physics (IBP), Stuttgart

Erhorn, H., Reiss, J., Kluttig, H. and Hellwig, R. (2000) 'Ultrahaus, Passivhaus oder Null-Heizenergiehaus?' ['Ultra, passive, or zero energy buildings?']: Eine Statusanalyse anhand praktisch realisierter Energiesparkonzepte', *Bauphysik* vol 22, vol 1, pp28–36, www.wiley-vch.de

Baden-Wuerttemberg (2000) *Energiesparen im Altbau [Saving Energy in Existing Buildings]*, Landesgewerbeamt Baden-Wuerttemberg, Informationszentrum Energie, Baden-Wuerttemberg.

Internet links

BASF Aktiengesellschaft www.basf.de
FHBB Institut für Energie www.vip-bau.ch
Fraunhofer Institut für Solare Energiesysteme (ISE)
    www.ise.fhg.de/english/press/pi_2001/pi05_2001.html
IVPU-Industrieverband Polyurethan-Hartschaum e.V. www.ivpu.de
Knauf Marmorit GmbH www.marmorit.de
Sto AG: www.sto.de
Wienerberger Ziegelindustrie GmbH www.wienerberger.de

9.2 Thermal bridges in building constructions

Gerhard Faninger

9.2.1 Cause and effect of thermal bridges

Thermal bridges in building constructions are part of the building envelope with disproportionately high heat losses. Typical problem areas include window and door frames, balconies, and the junction between the ground floor and basement, between intermediate floor and wall, wall to roof and wall corners.

9.2.2 Calculation of heat transmission losses through thermal bridges

The heat losses from thermal bridges can be calculated for transient or steady-state heat conductions in two or three dimensions (see Blomberg, 1996; Panzhauser, 1997). A useful computer program, *Eurokobra/Austrokobra*, was developed within a project among European Union (EU) member countries in 1997. With this PC tool, thermal bridges such as heat transfer through corners of windows and heat loss from a house to the ground can be analysed, making it easy to solve ordinary construction problems. The user is helped in designing building constructions with minimized thermal bridges. A database for typical building construction parts (outside walls, floors, window frames, balconies, cellars, etc) is included. It provides the user with default values for defining the constructions (thickness of material layers, horizontal and vertical) and materials (characterized by their heat conductivity in W/mK). The results are isotherm lines in the building construction with condensation problems identified. The heat losses of the thermal bridges are characterized by Ψ–values. Tables 9.2.1 and 9.2.2 show examples of such Ψ–values. The U-values of windows are increased through thermal bridges between the glass and frame by about 0.05 W/m²K (high-performance window) up to 0.19 W/m²K (standard window).

9.2.3 Influence on transmission losses

Calculation results of the effect of thermal bridges on heat transmission losses in housing with different envelope insulation standards are illustrated in Tables 9.2.3 to 9.2.5 (single family detached house, row house and apartment building). The contribution of thermal bridges to the transmission heat losses are up to 25 per cent. The target for the heat transmission through thermal bridges in Passivhaus constructions is below 4 per cent.

In highly insulated house construction, thermal bridges can have a disproportionately negative influence on the actual energy performance compared to conventional construction. Therefore, it is essential to pay careful attention to classical thermal bridge situations and to conduct an analysis of the solutions using tools mentioned above.

Table 9.2.1 *Typical guide values for thermal bridges in building constructions*

Building envelope	Ψ-values (W/mK)		
	Standard house	Low energy house	Passive house
Highest floor/roof/attic	0.20	0.12	0.008
Outside wall/ceiling/floors	0.20	0.10	0.008
Outside wall/balconies	0.30	0.15	0.008
Outside wall/window frame	0.20	0.20	0.040
Outside wall/basement	0.20	0.10	0.050

Table 9.2.2 *Guide values for thermal bridges between the window frame and window glass (ÖNORM B 8110-1)*

Window frame	Ψ_g-values (W/mK)	
	Double and triple glazing without coating	Double and triple glazing with coating sealed units
Wood and plastic frame	0.04	0.06
Metal frame	0.06	0.08
Metal frame with insulation	0.00	0.02

Table 9.2.3 *Transmission losses in housing with different envelope insulation standards: Detached single family house*

Building insulation standard	Standard house		Low energy house		Passive house A		Passive house B	
	W/m²K	W/mK	W/m²K	W/mK	W/m²K	W/mK	W/m²K	W/mK
Upper floor/roof/attic	0.50	0.20	0.15	0.12	0.10	0.05	0.10	0.008
Exterior wall	0.40	0.20	0.20	0.10	0.12	0.08	0.10	0.008
Window	1.80	0.20	1.10	0.10	0.70	0.10	0.70	0.010
Basement/ceiling	0.50	0.30	0.20	0.10	0.10	0.10	0.10	0.050
Thermal conductance (W/K)	37.6		17.3		14.0		3.1	
Total transmission losses (kWh/m²a)	88.7		37.7		23.4		18.2	
Transmission losses through thermal bridges (kWh/m²a)	14.7		6.8		5.5		1.2	
$Q_{thermal\ bridges}/Q_{total}$ (per cent)	16.6		18.0		23.5		6.8	

Table 9.2.4 *Transmission losses in housing with different envelope insulation standards: Row house*

Building insulation standard	Standard house		Low energy house		Passive house A		Passive house B	
	W/m²K	W/mK	W/m²K	W/mK	W/m²K	W/mK	W/m²K	W/mK
Upper floor/roof/attic	0.50	0.20	0.15	0.12	0.10	0.05	0.10	0.008
Exterior wall	0.40	0.20	0.20	0.10	0.12	0.08	0.10	0.008
Window	1.80	0.20	1.10	0.10	0.70	0.10	0.70	0.010
Basement/ceiling	0.50	0.30	0.20	0.10	0.10	0.10	0.10	0.050
Thermal conductance (W/K)	58.6		27.7		22.8		4.6	
Total transmission losses (kWh/m²a)	80.5		40.4		24.1		19.5	
Transmission losses through thermal bridges (kWh/m²a)	11.4		5.4		4.4		0.9	
$Q_{thermal\ bridges}/Q_{total}$ (per cent)	14.2		13.4		18.4		4.6	

Table 9.2.5 *Transmission losses in housing with different envelope insulation standards: Apartment building*

Building insulation standard	Standard house		Low energy house		Passive house A		Passive house B	
	W/m²K	W/mK	W/m²K	W/mK	W/m²K	W/mK	W/m²K	W/mK
Upper floor/roof/attic	0.50	0.20	0.15	0.12	0.10	0.05	0.10	0.008
Exterior wall	0.40	0.20	0.20	0.10	0.12	0.08	0.10	0.008
Window	1.80	0.20	1.10	0.10	0.70	0.10	0.70	0.010
Basement/ceiling	0.50	0.30	0.20	0.10	0.10	0.10	0.10	0.050
Thermal conductance (W/K)	195.6		95.1		83.2		12.2	
Total transmission losses (kWh/m²a)	74.5		36.1		23.2		17.9	
Transmission losses through thermal bridges (kWh/m²a)	11.8		5.2		5.0		0.74	
$Q_{thermal\ bridges}/Q_{total}$ (per cent)	15.8		15.8		21.6		4.1	

References

Astl, C., Grembacher, C., Wimmers, G., Crepaz, H. and Auer, K. (1999) *Wärmebrückenvermeidung*, Energie Tirol, Innsbruck, Austria, www.tirol.energie-tirol.at

Krapmeier, H. and Müller, E. (2003) *CEPHEUS Austria: Passivhaus konkret*, Energieinstitut Vorarlberg, Dornbirn, Austria, www.cepheus.at

Österreichisches Normungsinstitut (1999) *ÖNORM B 8110, ÖNORM EN 1190: Wärmeschutz im Hochbau*, Österreichisches Normungsinstitut, Wien, Austria

Panzhauser, E., Krek, K. and Lechleitner, J. (1998) *EUROKOBRA/AUSTROKOBRA: Das EDV Programm für den Baupraktiker – Dynamischer Wärmebrücken-Europa-Atlas im PC*, Technische Universität Wien, Institut für Hochbau für Architekten, Wien, Austria, www.hb2.tuwien.ac.at

Schwarzmüller, E. (1999) *Wärmebrücken, Luft- und Winddichte*, Energie Tirol, Innsbruck, Austria, www.tirol.energie-tirol.at

9.3 Doors and vestibules

S. Robert Hastings

9.3.1 Concept

The entry door of a house is a very strong selling point and, like windows, strongly influences how a homeowner feels about his or her house. However, the entrance is also an extremely weak point in the envelope of highly insulated buildings. A conventional door can lose as much heat as 20 m² of a well-insulated wall. Furthermore, given the importance of the air tightness of the envelope, the door is a major leakage source since gaskets and weather-stripping are subject to extensive wear.

This heat loss and leakage by the entry can be minimized, first, by where it is located. A good entry solution is a vestibule or air lock. Finally, high-performance certified doors are now on the market.

9.3.2 Door location

Often in high-performance houses, the entry is located on the north side. It opens into a foyer with adjacent closet, guest WC and kitchen. These spaces have a lower priority for south-facing windows than living and dining spaces – hence, the north side entry. However, this side of the house typically has the worst wind exposure, is always in shadow in winter and the micro-climate can be several degrees colder than the south side of the house. The north side of a house is, therefore, the worst direction in which to make a hole in the building envelope, nor is it a pleasant way to enter or exit the house. A wind-sheltered, sun-warmed south-facing entry is much more inviting. Plants and flowers can further enhance the entry experience. Indeed, many traditional house designs incorporate a ceremonial entry at the 'front' of the house for guests and an everyday entrance to the rear or through the garage.

9.3.3 Door constructions

A choice of highly insulating door constructions is available in the market. Of particular importance for high-performance housing is that the doors remain air tight over time (no warping of the door, durability of the weather stripping and air tightness reinforced by the hardware). Various door constructions meet these demands.

Wooden sandwich doors

Sandwich doors are built in a multi-layered construction. The visible outer faces are typically plywood with a high quality outer veneer or pattern treatment. The core of the door is a wooden frame construction reinforced with an aluminium profile or diaphragm to prevent warping. A plastic film may be added to ensure air tightness. The void space is filled with insulation with a very good lambda value. To achieve the required insulation levels, these doors must be comparatively thick, typically between 85 mm to 110 mm. The door frame is a thermal weakness in the system. Accordingly, the frame is also an important factor in selection criteria for a door.

Table 9.3.1 *Properties of a wooden sandwich door*

Thermal performance	U-value: 0.71 W/m²K
	Air tightness: V = 2.25 m³/hour linear m by 100 Pa
Ecology	Wood as a CO_2 neutral material is a favourable choice, except if the facings are of tropical woods. A typical value for the grey energy of a wooden sandwich door is 125 kWh.

Source: Alex Hastings

Figure 9.3.1 *Entry door*

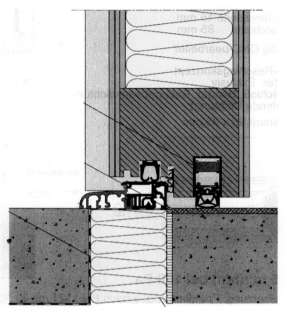

Source: VARIOTEC Sandwichelemente GmbH & Co,
www.variotec.de

Figure 9.3.2 *Wooden sandwich door*

Metal sandwich doors

The outer faces of sheet aluminium are stiffened with aluminium angles and the core is filled with a sprayed-in rigid insulation. The overall thickness is 80 mm. This type of door is very break-in resistant.

Source: Biffar GmbH, Edenkoben, www.biffar.ch

Figure 9.3.3 *Aluminium sandwich door*

Table 9.3.2 *Properties of a metal sandwich door*

Thermal performance	U-value: 0.8 W/m²K
	Air tightness: V = 1.3 m³/hour linear m by 100 Pa
Ecology	Aluminium is produced with a high percentage of renewable energy (hydro- or geothermal electric generation) and is easily recycled.

Vacuum insulation doors

Using a vacuum insulation panel instead of conventional insulation allows the door to be much thinner and still achieve the required U-value. A vacuum (0.1 to 20 mbar) eliminates heat transport by convection across the gap, which is filled with a micro-porous material to maintain the separation. As a result, vacuum panels achieve, with very little thickness, very high insulation levels. A vacuum panel at 1 mbar can have a Lambda-value of 4.8 mW/mK compared to closed-cell polyurethane, with 19 to 35 or expandable polystyrene with 36 mW/mK.

Source: VARIOTEC Sandwichelemente GmbH & Co, www.variotec.de

Figure 9.3.4 *Example of a vacuum-insulated door*

Table 9.3.3 *Properties of a door with vacuum panel insulation*

Thermal performance	U = 0.3–0.8 W/mK depending on glass area if there is an integrated viewing window
Ecology	The vacuum panel core consists typically of either an open-cell polyurethane (ICI) or polystyrene (Dow) foam, or carbon/silica aerogels. Neither is more environmentally detrimental than conventional insulation products, and the amount of material is very small compared to conventional insulation volumes.

Glass doors

Thermal glazing has been optimized to such an extent that a glass door offers one of the best solutions regarding insulation value for its thickness. The opaque part of the door and frame construction can be the same as that used for high-performance windows. Glass doors are offered in triple glazing. The weak point of the door is the threshold.

Table 9.3.4 *Properties of a window as a door*

Thermal performance	U_f = 0.6973 W/mK U_g = 0.7060 W/mK Ψ = 0.035 W/mK
Ecology	The coatings of thermal glazings are so thin that they pose no environmental hazard when the door is recycled

Source: VARIOTEC Sandwichelemente GmbH & Co, www.variotec.de

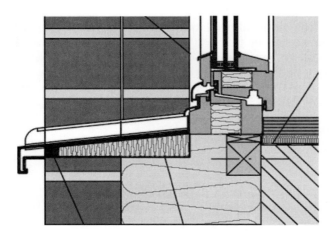

Figure 9.3.5 *Example of a high insulation glass entry door*

9.3.4 Storm vestibules (air lock)

When an entry door is opened, the room air exchange with the ambient can increase by a factor up to 50 compared to the natural infiltration of a house built to an airtightness of 0.6 air changes by 50 Pa. Considering this, a storm vestibule offers two important benefits compared to a single highly insulated door:

- it impedes the penetration of wind into the house, saving energy (assuming that the doors are opened consecutively); and
- it improves comfort in spaces adjacent to the entry that would otherwise be confronted by cold draughts when people come or go.

Source: Arkitekt Hans Eek, Alingsås

Figure 9.3.6 *Entry vestibule of row houses in Göteborg*

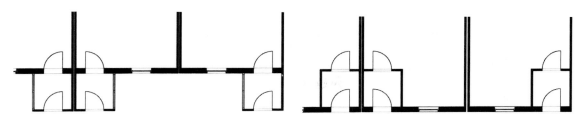

Source: Lars Junghans, AEU GmbH, Wallisellen

Figure 9.3.7 *Interior versus exterior vestibules:* (left) *Inset vestibule;* (right) *Exterior vestibule*

Various vestibule configurations were modelled with the programme DEROB-LTH to quantify the effect of its design and construction on the resulting energy savings of the heated house.

Placement of the vestibule

Placing the vestibule outside the heated house envelope logically should result in the greatest savings since this configuration has the least area of common wall between the cold vestibule and heated house volume (see Figure 9.3.7). However, compared to an interior vestibule, the difference is insignificant. The greatest benefit of the exterior versus interior vestibule could be seen for the cold climate (1.1 versus 0.9 kWh/m²a reduction of the house heating demand). In both the temperate and the mild climates, the energy savings of the vestibule, whether exterior or interior, were approximately 1 kWh/m²a.

The argument for the exterior vestibule is therefore primarily economic: space within the highly insulated envelope of the house costs much more than an inexpensive construction outside the heated envelope of the house.

Construction of an exterior vestibule

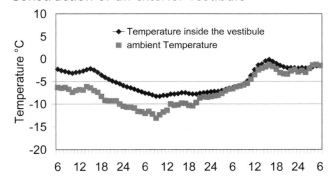

Source: Lars Junghans, AEU GmbH, Wallisellen

Figure 9.3.8 *Temperatures inside the vestibule compared to the ambient temperature*

Because the principle function of the vestibule is as a buffer and as wind protection, a low cost construction was assumed (walls and roof: U = 1.0 W/m²K; doors: U = 1.6 W/m²K; and glazing: U = 1.8 W/m²K). The temperature in the vestibule is consistently 3 K to 4 K warmer than the ambient temperature in all three climate types. Figure 9.3.8 shows the temperature profile over three very cold days in the temperate climate.

The extreme case of a fully glazed vestibule (all three walls) was compared to an insulated vestibule. Since the vestibule is not heated and is cool, the U-value of the construction is not important. The glass vestibule showed no difference in savings compared to the savings from the opaque insulated vestibule in the cold climate.

Location of the vestibule

The entry with vestibule was moved from the north to the south side of the house. All other conditions were kept the same. This had the negative influence of reducing the possible south-facing window area for direct solar gains into the heated living space. The result is that the positioning of the vestibule on the south side increased the space heating demand in all climates, as can be seen in Table 9.3.5.

Table 9.3.5 *Effect of a vestibule location on house heating demand (kWh/m²a)*

Climate	North side	South side
Cold	12.8	15.1
Temperate	12.9	15.0
Mild	12.7	14.5

A vestibule or a highly insulated door

Here a vestibule with two conventional doors is compared to the case of no vestibule and a single highly insulated door. In all three climates, the vestibule saves energy compared to the single door, as can be seen in Table 9.3.6.

Table 9.3.6 *Effect of a vestibule versus a super door on house heating demand (kWh/m²a)*

Climate	Vestibule	Super door
Cold	12.8	14.6
Temperate	12.9	14.9
Mild	12.7	14.4

Design recommendations

The entry door is a weak point in highly insulated houses and, as such, either a highly insulating door or a vestibule should be specified.

Table 9.3.7 *Requirements for a high-performance entry*

Property	Requirement
U-value	A value of 0.8 W/m²K or better should be achieved (conventional doors typically have U = 1.1 to 2.0 W/m²K).
Air tightness	The leakage should not exceed 2.25 m³ per m perimeter and hour by a pressure difference of 100 Pa. The tightness of the door is reported by its 'A-value' (hourly perimeter air leakage rate).
Form stability	This is essential because warping will increase air leakage.
Sound insulation	Since the ambient noise levels are lower in highly insulated houses, occupants are more sensitive to outside noise.
Cost	Better insulation, more precise hinging, compression locking and tighter weather stripping increase costs; but expensive doors are also tolerated in conventional houses for prestige.
Materials	Avoid foam insulation where FCKW (hydrofluorocarbons) is an output in the manufacturing.

The following advice is offered regarding location and construction:

• Incorporate an external vestibule, if possible, and include substantial glass with a normal U-value of 1.3 W/m²K to provide daylight in the vestibule (that is, 40 per cent to 60 per cent of the wall areas).
• The plane of the door should be towards the outside of the wall opening to minimize thermal bridging.

- The wall insulation could extend over the door jambs and head to further reduce heat loss, as is often done in window details.
- If the threshold is metal (aluminium), it should have a thermal break. The problem of thermal bridging at the hinges has not been solved.
- In no case should the door or entry have a mail slot!
- If there is a home automation system, the status of the door should be registered to provide a warning if the door is left ajar by accident or held open for an excessive time. A warning can also occur if it is left unlocked.

References

Glacier Bay (no date) *Vacuum Insulation Panels: Principles, Performance and Lifespan*, Glacier Bay, Inc., CA, www.glacierbay.com

Bavarian Center for Applied Energy Research (ZAE Bayern) (2005) Vacuum Insulation Panels in Buildings, Seventh International Vacuum Insulation Symposium, EMPA, Dübendorf, September 2005, www.vip-bau.de/technology.htm

Industry contracts

Biffar A.G., Schaffhauser Straße 118, 8057, Zürich, Biffer

Sigg GmbH & Co, KG, Allgäustrasse 155, A-6912, Hörbranz; (tel) +43/5573/82255-0; (fax) +43/5573/82255-4, www.sigg.at, manfred@sigg.at

Variotec GmbH & Co, KG, Weißmarterstr. 3, D-92318, Neumarkt, www.variotec.de

9.4 Transparent insulation

Werner Platzer and Karsten Voss

9.4.1 Basic concepts

The basic concept of transparent insulation is to reduce thermal losses, while at the same time allowing solar gains in order to optimize the energy balance of walls during the heating season. While opaque insulation just minimizes the heat losses approaching the ultimate limit zero, transparent insulation also considers solar gains to be utilized in the building during the heating season. The wall should be a net energy gainer during that time. Nevertheless, there will be some periods with very little sun where instantaneous losses may occur.

Solar wall heating

With a transparent insulation element covering the outside of a *massive* wall, this part of the building can be converted to a solar wall heating area. Solar energy is converted to heat at the absorber and conducted with a phase delay of some hours – depending on thickness and building material – through the massive wall into the interior. This is the reason why windows and solar wall heating with transparent insulation fit very well together: the solar gains of a south-oriented solar wall reach the room mainly at night time and thus extend the period with passive solar heating considerably.

Suitable wall materials have a high density that is correlated with good conductivity and high thermal capacity. Examples are concrete, limestone and low porosity bricks. Gaseous concrete, high porosity bricks or wooden constructions with a density below 1000 kg/m^3 are not suitable because the wall then cannot store enough heat, and only badly conducts the heat to the interior. This results in low efficiency and, worse, high absorber temperatures above 100°C, leading to thermal stresses and, eventually, destruction of the plastic transparent insulation materials.

The two principle variants of transparent insulation systems are shown in Figure 9.4.1. When a highly transparent exterior cover (type T for 'transparent') is used, most of the solar radiation is

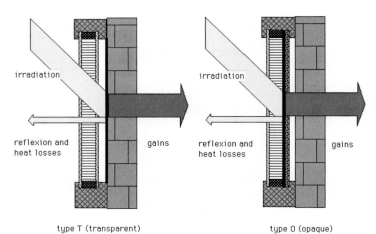

irradiation

reflexion and
heat losses

gains

irradiation

reflexion and
heat losses

gains

type T (transparent)

type O (opaque)

Source: Fachverband TWD e.V. Gundelfingen,
Germany

Figure 9.4.1 *Principle types T
and O for solar wall heating with
transparent insulation (type O can
be vented in summer for effective
overheating protection)*

absorbed on the surface of the massive wall behind. Here the wall should be painted with a dark paint (black, blue, green, dark red), thus influencing the system's performance with the choice of paint. A second opaque system (type O for 'opaque') includes the absorber similar to a thermal solar collector at the rear side of the product. The solar gains have to be transferred over an air gap, necessary because of building tolerances, to the wall by radiation and convection. The absorber colour cannot, then, be chosen freely.

Solar insulation

Non-transparent materials like cardboard structures or mineral wool can also be used in wall constructions for utilization of solar gains, when covered with a glazing instead of an opaque construction, see Figure 2.4.2. The efficiency of these systems is certainly rather low. The intention here is not to convert the wall into a solar collector but to use the solar gains to reduce the heat losses further down towards approaching the zero energy balance over the heating season. The absorbed solar energy is used mainly to raise the average temperature of the outer shell to the interior temperature level thus bringing down the average temperature gradient over the heating season. There will be no solar heating, but the insulation level will be increased without using too large material thickness.

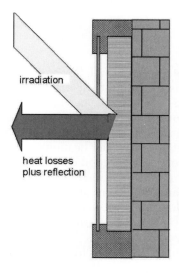

irradiation

heat losses
plus reflection

Source: Fachverband TWD e.V. Gundelfingen,
Germany

Figure 9.4.2 *Principle of solar
insulation: Solar gains and heat
losses balance each other over the
heating season*

9.4.2 Products

Transparent insulation products exist in a variety of designs, having different appearances and leading to various building construction principles. Very often, they consist of glass and plastic transparent materials. In the following sections the main types of transparent insulation products are briefly described.

Transparent exterior insulation finish system

This system (see Figure 9.4.3) is similar to opaque insulation: it is glued to the wall and is covered with an exterior finish. However, in this case, the absorber glue (1) is black, the insulation material (2) is a capillary structure and the finish (3) + (4) mainly consists of glass spheres. Shape and size are quite arbitrary. There is no frame needed; but the system is embedded in an opaque insulation finish system.

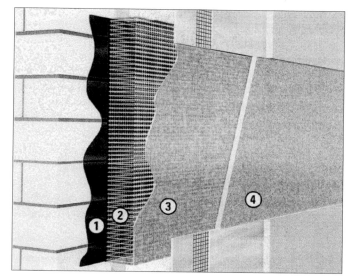

Source: www.umwelt-wand.de

Figure 9.4.3 *Schematic view of Sto Solar system*

Transparent insulation glazings

Most transparent insulation (TI) products can be described as glazings filled with transparent insulation material. There are some that, in addition, use the potential of low-e coating and noble gas fillings (see Figure 9.4.4); but many only rely on the insulation of air-filled structures. Glazings thicker than

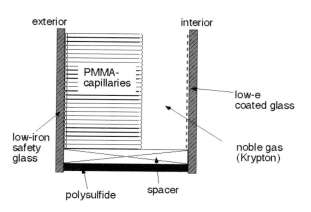

Source: Kapilux-H

Figure 9.4.4 *Cross-section of transparent insulation (TI)-insulated glazing, utilizing noble gas filling and low-e coatings*

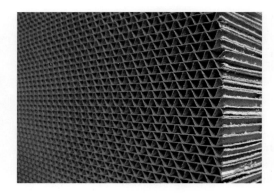

Figure 9.4.5 *View of thin cardboard honeycomb structure (gap solar)*

50 mm to 60 mm need a breathing opening and cannot be hermetically sealed. With a step rebate, these products may be integrated like slim glazings in ordinary profiles of transom-mullion constructions.

Opaque solar absorber modules

Instead of highly translucent materials, opaque materials such as cardboard structures or mineral wool can be used behind a glass pane to absorb the solar radiation. The Gap solar solarpanel (previously ESA Solarfassade; see Figure 9.4.5) and the Isover Design FP6 (no longer on the market) are such systems that can also be used in front of walls with low storage capacity and density.

Other products and overview

A product different from the type above is TI made from multi-channelled duct plates. The company GlassX AG in Zurich recently developed a complete glass element, including latent heat storage and seasonal shading using prismatic sheets. From some manufacturers, only the transparent insulation

Table 9.4.1 *Product characteristics (selection)*

Product	Type	Manufacturer	Product thickness D (mm)	Material thickness d (mm)	Thermal resistance R (m²K/W)	Total solar energy transmittance g_h (%)
Kapilux H	T	Okalux	49	30	1.08	61
Kapillarsystemglas	T	LES	58	50	0.57	67
LINIT-TWD	T	Lamberts	74	40	0.42	59
TWD Basic	T	Bayer Sheet Europe	100	100	1.14	40
TWD-G	T	Schweizer	146	120	1.40	53
TWD-M	T	Schweizer	136	120	1.28	65
Solfas	O	Schweizer	173	142	1.50	57
Sto Solar	O	Sto AG	105	100	0.97	41
K-Spezial	T	Termolux	50	40	0.78	34
Gap Solarpanel	O	gap solar	105	80	0.83	13
GlassXcrystal	O	GlassX	80	–	1.92	37
Double low-e argon	T	Generic	24		0.66	55
Triple low-e argon	T	Generic	36		1.25	42

Notes:

1 The total solar energy is for diffuse radiation – thus, it is much lower than for normal incidence!

2 Many manufacturers have several product variations with differing characteristics.

3 The product characteristics are typical values for these products.

4 The thermal resistance is given for 10°C average temperature; it is not a rated value that includes safety allowance.

material can be obtained. This can be used by architects or craftsmen to develop own solutions – for example, using wooden window technology or filling a timber framing construction. Humidity transport, ventilation and condensation have to be considered in such cases.

Table 9.4.1 gives a short overview of characteristic values for a range of selected products. Most values are measured values; but some are extrapolated from material composition and manufacturers' data. The data can be used for approximated design. When in doubt, manufacturers should be asked for more detailed data.

9.4.3 Energy performance and performance calculation

The energy performance of buildings with transparent insulation systems can be calculated in a similar manner to other buildings with monthly methods like the one proposed in the European standard EN832 (1998). First, the system parameters have to be determined from product characteristics; then the solar gains must be calculated for each month depending upon orientation; and, third, a utilization factor for these gains must be determined. For the last task, according to the standard, all gains (internal and through windows and solar walls) are summed up. However, due to the different dynamic storage effects, in reality, there should be a difference in calculating gains. The night-time discharging of solar wall heating, in particular, should have much higher utilization than instantaneous gains through windows. However, this can only be proven through dynamic simulation.

System characterization

For solar wall heating and solar insulation, the same methodology can be used for characterizing the wall construction. The U-value can be calculated according to ISO 6946 (EN ISO 6946, 1996). In general, the wall construction is an inhomogeneous building element consisting of wall material, transparent insulation product and frame part. Similar to a window, the solar gains are proportional to a total solar energy transmittance (g-value) of the complete system g_{SWH} – or, in collector terminology, a solar efficiency η_{SWH}. The basis for the determination of this parameter is the thermal resistance network of Figure 9.4.6: the solar energy transmitted is proportional to the g-value of the transparent insulation g_{TI} and the relation of the resistance from the wall surface to the exterior $R_{TI} + R_e$ to the total resistance R_{sys}:

$$g_{SWH} = \eta_{SWH} = g_{TI} \times \frac{R_{TI} + R_e}{R_{i+}R_{Wall} + R_{TI} + R_e} \qquad [9.1]$$

It is sometimes confusing that there are three different g-values: the one of the building product g_B as tested, the one of the TI construction, including absorber colour and air gaps g_{TI}, and the one of the total system, including the wall g_{SWH}. The calculation of the second quantity from the tested product quantities is different for the two types T and O, described in detail in (Platzer, 2000).

Moreover, the g-value for transparent insulation is very much dependent on incidence angle. In order to calculate the monthly effective values for different vertical orientations, only the values $g_{n,B}$ and $g_{h,B}$ for normal and diffuse hemispherical irradiation are needed (Platzer, 2000).

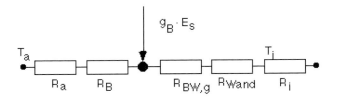

Source: Fachverband TWD e.V. Gundelfingen, Germany

Figure 9.4.6 *Thermal resistance network for system consisting of transparent insulation cover and wall (R_i, R_e: interior and exterior surface coefficients)*

Monthly calculation according to EN 832

For every month M and orientation O, the effective g-value gSWH,M,O has to be calculated (as a simplification, the constant value for hemispherical irradiation can be used). Then the solar gains are calculated exactly as the gains from windows, using a frame reduction factor. For the heat losses, the resistance of the TI section and the frame section have to be considered. In some cases, like the transparent exterior insulation finish system, the notion of 'frame' is ambiguous. 'Frame' and 'opaquely insulated wall' are identical. Furthermore, in transom mullion systems, frames might partly be used for transparent insulation and partly for glazings or operable windows. The definition should be consistent within one project.

Utilization and building standard

The utilization factor for gains in the monthly method of EN 832 depends on building thermal capacity and total thermal loss factor. The better the thermal insulation, the shorter the heating period for the building. Thus, there will be less and less utilizable solar gains for low energy houses and passive houses. However, if the difference between similar houses with and without TI is calculated with EN 832, the utilization of these small additional gains is insignificant.

Climate dependence

Similarly, the utilizable solar gains depend on climate: the longer the heating period, the better for the utilization. This is, of course, only true for identical buildings – as the reference buildings in Sweden are better insulated than the ones in Milan, this effect is reversed (see Figure 9.4.7). Thus, it is not certain that a sunnier climate is always best for solar wall heating.

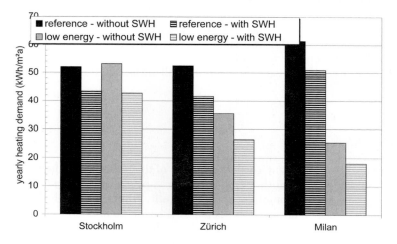

Source: Fachverband TWD e.V. Gundelfingen, Germany

Figure 9.4.7 *Solar gains dependent on climate for variable reference buildings and for constant low energy buildings – with and without 10 m² solar wall heating (SWH)*

Primary energy savings

For the different row houses in Zurich's climate, the space heating demand (see Figure 9.4.8) and primary energy savings were calculated (see Figure 9.4.9).

The lower the space heating demand, the higher the specific primary energy demand per kWh heating. For the reference house, a low temperature gas heating system with radiators was assumed; for the passive house standard, a heat pump mainly heating warm water and air was assumed. Since the tool used was a German tool (PHPP), the conversion factor for electricity is for the German energy mix. If the primary energy savings are related to the gross area of solar wall heating, this results in primary energy savings from 50 to 200 kWh (see Figure 9.4.9). It has to be kept in mind that the solar

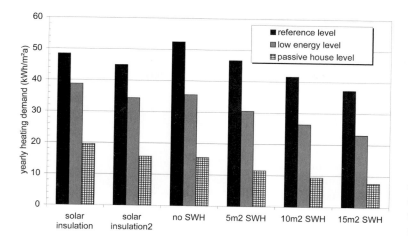

Source: Fachverband TWD e.V.
Gundelfingen, Germany

Figure 9.4.8 *Yearly space heating demand for different building standards and variable solar wall heating design (Zurich climate)*

wall was oriented to the south and shading from surrounding buildings was assumed to be minimal for windows and walls. It is obvious that for passive houses, the savings are much smaller than for houses without ventilation heat recovery.

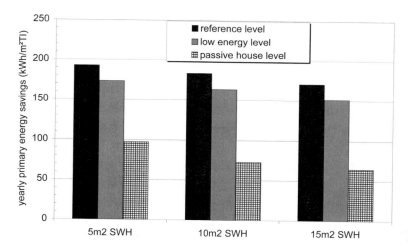

Source: Fachverband TWD e.V.
Gundelfingen, Germany

Figure 9.4.9 *Primary energy savings per gross area solar wall heating for the climate of Zurich and for different building insulation levels*

Conclusions

- Solar wall heating with transparent insulation can be used favourably in new building projects and renovation down to a low energy level. If ventilation heat recovery is employed, the utilizable solar gains are still significant, but the absolute values become much smaller.
- Typical collector areas of 0.1 m² per m² of living area give remarkable energy savings.
- The savings are more dependent on the building standard than on the climate if one stays in moderate zones.
- Solar insulation does not produce wall heating, but is an alternative for high-level insulation of very well-insulated buildings and light constructions.

9.4.4 Overheating protection and thermal comfort

Surface temperature and comfort temperature

If one considers the use of solar wall heating with transparent insulation, not only the solar gains are important. Due to the storage and conduction of absorbed heat in the wall element, the surface temperatures of the interior wall are raised. Due to the long-wave radiation exchange, the operative temperature increases as well. This results in enhanced comfort during the heating season. The effect can be called solar radiation heating. The surface temperature can temporarily reach 40°C to 50°C even in cold winter evenings (see Figure 9.4.10).

Source: Fraunhofer ISE, Germany

Figure 9.4.10 *Infrared picture of wall section with two TI elements in front of a 240 mm limestone wall (January, 9.00 pm; maximum surface temperature 32°C)*

Overheating protection by system design

During the summer, of course, surface temperatures above room temperature decrease the thermal comfort. Due to the high solar altitude, the g-value in summer is much smaller for south-east to south-west oriented walls. A second effect that reduces the efficiency is a comfortably raised room temperature of 24°C in summer. If only small areas of solar wall heating are used, the excessive gains can therefore be quite small. Another possibility is seasonal shading with building structure (balconies with a width larger than 1 m). Recently developed glass panes with prismatic surface structures can simulate this effect even without using overhangs (*Detail*, 2002). More than 50 per cent of the realized projects do not apply any solar protection devices.

Overheating protection by nighttime ventilation

Increased air change rates in summer (nighttime ventilation) by opening the windows in private houses can enhance thermal comfort considerably. This should be more effective for solar wall gains than for direct gains because of the nighttime disposal of heat. When surplus gains reach the room, the ambient temperatures are, in most cases, already low enough for cooling purposes. Results from dynamical simulations are compared showing the effects of overhangs and ventilation (see Figure 9.4.11).

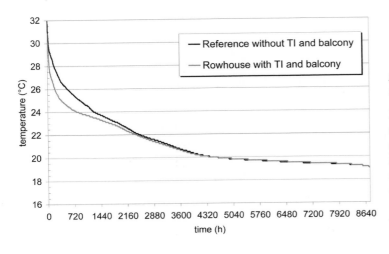

Source: Fachverband TWD e.V. Gundelfingen, Germany

Figure 9.4.11 *Room temperature distribution based on dynamical simulations of the reference row house with 10 m² high-performance TI with 1 m balcony compared to the house without TI and balcony (both nighttime ventilation with 2 air changes per hour)*

Overheating protection by solar shading

If the solar wall heating is designed for a large contribution to heating (large solar fraction), passive measures against overheating in summer might not be sufficient. In this case, active shading elements have to be used. This also occurs if inhabitants do not tolerate temperature swings (for example, in an office building). The costs for active shading are considerable. The reason is that either the shading device must be integrated within the transparent insulation product or an external robust shading device must be installed. Wiring, weather protection, control from inside and power connection for motor drives add to the cost of the façade. If possible, shading should be combined for both windows and transparent insulation to reduce extra costs. Active shading adds about €200 to €250/m² to the costs of the transparently insulated façade and should be avoided.

9.4.5 Outlook

In principle, solar wall heating is a good supplement to windows for passive solar heating due to the time shift for the solar gains. Because of the small market, there is little impetus for research and development to improve existing solutions. The concept can now be treated within the building standard EN 832 and the method will be updated for new versions. Most projects work only with natural ventilation and passive shading in summer. It is possible that construction combinations with latent storage materials will enter the lightweight building market in the near future.

References

Detail (2002) 'Solar house in Ebnat-Kappel', Detail, vol 6, pp736–737

EN 832 (1998) *Thermal Performance of Buildings: Calculation of Energy Use for Heating – Residential Buildings*, European standard, European Committee for Standardization (CEN), Brussels, Belgium

EN ISO 6946 (1996) *Building Components and Building Elements: Thermal Resistance and Thermal Transmittance – Calculation Method*, International standard, International Organization for Standardization (ISO), Geneva, Switzerland

Passivhaus Institut (2002) *Passivhaus Projektierungspaket (PHPP)*, Passivhaus Institut, Darmstadt, Germany

Platzer, W. J. (1998) *Energy Performance Assessment Method*, Proceedings of the Second International ISES Europe Solar Congress, Portoroz, Slovenia, 14–17 September 1998

Platzer, W. J. (2000) *Bestimmung des solaren Energiegewinns durch Massivwände mit transparenter Wärmedämmung*, Fachverband Transparente Wärmedämmung e.V., Gundelfingen, Germany

Website

Transparent Insulation Manufacturers' Association www.umwelt-wand.de.

9.5 Fenestration

Berthold Kaufmann and Wolfgang Feist

9.5.1 Concept

High-performance windows are important in order to minimize the space heating demand and space heating peak load, while also ensuring superior comfort. High inner-surface glazing temperatures also prevent condensation, which may damage the window and be a health risk (Recknagel et al, 1997; Fritz et al, 2000; Schnieders, 2000; Feist, 2001, 2003; Kaufmann et al, 2002, 2003).

Energy

High-performance windows ($U_W \leqslant 0.8$ W/m²K and $g \geqslant 50$ per cent), south oriented and not shaded,

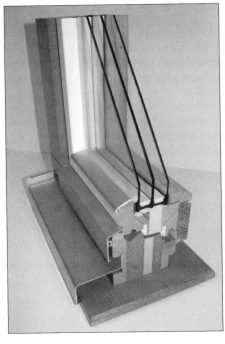

Source: www.passivehouse.com

Figure 9.5.1 *A high-quality window construction with thermal insulation layer in the multi-layer frame (three-pane glazing with thermal optimized edge system)*

can achieve a positive energy balance, even during the shortened heating period (typically November to March) of high-performance houses.

Solar gains through standard windows with double glazing and un-insulated frames ($U_W \geqslant 1.6$ W/m²K) are not sufficient to offset the window heat lost during the winter period. Such windows lose up to ten times more heat than the highly insulated opaque insulated walls (U-value 0.15 W/m²K) of high-performance housing. A superior window glazing and framing system is required, as illustrated in Figure 9.5.1.

This section is based on case studies in Germany, which has a similar climate to that of Central and Eastern Europe, and southern Scandinavia. In Southern and Western Europe, with Mediterranean or maritime climates, the heating season is less severe, so windows may more readily achieve a positive balance. The Passivhaus concept developed in Germany is one proven approach towards achieving very low energy housing with superior comfort (Truschel, 2002).

Comfort

In cold winter nights when the outside temperature drops below −10°C, the heat losses through the window glazing and the frame must be limited so that the mean inner surface temperatures of the window exceed 17°C. The warmer surface temperatures of the window reduce the long-wave radiation asymmetry of a room. This occurs when most room surfaces are much warmer than the window surface. Superior windows also reduce the discomfort risk of draughts caused by air cooling on the window surface and cascading to the floor. This is one reason why radiators were often placed under windows. With superior windows, this is no longer necessary.

Health

Finally, to avoid condensation and mould growing on some parts of windows (see Figure 9.5.2), the window in its entirety must stay above 13°C. Typical weak points are the edges of the glass and opaque panels beneath the window. The Passivhaus standard requirement of less than 0.85 W/m²K for the total window is based on such considerations.

Thermal optimization of windows

The thermal optimization of a window must address air tightness and the conductivity of the construction. To ensure air tightness, there should be at least two effective perimeter seals for an operable window sash and a reliable seal from the frame to the wall.

Source: www.passivehouse.com

Figure 9.5.2 *Condensation at the inner surface of a standard window with an aluminium edge system and small glazing rebate of only 15 mm*

Reducing conducted heat losses is more complex and involves the effects of the frame (U_f), glazing (U_g) and thermal bridge at the glass edge. This requires analysis using a two-dimensional thermal bridge calculation, described in ISO 10077 (2000). This calculation divides the window frame properties in two parts: the U-value of the frame (U_f) and the linear thermal bridge loss coefficient (Ψ_g). The properties of the window frames mentioned in this section were calculated using this method.

9.5.2 The glazing of high-performance windows

Triple glazing optimized for insulation can achieve Ug-values of 0.5 to 0.8 W/m²K. The value depends on the depth of the gap between the panes (8 mm to 16 mm) and which gas filling is used. Normally the noble gas argon is used. For very narrow spaces (8 mm to 10 mm), krypton is used, although this is rather expensive. Note that U_g describes the U-value in the centre of the glazing surface area. The heat lost at the edges is *not* included in this number and is significantly higher. These heat losses have to be considered by a two-dimensional thermal bridge calculation according to ISO 10077 (2000), which gives the Ψ_g-value.

The g-value (total direct and indirect radiated heat gain through the window compared to the amount of solar radiation striking the exterior surface) for common triple glazing is about 40 per cent to 60 per cent, depending on the coatings used and the glass transmittance. A rule of thumb based on simulations is that the glass 'g' value multiplied by a factor 's' should be equal or greater than the glass U-value:

$$g \cdot s \geq U_g \qquad\qquad\qquad [9.2]$$

For Central Europe s = 1.6 W/m²K.

If this rule is fulfilled, a south-oriented – and *not* shaded – glazing should provide a positive energy balance during the winter. This criterion may be checked easily with the data given from the manufacturer. It is important to check the energy balance for the whole house before making a final decision (PHPP, 2004).

Low-emissivity coatings

Highly insulated glazing typically has three panes, with two of the panes having a thin, soft metal coating. This low-emissivity (low-e) coating reflects the thermal radiation but transmits the visible light. The coating thus lets the sun shine in while keeping the resulting heat within the house. Different layers of the glazing may be coated, as can be seen in Figure 9.5.3.

Normally, the surfaces 2 and 5 (counted from the outside) are low-e coated, which leads to typical g-values of 52 per cent (Euronorm 410) and U_g-values of 0.5-0.6 W/m²K (Euronorm 673). Coating

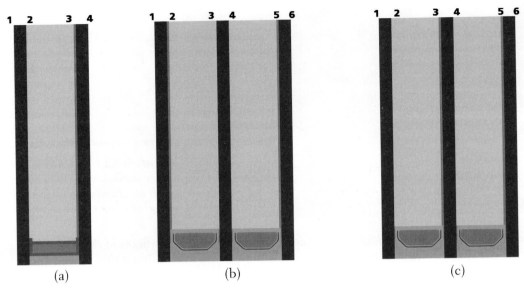

Source: www.passivehouse.com

Figure 9.5.3 *Different configurations of high-performance glazing: (a) double-glazing coating on surface 3; not suitable for passive houses; g = 64 per cent; $U_g \geq 1.1$ W/m²K; glazing rebate made of aluminium; (b) triple-glazing coating on surface 2 + 5; g = 52 per cent; $U_g = 0.6$ W/m²K; thermally separated glazing rebate – for example, of armed polycarbonate; (c) triple-glazing coating on surface 3 + 5; danger of rupture; use hardened safety glass for the middle pane; g = 54 per cent; $U_g = 0.6$ W/m²K; thermal separated glazing rebate – for example, of armed polycarbonate*

surfaces 3 and 5 yields a slightly higher g-value (54 per cent); but the middle pane must be hardened safety glass to prevent breakage from heat stress.

Condensation on windows is a potential problem and is more frequent on windows inclined skywards (Fritz et al, 2000). This can be observed on car windows that are frosted in early mornings after a clear night sky. This phenomenon may be less frequent with conventional double glazing because its greater heat loss may prevent frost. With superior glazing, frosting is more likely. Condensation can easily occur on the exterior surface because it will become colder since less room heat flows out. Such exterior condensation is a sign of good glazing insulation quality and not a defect.

Hard low-e coatings on the exterior surface of glazings also significantly reduce the radiation heat losses. Soft coatings cannot be used on external surfaces since they scratch easily. Hard-coated glass is preferably used with inclined roof windows. Hard coatings have, however, a somewhat higher emissivity than soft coatings and therefore cannot achieve the same low U-value as windows with soft coatings.

Special glazings

Sun-blocking glazings with a reduced g-value are unsuitable for high-performance housing. With such glazings, solar gains are reduced during the whole year. It is better to separate the two functions: maximizing passive solar gains and daylighting during winter, and preventing overheating during summer.

Electrochromic or gasochromic glazings offer an expensive alternative, where mechanical shadings are not possible. These glazings can vary the g-value and optical transparency by an internal two-phase material. The switching between the transparent and the opaque phase is provided by an applied electric voltage or by an additional H_2 gas filling. A better solution is to plan the housing so that it does not need such solutions.

Shutters at night?

The U-value for high-performance windows ($U_W \leq 0.85$ W/m²K) is more than a factor five worse than for opaque walls ($U_{wall} \leq 0.15$ W/m²K). Some experience with insulated shutters exists, typically about 4 cm thick and made of material with $\lambda = 0.04$ W/mK. If these shutters are closed and air tight during the night, the remaining heat losses may be reduced significantly (Feist, 1995). A detraction is the need for the occupants to open and close the shutters at night and in the morning. The promise of thermal shutters has been greatly diminished by today's highly insulating glazing.

9.5.3 The frames of high-performance windows

The heat losses of a conventional frame with $U_f = 1.5$–2 W/m²K are about double the losses of a typical triple glazing ($U_g = 0.7$ W/m²K); hence, these thermal losses are considerably high compared to other components of the building. The fraction of the frame area to the glazing area is typically about 25 per cent to 40 per cent. Obviously, the frame insulating qualities are also important! The frames can be improved in several ways.

First, the frame can be made thicker to accommodate an insulation material. A depth of 70 mm, which is typical for standard window frames, is too thin even if a highly insulating material is used. Insulated window frames available on the market typically are about 100 mm to 120 mm thick. The most important steps to thermally optimize window frames are described in Schnieders (2000) and Kaufmann et al (2002). Recent developments are available at www.passivehouse.com.

It is instructive to study the isothermal lines and heat flow lines of the thermally optimized frame construction (Schnieders, 2000). The insulating layer should lead through the frame section from top to bottom as straight as possible and should not be interrupted. Separate local insulating inserts are not very effective. In a thermally optimized frame, the isothermal lines are as 'short' as possible. The optimized frame on the right in Figure 9.5.4 is thicker (120 mm), has a deeper glazing rebate (20 mm to 30 mm) and the glazing separators are reinforced polycarbonate instead of aluminium.

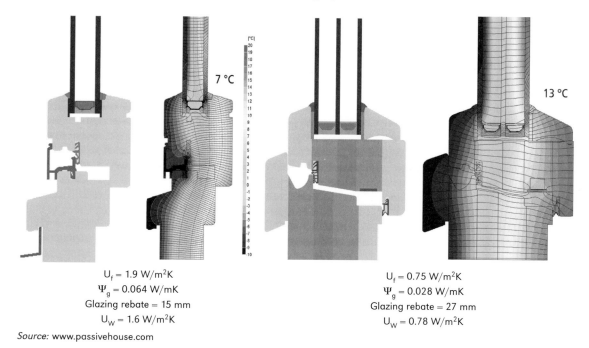

$U_f = 1.9$ W/m²K
$\Psi_g = 0.064$ W/mK
Glazing rebate = 15 mm
$U_W = 1.6$ W/m²K

$U_f = 0.75$ W/m²K
$\Psi_g = 0.028$ W/mK
Glazing rebate = 27 mm
$U_W = 0.78$ W/m²K

Source: www.passivehouse.com

Figure 9.5.4 *Standard wooden window frame (70 mm) (left) compared to a thermally optimized frame (right), shown together with a graph of isothermal and heat flow lines*

Deepened glazing rebate and less conducting glazing layer separators

In standard window frames, the rebate depth for the glazing is only 15 mm. Furthermore, in conventional double glazing the edge system is made of aluminium, which has very high thermal conductivity. The resulting heat lost at the edge of the glazing may be as great as that lost over the total glass surface.

This can be reduced if the glass is set deeper into the frame (that is, 25 mm to 30 mm). In addition, the glazing spacer should be a less conductive material than the commonly used aluminium. Spacers are made from reinforced polycarbonate or thin stainless steel sheet metal less than 0.2 mm thick (see Figure 9.5.5).

The heat losses through the window can be reduced by about 8 per cent with these measures without changing the geometry of the frame cross-section. Accordingly, a thermal separated spacer is also cost effective and suitable for standard windows.

Examples of super-insulated window frames

Some popular highly insulated window frame constructions on the market include the following:

- Frames made of prefabricated sandwich structures of wood/polyurethane/wood or wood/cork/wood. These materials are available today and there is no difference in the production compared to a standard wooden frame, except for the depth of the frame (see Figure 9.5.5).
- Basic wooden frames with an additional separate shell made of cork, PU, expanded polystyrene insulation (EPS) or plastic profile filled with thermal insulating material. These shells are mounted on the external side of the wooden construction. The shell is not glued onto the wood and, hence, can easily be separated at the end of its lifetime for waste disposal (see Figure 9.5.6).

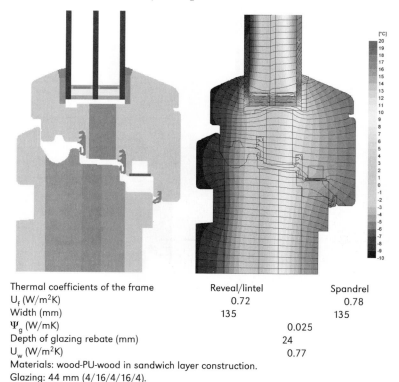

Thermal coefficients of the frame	Reveal/lintel	Spandrel
U_f (W/m^{2}K)	0.72	0.78
Width (mm)	135	135
Ψ_g (W/mK)	0.025	
Depth of glazing rebate (mm)	24	
U_w (W/m^{2}K)	0.77	

Materials: wood-PU-wood in sandwich layer construction.
Glazing: 44 mm (4/16/4/16/4).
Glass edge system: reinforced polycarbonate with embedded stainless steel layer (0.1 mm).
Frames of this type are also available with aluminium clad at the outer surface.

Source: www.passivehouse.com

Figure 9.5.5 *Window frame made of a wood–polyurethane–wood sandwich plate*

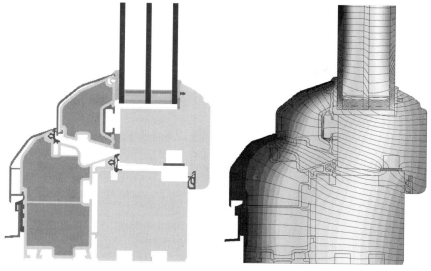

Thermal coefficients of the frame	Reveal/lintel	Spandrel
U_f (W/m²K)	0.76	0.76
Width (mm)	148	148
Ψ_g (W/mK)	0.035	
Depth of glazing rebate (mm)	23	
U_w (W/m²K)	0.80	

Materials: wood-PU-wood in sandwich layer construction.
Glazing: 44 mm (4/16/4/16/4).
Glass edge system: reinforced polycarbonate with embedded stainless steel layer (0.1 mm).

Source:
www.passivehouse.com

Figure 9.5.6 *Wooden frame with an additional thermal insulating shell*

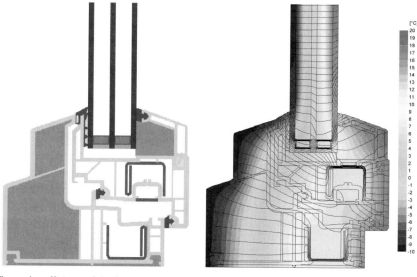

Thermal coefficients of the frame	Reveal/lintel	Spandrel
U_f (W/m²K)	0.71	0.71
Width (mm)	120	120
Ψ_g (W/mK)	0.035	
Depth of glazing rebate (mm)	30	
U_w (W/m²K)	0.79	

Materials: plastic (PVC) profiles filled with thermal insulating foam.
Glazing: 36 mm (4/12/4/12/4).
Glass edge system: profile made of thin stainless steel sheet (0.2 mm).

Source:
www.passivehouse.com

Figure 9.5.7 *Thermally insulated plastic profile*

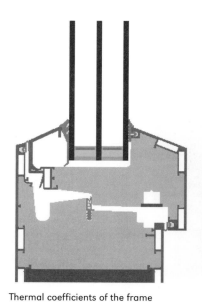

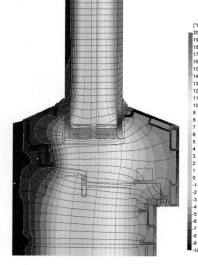

Source: www.passivehouse.com

Figure 9.5.8 *Thermally separated aluminium frame with minimal thermal bridges*

Thermal coefficients of the frame	Reveal/lintel	Spandrel
U_f (W/m²K)	0.71	0.71
Width (mm)	125	125
Ψ_g (W/mK)	0.038	
Depth of glazing rebate (mm)	32	
U_w (W/m²K)	0.80	

Materials:
Shell: aluminium.
Core: tight PU foam (Ï = 0.06 W/mK) with minimal thermal bridges.
Glazing: 44 mm (4/16/4/16/4).
Glass edge system: reinforced polycarbonate with embedded stainless steel layer (0.1 mm).

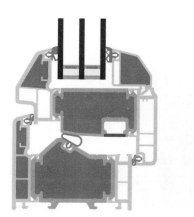

Thermal coefficients of the frame	Reveal/lintel	Spandrel
U_f (W/m²K)	0.79	0.79
Width (mm)	127	127
Ψ_g (W/mK)	0.029	
Depth of glazing rebate (mm)	25	
U_w (W/m²K)	0.80	

Materials: plastic (PVC) profiles filled with thermal insulating foam. Glass fibre reinforced profile instead of steel.
Glazing: 36 mm (4/12/4/12/4).
Glass edge system: reinforced polycarbonate with embedded stainless steel layer (0.1 mm).

Source: www.passivehouse.com

Figure 9.5.9 *Plastic profile and glass fibre-reinforced profile instead of steel profile*

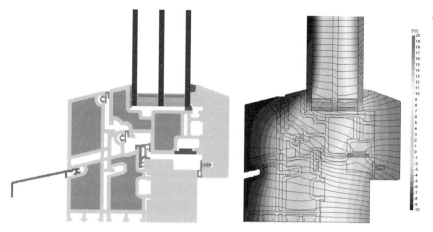

Thermal coefficients of the frame	Reveal/ lintel	Spandrel
U_f (W/m²K)	0.81	0.81
Width (mm)	108	108
Ψ_g (W/mK)	0.028	
Depth of glazing rebate (mm)	18	
U_w (W/m²K)	0.80	

Materials: wood fibre-reinforced profiles filled with thermal insulating foam, wooden shell inside.
Glazing: 44 mm (4/16/4/16/4).
Glass edge system: reinforced polycarbonate with rolled stainless steel layer on surface (0.025 mm)

Source:
www.passivehouse.com

Figure 9.5.10 *Wood fibre-reinforced plastic profile; no steel for stiffening is necessary*

Plastic frames are made of extruded profiles, mainly out of PVC. Here the main chambers have to be filled with polystyrene, PU or other thermal insulating materials, or they have to be very narrow ($\leqslant$ 5mm diameter) (see Figure 9.5.7). Conventional plastic frames lack these insulation properties.

- Thermally separated frames with aluminium shells are available. This frame has the functionality and appearance of an aluminium window, but the core is completely made of tight polyurethane foam with $\lambda = 0.06$ W/mK and with minimal thermal bridges in the construction (see Figure 9.5.8).
- Further developments will be highly strong profiles, which will not need to be reinforced by steel. Profiles made of glass fibre, reinforced materials (see Figure 9.5.9) or wood fibre-reinforced materials (Figure 9.5.10) are now ready for production.

9.5.4 Positioning of highly insulated windows in a super-insulated wall

When placing the window in the wall, an extra thermal bridge effect has to be taken into account. Typical thermal bridge coefficients (Ψ_{pos}) with optimally designed positions are about $\Psi_{pos} = 0.01$–0.03 W/mK. The value is higher at the spandrel, for here the frame cannot be covered by an insulation layer because of the weep outlet. At the reveal of the window the frame is normally covered by thermal insulation and the thermal bridge effect can be almost diminished ($\Psi_{pos} = 0$).

The limit of heat losses for windows in passive houses should be $U_{W,pos} \leqslant 0.85$ W/m²K (Central Europe), including the thermal bridge effect of positioning the window in the wall. The indicated values of æpos refer to a super-insulated wall with $U_{wall} \leqslant 0.15$ W/m²K. Many conventional positioning design details result in large thermal bridge effects (Hauser and Stiegel, 1992, 1997; Hauser et al, 1998; Hauser et al, 2000).

In highly insulated walls, windows are often deeply inset in the wall opening (that is, 30 cm to 40 cm). This can result in the wall section shading the window from solar gains and daylight. One solution to reduce this effect is to bevel the sides of the opening (see Figure 9.5.12). This solution has been applied for centuries – for example, in the Swiss Graubünden region.

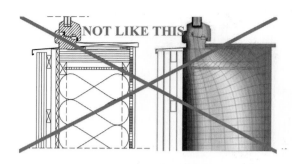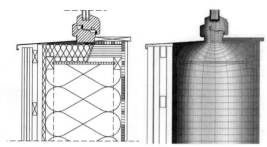

Not like this: unfavourable positioning causes high thermal bridge effects and increases the thermal losses dramatically (Ψ_{pos} = 0.06 W/mK; $U_{W,pos}$ = 0.93 W/m^{2}K).

Optimal: the window is placed in the middle of the thermal insulation layer of the wall; framing should be minimized by careful structural engineering (Ψ_{pos} ≤ 0.014 W/mK; $U_{W,pos}$ = 0.82 W/m^{2}K).

Note: U_{Wall} = 0.12 W/m^{2}K; the U-value of a single window is, in both cases, the same: Uw = 0.78 W/m^{2}K:

Source: www.passivehouse.com

Figure 9.5.11 *Design details for positioning a window in a wall*

Roof windows

Skylights must be positioned to the exterior of the roof section (that is, in the plane of roofing tiles). This contradicts the previous section on advice for positioning windows in walls; indeed, the thermal bridge effects at the skylight edges are rather high. This, combined with the direct exposure to the cold night sky, results in roof glazing losing much heat. Some skylight products use double glazing together with a third hard low-e coating on the exterior surface of the outer glazing. The resulting U_g-value is about 1 W/m^{2}K. Rooms with tilted windows need more heating power in winter and tend to overheat more in summer. Nevertheless, the daylight benefit for such rooms can be substantial. The overheating problem can be reduced with an effective solar shading, which should be on the exterior.

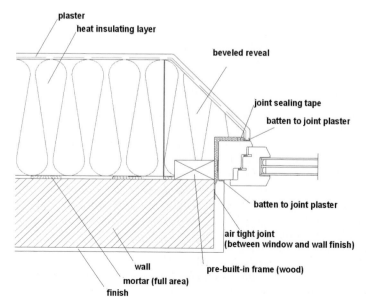

Source: G. Lude, ebök

Figure 9.5.12 *Bevelled wall openings to increase solar gains; the aspect ratio in this example is as good as in standard walls without any thermal insulation*

Double-sash windows (an outer and inner window) may achieve U_g and g-value equivalent or superior to triple glazing, but also at a high price. Here, as was done in old farmhouses, the inner window should be more air tight than the outer window to minimize condensation. The gap between the windows is a sheltered place for sun shading. This construction also provides good sound isolation. Some constructions are commercially available (see www.passivehouse.com).

9.5.5 Economics

Standard windows with double glazing and wooden or plastic frames are available today for about €200 to €300/m². High-performance windows as described in this section are available for about €350 to €500/m² for small quantities (that is, single family houses in Germany). High-performance windows for office buildings can easily cost €340/m². Obviously, windows are, at present, a high-cost item; but there is great potential for price reductions as the number of high-performance window units increases.

Furthermore, in such high-performance housing, there can be considerable savings in the reduced heating system costs. For example, there is no longer a need to place radiators under windows. For this reason, the economics of high-performance windows must be evaluated in the context of the whole building and not as a single component.

9.5.6 Outlook

Vacuum glazing may be a further development to obtain lower U-values ($U_g \leq 0.4$ W/m²K) with double glazing, separated by a thin evacuated space of 0.5 mm to 1.0 mm. Vacuum glazing is already used for freezers and refrigerators that need (small) windows. This technology requires large numbers of produced units at moderate costs.

High-performance housing and its corresponding components, such as windows, described in this section, are a challenge for the building industry during the next few years. The possibility of achieving buildings that are almost independent from the delivery of fossil fuels is fascinating. The extra costs that have to be spent are an investment in a local market and a local industry such as handicraft and trade, which feeds many people. Furthermore, this is an investment in a future of low and decentralized power distribution, which will be less sensitive and less dependent on the delivery of fossil fuels.

Links

Passivhaus Institut, Darmstadt, Germany: www.passivehouse.com. A list of projects and product manufacturers for passive houses is presented and kept up to date. This list contains information on, for example, window frames, prefabricated constructions and mechanical ventilation systems.

References

Feist, W. (1995) *Gedämmte Fensterläden im Passivhaus*, Passivhaus Bericht no 9, Institut Wohnen und Umwelt GmbH, Darmstadt, Germany

Feist, W. (2001) *Passivhaus Sommerfall, Arbeitskreis kostengünstige Passivhäuser*, Protokollband no 15, Passivhaus Institut, Darmstadt, Germany

Feist, W. (2003) *Arbeitskreis kostengünstige Passivhäuser*, Protokollband no 22, Sommerlicher Wärmeschutz, Passivhaus Institut, Darmstadt, Germany

Feist, W. and colleagues (2004) *Passivhaus-Projektierungs-Paket (PHPP) [Passive House Planning Tool]*, Spreadsheet calculation tool based on EN 832, developed at PHI, Darmstadt, Germany

Feist, W., Peper, S. and Oesen, M. (2001) *Klimaneutrale Passivhaussiedlung Hannover-Kronsberg*, CEPHEUS-Projektinformation no 18, Hannover, Germany

Fritz, H. W., Sell, J., Graf, E., Tanner, C., Büchli, R., Blaich, J., Frank, T., Stupp, G. and Faller, M. (2000) *Die Gebäudehülle, konstruktive, bauphysikalische und umweltrelevante Aspekte*, EMPA-Akademie, Eidgenössische Materialprüfungs- und Forschungsanstalt, Dübendorf, Switzerland, www.empa-akademie.ch

Hauser, G., Otto, F., Ringeler, M. and Stiegel, H. (2000) *Holzbau und die EnEV*, Informationsdienst Holz, Holzbau Handbuch, Reihe 3, Teil 2, Folge 2, DGFH, München, Germany

Hauser, G. and Stiegel, H. (1992) *Wärmebrückenatlas für den Holzbau*, Bauverlag, Wiesbaden and Berlin, Germany

Hauser, G. and Stiegel, H. (1997) *Wärmebrücken*, Informationsdienst Holz, Holzbau Handbuch, Reihe 3, Teil 2, Folge 6, DGFH, München, Germany

Hauser, G., Stiegel, H. and Haupt, W. (1998) *Wärmebrückenkatalog*, CD-ROM, GmbH, Baunatal, Germany

ISO 10077 (2000) *Thermal Performance of Windows, Doors and Shutters – Calculation of Thermal Transmittance – Part 1: Simplified Method (ISO 10077-1:2000); Part 2: Numerical Method for Frames*, International Organization for Standardization (ISO), Geneva, Switzerland

Kaufmann, B., Feist, W., John, M. and Nagel, M. (2002) *Das Passivhaus – Energie-Effizientes-Bauen*, Informationsdienst Holz, Holzbau Handbuch, Reihe 1, Teil 3, Folge 10, DGfH, München, Germany

Kaufmann, B., Feist, W., Pfluger, R., John, M. and Nagel, M. (2003) *Passivhäuser erfolgreich planen und bauen, Ein Leitfaden zur Qualitätssicherung von Passivhäusern*, Landesinstitut für Bauwesen des Landes Nordrhein-Westfalen, Aachen, Germany

Kaufmann, B., Schnieders, J. and Pfluger, R. (2002) *Passivhaus-Fenster*, Proceedings of the Sixth European Passive House Conference, Basel, Switzerland, p289

Lude, G. (no date) Design study and development on behalf of Marmorit, Ingenieurbüro ebök, Tübingen, Germany,

Peper, S., Feist, W. and Kah, O. (2001) *Klimaneutrale Passivhaussiedlung Hannover-Kronsberg, Meßtechnische Untersuchung und Auswertung*, CEPHEUS-Projektinformation no 19, Hannover, Germany

Pfluger, R. and Feist, W. (2001) *Kostengünstiger Passivhaus-Geschosswohnungsbau in Kassel Marbachshöhe*, CEPHEUS-Projektinformation no 16, Endbericht, Fachinformation PHI-2001/3, Passivhaus Institut, Darmstadt, Germany

Recknagel, H., Sprenger, E. and Schramek, E. R. (1997) 'Thermische Behaglichkeit', in *Taschenbuch für Heizung und Klimatechnik*, R. Oldenburg-Verlag, München, Germany, Chapter 1.2.4

Schnieders, J. (2000) *Passivhausfenster*, Fourth Passive House Conference, Kassel, March 2000

Schnieders, J., Feist W., Pfluger, R. and Kah, O (2001) *CEPHEUS – Projektinformation Nr 22, Wissenschaftliche Begleitung und Auswertung*, Endbericht, Fachinformation 2001/9, Passivhaus Institut, Darmstadt, Germany

Truschel, S. (2002) *Passivhäuser in Mitteleuropa*, Thesis, FHT Stuttgart, Germany, in collaboration with Passivhaus Institut, Darmstadt, Stuttgart, Germany

9.6 Shading devices

Maria Wall

9.6.1 Concept

In spring and autumn, when a standard house requires heating and solar gains are useful, the solar gains through windows in a high-performance building may overheat rooms. During this time of the year the solar altitude is still relatively low, especially in northern latitudes. Therefore, the solar transmittance through windows will be high due to near perpendicular incidence, and a fixed overhang, such as a roof, will not even shade a south window efficiently. Solar control and overheating protection in high-performance houses must be rethought.

Overview of shading types

The three main groups of shading devices are:

1   exterior devices, such as overhangs, awnings, Venetian blinds, fabric screens, shutters and solar control film on glass;

2   interpane shading devices inside the window construction between two panes or, in some cases, inside a sealed glass unit – examples of interpane sunshades are Venetian blinds, fabric screens, pleated curtains and roller blinds;
3   interior devices such as Venetian blinds, pleated curtains, fabric screens, roller blinds and solar control film on glass or as roller blinds.

Characterization of the shading performance

The total energy transmittance g is defined as the directly transmitted radiation plus the secondary transmitted heat (absorbed energy going inwards).

The total transmittance for the window with shading, g_{system}, is the product of the transmittance for the different parts of the system:

$$g_{system} = g_{sunshade} \cdot g_{window} \qquad\qquad [9.3]$$

A low g-value thus means a high shading performance. Note that the $g_{sunshade}$-value depends on the type of window used and also on the position of the shading device (interior, interpane or exterior). The g-value is neither constant over the year, nor constant for a product.

If the window is double glazed with clear glass, $g_{sunshade}$ is the same as the shading coefficient, which is a designation sometimes used in connection with sunshades. In Sweden, a double-pane window is normally used as a reference for the shading coefficient. However, some countries use a single clear glazing as a reference, which then gives shading coefficients that are not comparable. The g-value is therefore a more straightforward measure of the solar transmittance.

Position and properties of the shading device

Exterior shading devices are more effective since the absorbed heat is largely dissipated to the outdoor air. For interior-placed shading, it is essential to try to reflect the shortwave solar radiation since the heat absorbed in the sunshade is trapped by the window and, hence, heats up the room. However, depending on colour, slat angle position, etc., there is a large performance variation among exterior, interpane and interior sunshades. Figure 9.6.1 shows measured $g_{sunshade}$ for different shading devices. For interior shading devices, the reflectance of the fabric is the most important parameter in obtaining low g-values. This is contrary to exterior shading devices. For example, dark-coloured awnings (with low reflectance and high absorptance) provide lower g-values than light ones. On average, exterior shadings are twice as effective as interior shadings in reducing peak cooling loads.

Two additional issues in selecting shading devices are the effect of the devices on transmitted daylight and the view out. Interior shading yielding low g-values admit almost no daylight into the room and totally obstruct the view out, two of the main reasons for having a window.

Figure 9.6.2 shows the total solar transmittance (g_{system}) for a window with a beige shading screen. The results are from simulations with the program ParaSol. Monthly means during a year are shown for the cold climate (Stockholm). The window is a sealed, triple-glazed unit with low-e coatings on the inner and the outer panes and filled with argon between the panes. The bare window has a g-value of around 31 per cent to 39 per cent. If the screen is added on the interior side, the g_{system} decreases to 26 per cent to 32 per cent. Note that for this position, the gap between window and screen is assumed ventilated to the room (convection). If the screen is positioned between the inner-most pane and the mid pane (gap 2), the g_{system} is 20 per cent to 24 per cent. If the screen is positioned between the mid pane and the outermost pane (gap 1), the g_{system} is 12 per cent to 14 per cent. The best performance is achieved by placing the screen on the exterior side. The total transmittance for the system of window and screen is then only around 6 per cent. Note that vertical shading has a rather constant performance over the year.

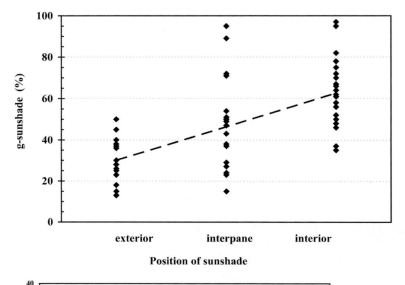

Source: measurements from Lund, Sweden, in Wall and Bülow-Hübe (2003)

Figure 9.6.1 *Measured g-values of different shading devices in combination with a double clear glazing*

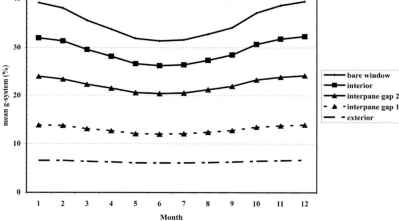

Source: Maria Wall

Figure 9.6.2 *The influence of the position of a beige shading screen: The g-value is shown for the system of shading and window; the g-value for the bare window is also shown (south orientation in a cold Stockholm climate)*

Fixed or moveable shading device

One major problem with fixed shading devices is that they will also shade the windows when there is a heating need or when daylight would be welcome. A moveable shading device is therefore ideal. Automatic control is beneficial if the occupants are not at home during the daytime. However, the occupants should still be able to override the automation.

9.6.2 Exterior shadings

Exterior shadings are very effective. However, they must be robust to withstand the elements and therefore cost more. External shadings such as awnings must be withdrawn when there are strong winds, which can conflict with the need for solar control.

Penetration through the building envelope, necessary for mechanical operation, is in conflict with the need for air tight envelope construction.

Awnings

- Tall windows need an awning that projects far out, which is therefore more exposed to wind damage. In addition, the further the projection, the greater the side opening through which solar radiation is admitted.
- The awning should be 15 cm to 20 cm wider than the window opening to reduce sun penetration from the sides.
- Italian awnings are more suitable for tall windows. The top part is located in side runners and the bottom part projects outwards in the same way as an ordinary awning (see Figure 9.6.3).
- Awnings are more efficient if they have a dark colour. A light colour will increase the primary solar transmittance of the fabric and also increase the solar gains reflected from the light backside of the awning into the room. A very light-coloured awning captures reflected solar radiation from the façade and the ground.
- Awnings are more efficient on a south façade than on a west or east façade.

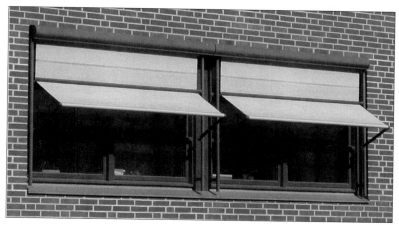

Source: Helena Bülow-Hübe

Figure 9.6.3 *Italian awning*

Exterior Venetian blinds

- A standard construction has aluminium slats in widths from 50 mm that can be tilted. Slats wider than 50 mm are stronger and have a stiffened edge. The shading performance is not very different due to the slat width. The slats are located in side runners to make the blind quieter and better able to resist strong winds. The exception is the 50 mm slat that can be guided at the sides with a plastic-coated wire.
- There should be sufficient space above the window to allow full access to winter sun when the blinds are retracted. When retracted, the external Venetian blind should be protected by a cassette.

Horizontal overhangs

- A horizontal slatted baffle should be capable of supporting snow loading.
- A sloped roof above a horizontal slatted baffle should have cleats to prevent snow avalanches from destroying the shading system.
- Slatted baffles may be combined with an inclined or vertical mantle.

Roller screens

- Roller screens are external screens that can be rolled up or down. The screen is guided by side runners in a track. The fabric is translucent PVC-coated polyester or glass fibre.

Source: Björn Karlsson

Figure 9.6.4 *A horizontal slatted baffle combined with photovoltaics on the vertical mantle*

- The fabric is 'transparent' from the dark side to the light side. The screens provide a relatively good view out but less privacy at night. In districts where dust particles, sand or similar substances are numerous, these may clog up the fabric, with the result that it is less transparent and the view of the outside is restricted. However, the fabric is easy to clean.
- A screen requires less room above the window than, for example, an external Venetian blind.

Energy performance for external shadings

In Figure 9.6.5, examples of g-values for external shadings in combination with a triple-glazed window (with argon and two low-e coatings of 4 per cent) are shown. This window has a centre-of-glass U-value of 0.69 W/m^{2}K. The window is facing south in a cold climate. The window is 1.2 m x 1.2 m and 0.9 m above the floor. The awnings are projected 70 cm down and 70 cm out from the window; thus, the awning angle is 45°. The awnings are 15 cm wider than the window on each side in order to increase efficiency.

For this example, fully closed grey blinds, a beige screen, grey blinds of 45° and a dark awning are the most effective from spring to autumn. The colour of the awning is important. As can be seen, the window with a blue awning has a g-value of approximately 9 per cent during the summer period. The window with a beige awning has a g-value of 16 per cent during the same period.

A horizontal slatted baffle is not a good choice. The slats are horizontal in this example. This baffle gives a similar shade as a roof overhang or a balcony above a window. Since a baffle or overhang is not retractable, it will also shade the window during early spring and late autumn. A 1 m overhang is more effective than only 0.5 m. But to increase the overhang to more than 1 m is not effective in this climate.

Figure 9.6.6 shows the corresponding performance for a westerly orientation in a cold climate. Here it can be seen that horizontal shading – for example, a slatted baffle – results in poor performance. Vertical shadings are not as influenced by the orientation. They are, therefore, preferable for west or east orientations.

The corresponding performance for the temperate climate (Zurich) is shown in Figures 9.6.7 and 9.6.8. During wintertime, the sunshades are more effective in the temperate climate for a south orientation. However, during the summertime, they are slightly more effective in the cold climate except for the beige screen and fully closed Venetian blinds. For a westerly orientation, the sunshades perform somewhat better in the temperate climate.

Figures 9.6.9 and 9.6.10 show the corresponding performance for the mild climate. The performance is almost the same as for the temperate climate.

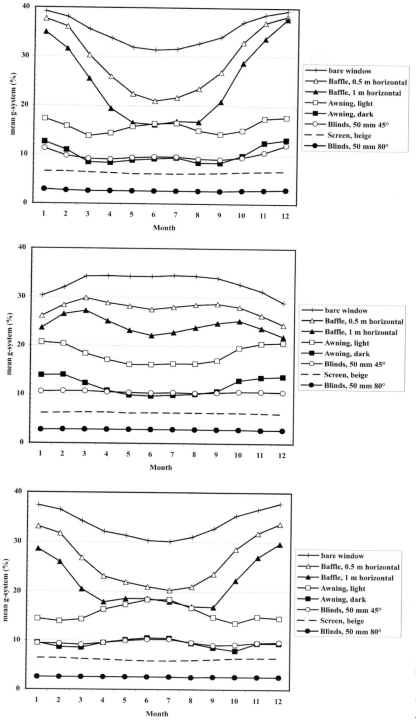

Source: Maria Wall

Figure 9.6.5 *Monthly mean g-values for the combination of window and exterior shading: Triple-glazed window with argon (12 mm) and 2 low-e coatings (4 per cent); south orientation in a cold Stockholm climate*

Source: Maria Wall

Figure 9.6.6 *Monthly mean g-values for the combination of window and exterior shading: Triple-glazed window with argon (12 mm) and 2 low-e coatings (4 per cent); west orientation in a cold Stockholm climate*

Source: Maria Wall

Figure 9.6.7 *Monthly mean g-values for the combination of window and exterior shading: Triple-glazed window with argon (12 mm) and 2 low-e coatings (4 per cent); south orientation in a temperate Zurich climate*

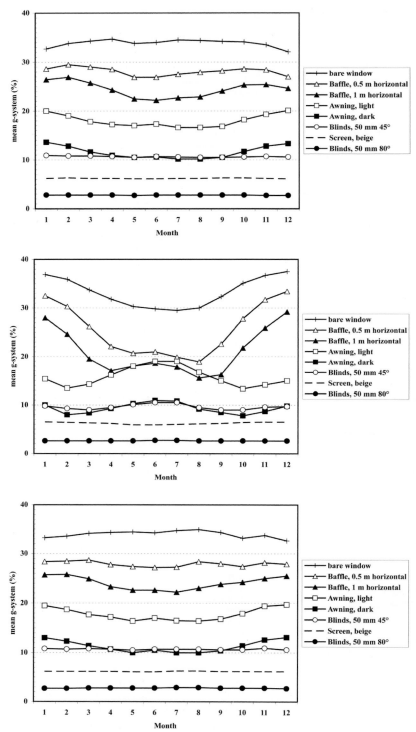

Source: Maria Wall

Figure 9.6.8 *Monthly mean g-values for the combination of window and exterior shading: Triple-glazed window with argon (12 mm) and 2 low-e coatings (4 per cent); west orientation in a temperate Zurich climate*

Source: Maria Wall

Figure 9.6.9 *Monthly mean g-values for the combination of window and exterior shading: Triple-glazed window with argon (12 mm) and 2 low-e coatings (4 per cent); south orientation in a mild Milan climate*

Source: Maria Wall

Figure 9.6.10 *Monthly mean g-values for the combination of window and exterior shading: Triple-glazed window with argon (12 mm) and 2 low-e coatings (4 per cent); west orientation in a mild Milan climate*

9.6.3 Shading devices inside the window construction

Interpane shadings are less effective than exterior devices. While they are well protected between the panes, the types of shading devices are limited by the width of the air gap. Venetian blinds, screens, roller blinds and pleated curtains are used. In case of a triple-glazed window, the shading is more effective if it is placed in the outermost gap.

Energy performance for interpane shadings

Figure 9.6.11 shows g-values for a south-oriented window with interpane shadings in a cold climate. The triple-glazed window consists of a double-glazed sealed unit with a low-e coating (4 per cent) and argon, and, on the outside, an 84 mm air gap (including sunshade) and a single glazing with a low-e coating (16 per cent). Such a triple-glazed unit has a centre-of-glass U-value of 0.79 W/m²K. The g-value for the bare window is somewhat higher (38 per cent to 46 per cent) than for the window used for the external sunshades.

Most of the interpane shadings in Figure 9.6.11 show a similar performance: g_{system} between 15 per cent and 20 per cent. Two white products – closed (= 80°) white Venetian blinds and a white screen with a high reflectance – have a better performance. The total transmittance, g_{system}, is approximately 7 per cent to 10 per cent for these products. It is thus essential that interpane products have a high reflectance. When included in the outermost air gap (as shown here), they obtain quite high shading performance, even better than some of the exterior ones.

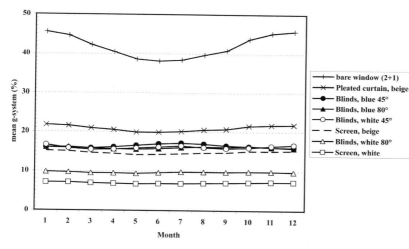

Note: Different shadings are included in the outermost air gap; south orientation in a cold Stockholm climate.

Source: Maria Wall

Figure 9.6.11 *Monthly mean g-values for the combination of a triple-glazed window and inter-pane shading: Double-glazed sealed unit with argon (12 mm) and a low-e coating (4 per cent) plus an air gap (84 mm) and clear glass on the outside with a low-e coating (16 per cent)*

9.6.4 Interior shading devices

Interior shading devices can reduce glare and obstruct the view into the room but are least effective in preventing overheating.

Energy performance for interior shadings

Figure 9.6.12 shows the performance of some internal shading devices. The white roller blind with high reflectance (83 per cent) shows the best performance with a g_{system} of 22 per cent to 26 per cent. The beige screen (reflectance 52 per cent) has a g_{system} of 26 per cent to 32 per cent. White Venetian blinds are effective and better than blue ones. Note that for the two screens, the gap between window and screen is assumed ventilated to the room (convection).

In general, interior sunshades are better when they are in a light colour, reflecting more of the shortwave radiation to the outside. This is especially true for highly insulating windows that can

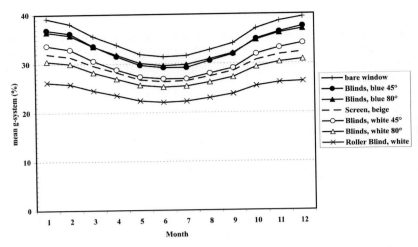

Source: Maria Wall

Figure 9.6.12 *Monthly mean g-values for the combination of window and interior shading: Triple-glazed window with argon and 2 low-e coatings (4 per cent); south orientation in a cold Stockholm climate*

reflect shortwave solar radiation back out, but more effectively trap long-wave heat inside the room. The purpose of low-emissivity coatings, often used in high-performance windows, is to reduce heat losses and thus give rise to a low U-value. A drawback is that heat absorbed in the interior shading will be hindered in retransmitting to the outside. This is also the case for interpane shading when a low-e coating is positioned outside the shading, on the outmost glass pane.

Figure 9.6.13 shows values for g_{system} for different interior sunshades in relation to the reflectance of the sunshade. There is a strong correlation between the reflectance of the sunshade and the g-value.

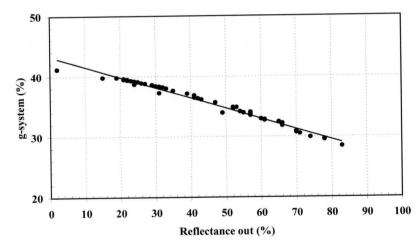

Source: Maria Wall

Figure 9.6.13 *G-values for the combination of window and interior shading in relation to the reflectance of the fabric: Triple-glazed window with argon and 2 low-e coatings (4 per cent); south orientation in a cold Stockholm climate*

9.6.5 Design advice

Exterior shading devices are the most effective solution to avoid overheating. Architectural overhangs are less efficient, cannot be retracted and should be avoided because they are less effective in preventing overheating than other devices and they block daylight all year. For a south orientation, a dark awning, external Venetian blinds or screen are good choices. For a west- or east-oriented window, vertical sunshades (parallel to the window) are the most effective.

Interpane sunshades are an acceptable alternative, especially when they are placed in the outer-most air gap. Especially for windy sites, they are a good alternative and could perform even better than some exterior shadings. The interpane sunshades should have a high reflectance facing out.

If interior sunshades must be used, it is even more important that they should have a high reflectance. Even so, they offer a poor overheating protection and are, at best, only good at reducing glare and providing privacy.

References

Kvist, H., Hellström, B. and colleagues (2006) *ParaSol version 3.0*, Simulation tool for performance studies of windows and shadings, Energy and Building Design, Lund University, Sweden, www.parasol.se

Wall, M. and Bülow-Hübe, H. (eds) (2001) *Solar Protection in Buildings*, Report TABK- 01/3060, Energy and Building Design, Department of Construction and Architecture, Lund Institute of Technology, Lund University, Sweden

Wall, M. and Bülow-Hübe, H. (eds) (2003) *Solar Protection in Buildings. Part 2: 2000–2002*, Report EBD-R–03/1, Energy and Building Design, Department of Construction and Architecture, Lund Institute of Technology, Lund University, Sweden

10

Ventilation

10.1 Ventilation fundamentals

Frank-Dietrich Heidt

In cold and temperate climates, ventilation and infiltration are a major part of the heating load of high-performance housing. The heat required, HV (Wh), due to any air change rate n (h–1) is:

$$HV = n \cdot V \cdot (\rho c)_{air} \cdot 24 \text{ h/d} \cdot DD \qquad [10.1]$$

where:

- V = volume of exchangeable indoor air in m^2;
- $(\rho c)_{air}$ = volumetric specific heat of air (= 0.34 Wh/m^3K); and
- DD = degree days in Kd (1 d = 24 h).

An air change rate of 0.5 h-1 in such housing in a climate with 3500 Kd (Kelvin degree days) would result in a heating demand of nearly 36 kWh/m^2a. Increasing the air change rate (due to ventilation or leakage) by a mere 0.1 h-1 would increase this by an additional 7.2 kWh/m^2a. Accordingly, in the interest of minimizing energy consumption for heating and also in moving air, the lowest air change rate possible to achieve desirable air quality is the goal. Three qualities of indoor air are the oxygen and carbon dioxide (CO_2) levels, the humidity and the concentration of pollutants.

10.1.1 Oxygen and CO_2 levels

Occupants breathing and depleting oxygen is never a condition for setting the ventilation rate of housing. A person requires between 0.005 and 0.0075 litres of O_2 per second. Because air consists of nearly 22 per cent oxygen, the required flow rate of O_2 is adequate with a mere air exchange rate of 0.082 to 0.123 m^3/h per person. This is a factor 300 to 400 smaller than the 20 to 40 m^3/h of fresh air per person commonly recommended. This latter recommendation is derived from the so-called Pettenkofer limit (Max von Pettenkofer was a well-known researcher on human physiology at the University of Munich in about 1870), postulating that about 1000 ppm (volume) of CO_2 as indoor air concentration is an upper tolerable limit for comfortable indoor air quality. The corresponding value of the overall air exchange rate depends on the outdoor air concentration of CO_2, which is actually at about 360 ppm (volume). With an average indoor air volume per person between 75 m^3 and 100 m^3 (German dwellings), the above-mentioned volume rates of air exchange per person are equivalent to air change rates between about 0.25 h^{-1} and 0.50 h^{-1}.

This same air exchange rate not only supplies (much more than required) O_2 to the system and maintains its CO_2 concentration within the desired range of values, but it also removes much of the water vapour that is produced inside dwellings.

10.1.2 Humidity

The amount of water vapour removal depends on the relative humidity and temperatures of indoor and outdoor air. It is critical to maintain a comfortable level of humidity in winter (indoor: temperature 20°C, relative humidity (rh) 60 per cent; outdoor: temperatures between 0°C–10°C, rh 70 per cent). In this case, the exfiltration rate of water vapour mass MR varies between:

$$3.8 \text{ g m}^{-3} \cdot \text{VR (m}^3 \text{ h}^{-1}) \leqslant \text{MR} \leqslant 7.0 \text{ g m}^{-3} \cdot \text{VR (m}^3 \text{ h}^{-1}) \qquad [10.2]$$

where VR = n • V is the volume rate of the exchanged air.

The lower limit correlates to 10°C outdoor air temperature, the upper value describes the case for 0°C. Correspondingly, an air exchange rate per person of 30 m^3/h will remove between 110 g/h and 210 g/h of water vapour. This rate of removing water vapour is quite sufficient for most of the cases where humidity is generated in dwellings. Only for more intensive showers, cooking, cleaning, washing and drying activities will higher humidity loads occur, which have to be removed by additional ventilation measures (intended actions such as opening of windows, setting the highest possible mechanical ventilation rate and activation of an extra fan). Table 10.1.1 gives the typical emission rates of water vapour due to various sources.

Table 10.1.1 *Typical emission rates of water vapour for some sources*

Source of water vapour	Evaporation rate (g/h)
Persons (sedentary activity)	40–60
Persons (average activity)	60–120
Persons (exhausting activity)	120–200
Pets (dog, cat)	5–10
Bath	approximately 700
Shower	approximately 2500
Cooking	600–1500
Potted plants	7–15
Drying laundry (4.5 kg washer drum), spinned dry	50–200
Drying laundry (4.5 kg washer drum), dripping wet	100–500
Aquarium (per m² water surface)	30–50

In a typical household with 4 individuals, approximately 12 kg of water vapour is emitted over 24 hours.

10.1.3 Pollutants

Whenever the emission rate Q (m^3/h) of any 'contaminating' substance of the indoor air (CO_2, water vapour, other substances) is given, the asymptotic ('after a long period of time') equilibrium concentration C_∞ (dimensionless) of this substance is:

$$C_\infty = C_{amb} + Q / (n \cdot V) \qquad [10.3]$$

where C_{amb} is the (dimensionless) concentration of the contaminant in the ambient air and V means the indoor air volume of the considered building. C_∞ has to be compared with the desired or just allowed value (in Germany: MAK – value = maximum allowed concentration at working place).

If the concentration of the diluted matter is given as a mass concentration ρ (in kg/m^3), the corresponding final value of it is:

$$\rho_\infty = \rho_{amb} + S / (n \cdot V)$$

[10.4]

where ρ_{amb} (in kg/m^3) is the mass concentration of the contaminant in the ambient air and S (in kg/h) is the local source strength within the room.

Corresponding values of air change rates are given for every kind of room as the maximum of the:

- required air supply, which depends on the number of individuals present (typically about 30 m^3/h per person);
- recommended volume rates of exhaust air for several functional rooms; and
- minimum air exchange rate of n = 0.3 h-1, which accounts for indoor air pollution without any persons or functional activity; this value considers the fact that indoor equipment and appliances are permanently releasing gaseous matter, which contaminates the indoor air and has to be removed by dilution with fresh air.

10.1.4 Design advice

The recommended volume rates of exhaust air are listed in Table 10.1.2. These data can serve as a reasonable guideline for providing preliminary answers to such questions as how much fresh air is needed altogether and how much fresh air is needed for each room?

Table 10.1.2 *Recommended nominal air flow rates for rooms with various functions*

Room function	Air flow rate (m^3/h)
Kitchen	60
Bathroom	40–60
Toilet	30
Housework, storage	20–30

References

Heidt, F. D. (1994) 'Lüftung', in Maier, K. H. (ed) *Der Energieberater. Kap.*, 5.1.1.6, S. 1-60, Verlag Deutscher Wirtschaftsdienst GmbH, Köln, Germany

Liddament, M. (1996) *A Guide to Energy Efficient Ventilation: The Air Infiltration and Ventilation Centre*, University of Warwick Science Park, UK

10.2 Ventilation typology

Frank-Dietrich Heidt

The air movement through a building's envelope is driven by a pressure difference created by wind and indoor air to outdoor air temperature differences. It also depends on the air exchanging openings of a building's envelope, which may be intentional (such as windows, inlet valves or ducts) or not (for example, porosity, cracks or leakage). This means that natural ventilation rates are very unpredictable, given the unknowns of weather, the size and location of leakage in the building envelope and the behaviour of the occupants (opening windows and doors). These factors are additive and define the natural air exchange rate n_{nat}:

$$n_{nat} = n_{inf} + n_{user} \qquad\qquad [10.5]$$

with n_{inf} as the air change rate due to infiltration/exfiltration and n_{user} as the air change rate due to the user-intended opening of windows, door(s) and other appliances.

Mechanical ventilation always acts in addition to the already existing natural ventilation and should dominate the air exchange rate. The overall air change rate is then a superposition of natural and mechanical ventilation:

$$n = n_{nat} + n_{mech} \qquad\qquad [10.6]$$

with n_{nat} as defined above and n_{mech} as an air exchange rate (in 1/h) due to motor-driven air movement. For energy-related considerations, the electrical power for fan operation and control has to be accounted for.

Natural ventilation is totally inadequate during winter in the tight envelope construction of high-performance housing, where the heating energy consumption is less than 25 kWh/m²a. It must, however, be considered during planning in order to ensure that this heating target is not exceeded. Equally important, natural ventilation should be adequate in summer so that if the occupants desire, the mechanical ventilation can be shut down.

10.2.1 Natural ventilation

Natural ventilation is commonly classified into three types:

1   crack ventilation;
2   stack ventilation; and
3   window ventilation.

Crack ventilation (or infiltration/exfiltration) occurs through all leakage of a building envelope, mainly through the joints and slits of windows and doors. It is uncontrolled and usually does not correspond to actual ventilation needs. Especially for older buildings with only limited air tightness during winter time, considerable heat losses can occur with the additional appearance of uncomfortable draught. This is one reason why new buildings have to meet a level of air tightness that restricts the air change rate due to infiltration/exfiltration to less than about 0.1 h⁻¹ to 0.2 h⁻¹.

Even small driving forces (pressure difference from the wind passing over a building) can move substantial volumes of air through windows or vent openings. If the outdoor air is colder than the indoor air, it flows across the lower part of the window into the building. Warmer indoor air exits via the upper part of the window, even if there is no wind present. In winter, the resulting draughts pose a comfort problem and, in the case of permanently tipped windows, a serious heat loss. Ideally, windows should be opened fully, briefly, resulting in a flushing of the house air. Table 10.2.1 lists typical ranges of resulting air change rates for different states of window openings.

Table 10.2.1 *Estimated ranges of air change rates for different states of window openings*

Status of window opening	Range of air change rates (h⁻¹)
Windows and doors closed	0.1–0.4
Windows tilted	0.5–4
Windows open	5–15
Cross-ventilation/opposite windows	up to 40

Stack ventilation can be achieved with ducts that penetrate a room at ceiling level and terminate at roof level. In high-rise buildings, the resulting buoyancy can provide a strong air extraction rate – for example, from kitchen, bathroom or washing rooms that are often without windows. Every room type needs a separate stack.

Window ventilation offers the following advantages:

- An 'open window' environment is popular.
- Natural ventilation costs less than mechanical systems.
- There is almost no maintenance required (work, costs).
- Natural ventilation needs no additional space for machinery.
- If there are enough openings, high air flow rates for cooling and purging are possible.

On the other hand, natural ventilation also shows some major disadvantages:

- Air flow rates and the patterns can be excessive or inadequate, varying unpredictably during the day and season. The result can be poor indoor air quality and high heat losses.
- Natural ventilation is unsuited for noisy and polluted locations.
- Filtration or cleaning of incoming air is usually not feasible.
- Occupants must constantly adjust openings to suit the prevailing demand.

10.2.2 Mechanical ventilation

Mechanical ventilation by electricity-powered fans can provide fresh air for a whole building or for special rooms only. In the latter case, such 'decentralized ventilation units' are not treated here. This section describes 'central ventilation systems' for a house, apartment or whole apartment building.

In the case of the simplest mechanical ventilation, air is extracted only. This creates an internal under-pressure that draws supply air through planned openings in the building envelope. At the next level, fresh air is mechanically supplied and 'used' air is extracted.

Mechanical extract ventilation permanently ensures the required air change rate independent of occupants opening windows and independent of the weather. As a result, building condensation of humid air inside of exterior walls can be avoided, contaminants are removed and outside noise can be kept outside. During summer nights, the housing can be flushed with cool, fresh outdoor air. The fresh air is supplied to the living and sleeping zones, flows across the entrance hall and is exhausted via the kitchen, the bathroom and the toilets. For multi-family dwellings, every apartment should have its individual extract ventilation system to avoid transmission of noise and/or odour among neighbours.

The under-pressure caused by the fans should be adequate to dominate over wind and stack effects. However, the negative pressure difference between the building and its environment should not be excessive – otherwise, high velocity draughts in the indoor air and/or back-draughts from the outside air may occur. Additionally, buildings with a mechanical extract system have to be as air tight as possible in order to avoid air flows through other openings than those which are provided for that purpose.

In summary, the advantages of mechanical extract ventilation are:

- controlled ventilation rates are possible;
- when carefully designed, the air flows along the planned paths;
- pollutants can be extracted at their source and entry into occupied spaces can be avoided;
- condensation of water vapour inside exterior walls is likely eliminated; and
- heat recovery from the exhaust air stream is possible by using a heat pump.

Disadvantages include that:

- investment costs are higher compared to natural ventilation;
- electrical energy is needed for system operation;
- system noise may be a problem;
- regular cleaning and maintenance are necessary;
- extreme wind may affect the adequacy of the ventilation because intakes and exhaust vents are at fixed locations on the building;
- there is a risk of back-draughts from flues or the intake of radon (or any other soil gas) being drawn from the below-grade spaces; and
- occupants adjusting individual air inlets can affect the air flow through other branches of the system.

Mechanical supply ventilation drives the outdoor air mechanically into the building where it mixes with the existing air. This process creates a positive pressure difference against the atmospheric pressure, which inhibits the entry of infiltration air from outdoors. In this way, all incoming air can be precleaned and thermally conditioned. Such systems are mainly used in areas where the outdoor air is polluted (for example, in city centres), for industrial clean rooms or for occupants with allergies. This system type is usually not recommended for dwellings since it increases the risk of indoor-generated water vapour penetrating and condensing in the exterior walls and roof insulation.

Mechanical balanced ventilation combines extract and supply systems that are implemented as two separately ducted networks. Typically, the air is supplied and mixed into the 'dry' or 'occupied' zones (living rooms, bedrooms and study rooms) and is extracted from the 'wet' or 'polluted' zones (kitchen, bathrooms and toilets). An air flow pattern is established between the supply to the extract areas, which should be supported by appropriately sized air slots between these rooms. This may occur under doors, or, for acoustical reasons, special sound-deadening slots can be built in.

Systems with an accurate balance of mass flows are usually 'pressure neutral' and, therefore, not resistant to infiltration/exfiltration driven by wind velocity and temperature differences. Consequently, the building must be air tight to ensure that the air flow volume and direction occur as planned. There are systems available on the market that are able to maintain an almost perfect mass balance either by velocity sensors or by using the characteristics of built-in fans (power versus flow rate). Sometimes an intentional imbalance of air flows is introduced to put the building in a slight negative pressure, with the extraction rate up to 10 per cent higher than the supply rate (for dwellings). This allows for some limited infiltration and prevents moisture migration into the exterior walls and interstitial condensation there.

Mechanical balanced ventilation systems offer the same advantages as mechanical extract ventilation regarding a guaranteed supply of fresh air and avoidance of excessive ventilation heat losses (as can occur with uncontrolled natural ventilation). Moreover, direct heat recovery from the exhaust air to the supply air by heat exchangers can drastically reduce the amount of purchased heat, which must be provided to temper incoming air. Furthermore, filtering and thermal conditioning of the supply air improve indoor air quality and comfort. These arguments can help to justify the additional capital investment and operating costs of such a ventilation system.

The disadvantages of mechanical balanced systems are similar to those of a mechanical extract system. The problem of noise (here with two fans) can be minimized by installing the ventilation units away from the living and sleeping zones near functional rooms such as the kitchen or bathroom. The air handling unit can be sound insulated. Impact sound has to be reduced by mounting the units with sound-absorbing materials. In any case, the sound level in living or sleeping rooms should not exceed 30 dB(A) according to German codes (DIN 4109, Part 5 and VDI Richtlinie 2081). In high-performance houses, an even lower sound level of 25 dB(A) is recommended. For single family houses, suitable space in the attic or the basement can often be found for the central ventilation unit.

In these cases, however, the duct runs for supply air as well as for exhaust air may be longer and, in any case, the duct runs in unheated spaces have to be kept short and well insulated.

References

Heidt, F. D. (1994) 'Lüftung', in Maier, K. H. (ed) *Der Energieberater. Kap.*, 5.1.1.6, S. 1-60, Verlag Deutscher Wirtschaftsdienst GmbH, Köln, Germany

Liddament, M. (1996) *A Guide to Energy Efficient Ventilation: The Air Infiltration and Ventilation Centre*, University of Warwick Science Park, UK

10.3 Ventilation systems for high-performance housing

Frank-Dietrich Heidt

10.3.1 Basics of ventilation for high-performance housing

The conventional ventilation systems described in the previous sections potentially cause high heat losses corresponding to the air change rate n. The only difference between natural and mechanical ventilation is that the mechanical ventilation rate n can be known ($n = n_{mech} + n_{inf}$), whereas for the natural ventilation it is largely unknown. Keeping in mind that the air change rate required for hygiene and resulting from leakage totals at least 0.5 h^{-1}, this results in ventilation heat losses of about 36 kWh/m^2a. This is a high value, given that the target heating demand for high-performance housing is 25 kWh/m^2a or less. Accordingly, a ventilation system with heat recovery is necessary to meet the target. Heat recovery can be accomplished by:

- mechanical extract ventilation with a heat pump;
- mechanical balanced ventilation with a heat exchanger;
- mechanical balanced ventilation with heat exchanger and ground heat exchanger; and
- mechanical balanced ventilation with all of the above.

For any of these systems to operate effectively, two prerequisites must be fulfilled:

- an air tight building envelope; and
- an 'all-inclusive' planning concept for the ventilation system.

Building air tightness is measured by the so-called n50 value. This is the average air change rate of a building that has a positive and negative pressure difference of 50 Pa against atmospheric pressure. The common measuring technique is by fan pressurization (blower door). The infiltration rate n_{inf}, which is achieved for natural pressure differences (typically between –10 Pa and +10 Pa) is estimated from the n50 value by:

$$n_{inf} = e \cdot n50$$

[10.7]

where the factor e describes how exposed the building is to its surrounding wind field. The following values for e can be assumed (German DIN 4108, Part 6):

- 0.10 for a wind-exposed site;
- 0.04 for a sheltered site; and
- 0.07 for moderate conditions.

A measured n50 value of 3.0 h^{-1} for a moderate site can accordingly be expected to have an air exchange rate due to infiltration of about 0.2 h^{-1}. The European standard EN 832 also offers values for the wind factor.

Air tightness ensures that:

- draughts due to external wind and temperature differences are prevented;
- noise and odour transmissions through the exterior walls are minimized;
- indoor-generated water vapour does not migrate into the exterior walls; and
- the air change rate and indoor air flow directions are under mechanical control and minimally affected by weather.

Moreover, some countries (for example, Germany, Switzerland, The Netherlands, Belgium, Sweden, Norway and Canada) have introduced air-tightness requirements as best practice standards.

Tight envelope construction is essential for the proper functioning of heat recovery in a mechanical ventilation system. If ε_{HR} is the effectiveness of heat recovery and only some fraction of the total exchanged air flow is driven through the corresponding devices, the effectiveness of this real system $\varepsilon_{HR,REAL}$ is only:

$$\varepsilon_{HR,REAL} = \varepsilon_{HR} \cdot (1 - n_{inf} / n)$$ [10.8]

This means that if 25 per cent of the total air exchange rate n occurs via the infiltration path ($n_{inf} = 0.25 \cdot n$), it will reduce the nominal heat exchanger effectiveness ε_{HR} to a real value of $\varepsilon_{HR,REAL} = 0.75 \cdot \varepsilon_{HR}$.

The decision to make the building tight and to have mechanical ventilation has several planning consequences. Due to the volume taken up by air ducts, their placement must be considered early in the design phase. The space and volume needed where all the ducts come together – namely, the equipment room – must also be planned for.

10.3.2 Conceptual planning

The conceptual planning of a ventilation system for high-performance housing includes the following.

Definition of ventilation/air quality requirements. This joint action by the planner and client establishes the purposes and the expected properties of the ventilation system and sets the boundary conditions. Standards and applicable codes have to be clarified. The conclusions of this process should remain constant for the rest of the planning process.

Specifying zones by air quality and temperature requirements. Fresh air should always be supplied to the living and sleeping spaces (for example, living rooms, children's rooms, study room, bedrooms). From there it flows through circulation spaces (corridors, entry hall or stair) to wet rooms (kitchen, bathrooms, toilets, utility rooms) where it is extracted. Placement of the supply and exhaust ducts to serve these zones has to be considered with the goal of keeping duct runs as short as possible.

Determining the nominal air flow rates and distribution. The total air change rate comes from the addition of all supply rates (or exhaust rates) for the interconnecting rooms between the point of supply and extraction. Measures have to be provided that allow for such air flows. Supply rate and extraction rates should be balanced.

Deciding on the level of air filtration (normal or for allergies). Different classes of air filters concerning efficiency, pressure drop and dust holding capacity are defined in ventilation standards (for example, the German DIN EN 779). The lowest acceptable filter class is G3 for coarse dust. To prevent pollution by very fine dust (down to about 1 μm), filter classes F6, F7 or F8 should be applied (see Table 10.3.1). The cleaning of air by filters is necessary when high concentrations of particles are present or when the outside air is contaminated. As the ambient air is usually rather clean, filtration of outdoor air serves mainly to keep the supply branch of the duct free from dust. If the indoor air contains pollutant aerosols (fat particles, tobacco smoke, etc), filters are also mounted in front of exhaust ducts, fans and heat exchangers, as the exchange of filters is cheaper than cleaning the ducts. On the other hand, filters cause pressure drop (typically 50 Pa to 300 Pa) and thus increase the electrical power demand of fans. Careful dimensioning is required to maximize the useful operating time of the filters while keeping the pressure drop to acceptable values. Because filters have to be inspected, cleaned or exchanged about every three to six months, they have to be easily accessible.

Table 10.3.1 *Air filter classes (degree of retention versus particle size)*

Particle size	Percentage of retention							
	G 1	G 2	G 3	G 4	F 5	F 6	F 7	F 8
0.1	–	–	–	–	0–10	5–15	25–35	35–45
0.3	–	–	–	0–5	5–15	10–25	45–60	65–75
0.5	–	–	0–5	5–15	15–30	20–40	60–75	80–90
1	–	0–5	5–15	15–35	30–50	50–65	85–95	95–98
3	0–5	5–15	15–35	30–55	70–90	85–95	> 98	> 99
5	5–15	15–35	35–70	60–90	90–99	95–99	> 99	> 99
10	40–50	50–70	70–85	85–98	> 98	> 99	> 99	> 99

Average values of dust concentrations in urban outdoor environments vary between 0.1 mg/m^3 and 0.5 mg/m^3, and particle sizes with maximum concentration range between 7 μm and 20 μm. For rural outdoor environments, dust concentrations are much less, ranging from 0.05 mg/m^3 to 0.10 mg/m^3, with most existing particles being smaller than 1 μm to 2 μm.

Specifying the duct geometry and construction. The ductwork geometry strongly influences the required fan power, as well as the sound level of the ventilation system. Duct cross-sections should be chosen to allow as slow an air velocity as possible so that it never exceeds 3 m/s. This is in order to limit pressure drops, electrical consumption and noise production. Space limitations or costs often lead to small diameter ducts. This results in turbulent air flow with all of the above disadvantages. Duct lengths should be kept short and with minimal bends. The duct interior should be smooth. Folded spiral seam tubes of tin-plated sheet steel are acceptable. Flexible spiral tubes made of aluminium are less favourable. They require special attention during installation to avoid pinch blockages. Spiral tubes of synthetics should be avoided. For straight ducts, a pressure loss of less than 0.5 Pa per metre length is desirable. The air ducts should be air tight in order to prevent penetration of external dust and to avoid heat losses in between the heated zone and the heat exchanger. Particularly during the building construction, ducts must be kept sealed.

Locating the outside air intake, distribution and room air extraction. Obviously, outside air should be taken where the best air quality is available (distant from sewer vents, chimneys, exhaust air vents, waste containers, car parking, etc). The fresh air intake should be protected, ideally inaccessible to avoid manipulations and to be shielded from heavy rain. The opening geometry should minimize pressure losses. The path from the point of supply in the living spaces to the point of extraction must also be ensured by closed doors. This can be achieved by horizontal slits at the upper or lower part of the door leafs or built-in air grilles. They should be designed so that pressure drops across the doors should not exceed approximately 1 Pa and air velocities should be under 1 m/s (to avoid air draught and noise). These pressure differences should be almost the same between all rooms of the supply zone and the transition zone, as well as between this zone and all rooms that belong to the extract zone of a building. This ensures the same quality of fresh air supply for all rooms. For volume rates up to 40 m^3/h, a horizontal slit with 15 mm height is sufficient. The exhaust vents should also cause minimal pressure losses (being adjustable along a correlation between volume rate and pressure drop). They should be mounted well away from heating appliances and should avoid short-circuiting with the air supply inlets. In rooms with high humidity, the exhaust vents should be located near the ceiling. In the kitchen area, a separate exhaust hood with volume rates between 150 m³/h to 200 m³/h is recommended to capture high water vapour and fat particles. During the operation of kitchen hoods, when exhausting air directly to the outside, the supply rate for the overall ventilation system has to be increased to keep the house balanced, otherwise a lower pressure within the building would increase the uncontrolled infiltration of air from outside. Prevention and suppression of noise is a common engineering task for the entrance, distribution and removal of air. For that, specific data and design advice are available from component suppliers.

Detailing thermal insulation. Cold and warm air ducts should ideally be within the tempered zone being served. Fresh cold air should not withdraw heat from the heated zone, and stale warm air should not lose heat to the colder ambient air. If this is not feasible, ducts must be insulated (thermal conductivity: 0.35–0.40 W/mK). This typically leads to an insulation thickness of between 5 cm and 10 cm. The central ventilation unit should be near where the ducts penetrate the boundary of the heated zone of the building – either just inside this zone or just outside. The central ventilation unit itself should be thermally insulated, too, to avoid the heat exchange between exhaust and supply ducts and the surroundings of the unit. Supply ducts providing heating should always be within the heated zone of the building.

Planning sound insulation, dampers and fire/smoke breaks. The sound level of the ventilation system should not exceed 25 dB(A) for the supply zone and 30 dB(A) for the rooms of the transition zone and the extract zone. These values are each better by 5 dB(A) (lower) than those required by the German standard DIN 4109. Experience has shown that designs just meeting the limits can lead to occupant complaints. To obtain such rather low sound levels, silencers have to be built into ducts between the fans and the served rooms. Depending on the ambient noise levels at the outside air intakes or air outlets, additional silencers may be needed. Rigid or flexible tubular silencers containing sound-absorbing material, which is covered on the inner surface of the tube by perforated metal sheets, are well suited for this purpose. The propagation of sound between rooms through the ducts or through slits or air grilles has also to be considered. Sound protection requires engineering! Finally, dampers, and fire and smoke protection have to be planned for local building codes.

Programming the control system. Optimization of indoor air quality with the constraint of ventilation heat losses requires the ability to control the ventilation system for the conditions that are occurring. The following aspects should be considered:

- Operation must be kept simple and easy to understand (user acceptance!).
- In multi family houses, air change rates should be adjustable individually for each apartment.
- For every apartment, the air change rate should be variable between several steps (for example, 'off', 'low', 'normal' and 'high'). This can be done manually or automated.
- Freeze protection of heat exchanger must not be achieved by switching off the supply fan, otherwise increased infiltration and ventilation heat losses, as well as cold air draughts, may result when the exhaust fan is still operating.
- Summer operation needs no heat exchanger. Therefore, either the system is switched off totally (window ventilation only), or there exists a bypass for the heat exchanger, or an interchangeable summer module for the ventilation unit is used.

Controls unfortunately require many sensors, actuators and other electronic equipment that cause additional pressure drop and electric power consumption. Moreover, additional costs arise due to investment, operation and maintenance. Therefore, the benefits of more sophisticated controls have to be traded off against these drawbacks.

Adjusting air flows and performance testing. Planning is one aspect; quality of workmanship is another! Therefore, prior to the call for tenders, a qualified procedure of acceptance tests has to be defined. This includes a complete system description, selected measurements, comparison with design targets, adjustments of devices and corresponding protocols for documentation. The main task is to establish the planned air change rates for every room and then, as part of the commissioning, test the functioning of the system and its controls and operating rules to verify that the requirements are fulfilled.

Documenting the operation and maintenance plan. Long-term performance depends on routine inspections and maintenance. A ventilation system has to be operated, inspected and maintained. Checking the operation is a short-term action and can happen in a sporadic way (for example, checking the power supply and on–off status of equipment). However, quality surveillance and maintenance must be carried out at regular intervals, at least every six months.

References

Heidt, F. D. (1994) 'Lüftung', in Maier, K. H. (ed) *Der Energieberater. Kap.*, 5.1.1.6, S. 1-60, Verlag Deutscher Wirtschaftsdienst GmbH, Köln, Germany

Liddament, M. (1996) *A Guide to Energy Efficient Ventilation: The Air Infiltration and Ventilation Centre*, University of Warwick Science Park, UK

10.4 Ventilation heat recovery

Frank-Dietrich Heidt

10.4.1 Characterization of performance

Given the magnitude of heat needed to temper ventilation air, it is essential in high-performance housing to recover as much heat as possible. The effectiveness of this heat recovery (HR) can be characterized by its coefficient of performance (COP). This is the ratio between the useful energy extracted from the system and the energy used in the extraction process. To give a fair picture, this should be calculated in terms of primary energy. For heat pumps (HPs), the COP is often presented as delivered thermal energy (or power) Q_{HEAT} divided by the required electric energy (or power) PEL:

$$COP\,(HP) = Q_{HEAT}/P_{EL} \qquad\qquad [10.9]$$

$$Q_{HEAT} = Q_{SOURCE} + P_{EL} \qquad\qquad [10.10]$$

where Q_{SOURCE} is the heat energy (or power) which is withdrawn from the heat source.

In this case, COP has to be divided by the primary energy factor PE for electricity in order to obtain COP. PE depends on the prevailing mix of power plants – that is, coal, oil, gas, nuclear, hydro, etc (see Appendix 1).

$$COP = COP\,(HP)/PE \qquad\qquad [10.11]$$

The COP (HP) of the installed device depends on its technical performance and operational conditions. From basic thermodynamics it can be learned that the COP HP can never exceed Carnot's value COP_{CARNOT} and is proportional to the inverse of the temperature difference between heat supply and heat source:

$$COP\,(HP) = f \cdot COP_{CARNOT} \qquad\qquad [10.12]$$

with typically $0.30 \leq f \leq 0.60$ and:

$$COP_{CARNOT} = T_{HEAT}/(T_{HEAT} - T_{SOURCE}) \qquad [10.13]$$

Accordingly, a heat pump works best when low heat temperature supply is required and high temperature heat sources are available.

Thermal efficiency. Thermal efficiency ε_{HR} relates to the proportion of waste or lost heat (sensible and latent) usefully recovered by the HR process. It is expressed as a percentage.

Latent heat recovery is the recovery of heat released by the condensation of (usually) water vapour.

Sensible heat recovery is the recovery of waste heat from dry air.

For the sake of simplicity, all subsequent explanations are restricted to the case of sensible HR only. The thermal efficiency is then:

$$\varepsilon_{HR} = (T_{SUPP} - T_{AMB})/(T_{ROOM} - T_{AMB}) \qquad [10.14]$$

where T_{SUPP}, T_{ROOM} and T_{AMB} are the temperatures of supply air, indoor air and fresh ambient air, respectively. If there is no heat loss of the HX unit to its surroundings, another expression for ε_{HR} is:

$$\varepsilon_{HR} = (T_{ROOM} - T_{EXH})/(T_{ROOM} - T_{AMB}) \qquad [10.15]$$

with T_{EXH} being the air temperature at the cold end of the exhaust air tract.
Equations 10.14 and 10.15 lead to:

$$T_{SUPP} = \varepsilon_{HR} \cdot T_{ROOM} + (1 - \varepsilon_{HR}) \cdot T_{AMB} \qquad [10.16]$$

$$T_{EXH} = \varepsilon_{HR} \cdot T_{AMB} + (1 - \varepsilon_{HR}) \cdot T_{ROOM} \qquad [10.17]$$

This means that T_{SUPP} and T_{EXH} are both weighted means of indoor air temperature TROOM and fresh ambient air temperature T_{AMB}. The better the efficiency ε_{HR} (approaching a value of unity of 1.0 from below), the closer T_{SUPP} comes to TROOM and the more T_{EXH} drops down to T_{AMB}. An almost perfect HR thermally isolates a house from the ambient environment with regard to ventilation heat losses.

Electrical efficiency. Electrical efficiency ε_{EE} is proportional to the pressure drop in a ventilation system and to the ratio between the air flow rate VR and the electric power PE that is needed to effect this flow (for the propagation of mass). Electrical efficiency is given as a percentage:

$$\varepsilon_{EE} \cdot P_E = VR \cdot \Delta p \qquad [10.18]$$

Values of this ratio ε_{EE} depend on equipment (fan quality, ductwork and control). DC-powered fans are usually much better than fans with AC supply.
The inverse of this ratio (power divided by flow rate) describes the *specific fan power* (SFP). The unit is Wh/m³. A survey of data for German ventilation systems indicates that for a pressure drop of about 100 Pa, the range of specific energy demand values is between 0.2 and 0.8 W·h/m³. These values are important in order to decide on the energetic and economic viability of technical solutions. In high-performance housing, the specific fan power should be 0.45 Wh/m³ or less (< 0.15 Wh/m³ for exhaust fans only).

10.4.2 Exhaust air heat pump systems

These systems extract heat from the exhaust air to produce useful heat for DHW or for space heating (or both) by means of electric power. Three configurations are common:

1   air-to-liquid systems for preheating the water supply for DHW and/or 'wet' central space heating;
2   air to both liquid and air for combined hot water heating and warm air space heating; and
3   air-to-air systems to supplement air-to-air heat recovery by a heat exchanger.

Often an 'air-to-liquid' heat pump is used in which the evaporator is located in the exhaust air stream to extract heat from the outgoing air, while the condenser is located in a reservoir tank, to boost water temperature. Sometimes the condenser may be located in a fan coil unit through which indoor air is continuously circulated and heated (an air-to-air heat pump system). To extract maximum efficiency, heat pump output may be split between space heating and DHW heating.

The advantages of a ventilation exhaust air heat pump are as follows:

• Heat may be recovered from the exhaust air without requiring a balanced supply air system.
• Ventilation system costs and the space required for ductwork are reduced.
• There is potential to upgrade exhaust systems or passive stack ventilation systems by incorporating a heat pump.

The disadvantages of ventilation exhaust air heat pump are:

• high investment costs; and
• COP HP need to be high for systems, probably greater than 4, to show true cost and primary energy benefits.

10.4.3 Air-to-air heat exchanger or heat recovery systems

Such systems are used to transfer heat from the exhaust air of a ventilation system to the supply air. Various approaches to air-to-air heat recovery are common. Some are able to transfer latent heat, while others can work in reverse mode and provide cooling. Air-to-air heat recovery systems are used in conjunction with mechanical balanced ventilation, incorporating separate supply and exhaust networks. There are four major technical types of heat exchangers on the market:

1   plate heat exchangers;
2   run-around coils;
3   heat wheel systems; and
4   heat regenerators.

Plate heat exchangers (HX) are static devices (that is, they contain no moving parts). They consist of layers of separated, interleaved flow channels through which the supply and exhaust air flows. The channel walls or plates are constructed from very high conducting material (usually metal, but also various types of plastic may be used) across which heat rapidly transfers.

The efficiency of a plate heat exchanger is primarily associated with the flow configuration of exhaust and supply air, the spacing between plates, the surface area and the type of surface (for example, roughness can promote turbulence and enhance heat transfer coefficients). Parallel counter-flow can produce a maximum theoretical heat recovery of 100 per cent (less fan energy), while performance is reduced to a maximum of 50 per cent if exhaust and supply air flow run in the same direction. For optimum HR, combined with ease of manufacture and installation, a cross-flow system is commonly used. These systems can have thermal efficiencies in excess of 70 per cent. Fans are usually located on the supply and extract side so that air is pulled through the heat exchanger. This minimizes the pressure difference between the two air streams and, therefore, reduces the risk of cross-contamination. Heat generated by the extract fan, however, is lost to the outgoing air stream. Plate heat exchangers are used in dwellings and in other environments in which the supply and exhaust ducts can be brought closer together. They are very popular in countries with severely cold climates, as in Scandinavia and Canada.

Run-around coils are comprised of two fin-type heat exchangers, one of which is installed in the supply air and the other in the exhaust air duct. A liquid (normally a water/glycol solution) is used as the heat transfer medium and is continuously pumped between the heat exchanger by using a circulation pump. Heat in the exhaust air stream is thus transferred to the supply air via the heat exchanger. Performance is primarily related to the number of coil rows although, eventually, there is a trade-off between the benefit of additional coil rows and the extra fan energy needed to overcome increasing pressure drop.

This fan-coil approach is useful when fresh air and exhaust ducts are not adjacent to each other and, hence, often has important retrofit applications. Multiple supply and exhaust systems can be combined by a single loop. The true benefit of this technique, however, refers to larger buildings and industrial applications.

The advantage of run-around coils is that:

- the supply and exhaust air streams are totally separated; therefore, the risk of cross-contamination is eliminated.

The disadvantages of run-around coils are that:

- this type of system can only generally transfer sensible heat and has a limited thermal efficiency of 40 per cent to 60 per cent;
- the additional energy needed to operate the circulation pump has to be offset against predicted energy savings; and
- the circulation pump presents additional maintenance requirements.

Heat wheel systems are comprised of a revolving cylinder divided into a number of segments packed with coarsely knitted metal mesh or some other inert material. The cylinder rotates between 10 and 20 times per minute, picking up heat in the warmer exhaust stream and discharging it into the cooler supply air stream. Some heat wheels contain desiccant materials that enable latent heat transfer to take place. This is especially useful in an air-conditioned environment where the system can be operated in reverse mode to dry and cool incoming air. Since it is not possible for the wheel to provide a perfect barrier between the exhaust and supply air, some cross-contamination is inevitable.

Heat wheel performance is strongly affected by the packing material. Different packing materials are applied according to need (for example, latent heat recovery). This is a unique benefit of thermal wheels combined with a low air-side pressure drop. Heat wheels tend to be preferred in large commercial or public buildings where they form an integral part of the heating, ventilating and air conditioning (HVAC) system, and high thermal efficiencies can be achieved. Smaller units have recently become available for residential applications.

Heat regenerators use two chambers with a significant thermal capacity and a switch to cycle the supply and exhaust flows between these two chambers. In the first part of the cycle, the exhaust air is flowing through the first chamber and heats up its thermal mass. After some time the switch is then moved so that the supply air now flows through the second part of the chamber, absorbing the heat from the structure and reducing its temperature for the beginning of the next cycle. Recovery of latent heat is possible. Thermal efficiencies can be quite high for these systems (up to 90 per cent).

10.4.4 Combined air-to-air heat exchanger and a heat pump

Some air-to-air HR units incorporate an additional HP for further exhaust air HR. These systems consist of a conventional balanced air-to-air HR unit combined with a balanced ventilation system. Inserted in the exhaust duct is the evaporator unit of an HP. This extracts further heat, which is transferred to the supply air stream via a condenser unit located in the supply duct. COP HP values for domestic systems of 3.0 and larger can be achieved. Output air temperatures range typically from 30°C to 50°C. Obviously, the air-to-air heat exchanger and the heat pump are competing for the same heat source. The heat pump typically comes after the heat exchanger, so its performance is reduced accordingly because it has a cooler heat source. The better the thermal efficiency of the air-to-air HR system, the worse the opportunities for HR by HP are.

Nevertheless, when used in an air tight, well-insulated building, this approach can offer additional useful heat gain and reduce the period in which auxiliary space heating becomes necessary. Efficient use depends on a good control strategy that prevents the operation of conventional space heating, while sufficient heat is being supplied by the HR unit. Air distribution must also be controlled for optimum performance. This means satisfying the ventilation needs of each room and providing sufficient air flow to meet thermal requirements.

The advantage of air-to-air HR with HP is that:

* additional, enhanced HR is possible from the exhaust air stream.

The disadvantages of air-to-air HR with HP are:

* as with air-to-air HR, air-tight construction is essential and costs in terms of operation and maintenance have to be considered; and
* extra capital costs and maintenance fees will be necessary.

10.4.5 Preconditioning of supply air by an earth-to-air heat exchanger (EHX)

Ventilation inlet air can be tempered if it passes through a buried pipe before entering the building. The thermal efficiency Â EHX of such a system is the ratio between the temperature difference between air entering and exiting the system $T_{OUTLET} - T_{INLET}$ and the temperature difference between the ground at that depth and the ambient $T_{GROUND} - T_{AMB}$:

$$\varepsilon_{EHX} = \varepsilon_{HR} = (T_{OUTLET} - T_{AMB})/(T_{GROUND} - T_{AMB}) \qquad [10.19]$$

T_{OUT} is the air temperature after having passed the EHX. It is equal to the air temperature at the inlet of the buildings ventilation system.

In winter, these systems gain heat from the heat stored in the ground, while in summer, the ground can absorb excess heat and cool the supply air. Applications are suitable for both small and large buildings with mechanical ventilation, adjacent to which preheating/precooling pipes can be buried. Special software for appropriate design is available on the market. Typical values of thermal efficiencies vary between 0.4 and 0.3.

A special benefit of EHX is to warm up the ambient fresh air beyond 0°C in order to prevent freezing out of humid air in the exhaust duct of the heat exchanger unit.

The advantage of ground 'preheat' recovery is 'free' heating and cooling from the ground. The disadvantages of ground 'preheat' recovery are:

* installation costs;
* extra fan capacity; and
* the requirement of a maintenance/replacement strategy.

These four heat recovery techniques, combined with mechanical ventilation, can provide about 5.5 W of heat (if latent heat is included up to about 7.8 W) per m² heated at a temperature level of 20°C (with an assumed air change rate of 0.4 h⁻¹). With a heated floor area of only 30 m², this is already more than enough for DHW preparation and can even contribute significantly to space heating. This is evident because the average heating power needed to heat DHW heating amounts to about 80 W/person (based on a hot water consumption of 40 litres per person per day and a temperature rise from 10°C to 50°C).

Systems with only a heat exchanger commonly use a cross-flow or counter-flow plate heat exchanger with thermal efficiencies between 60 per cent (cross-flow) up to slightly more than 90 per cent (only for counter-flow). Cross-contamination between the inlet and exhaust air paths must be strictly avoided. Leakage would compromise with fresh air supply and, perhaps also, the thermal efficiency. In Germany, especially for central ventilation units, examination procedures have been defined that test the air tightness of both air tracts against each other.

As already mentioned, the more that the exhaust temperature approaches the ambient air temperature, the better the thermal efficiency. Therefore, the exhaust air tract runs the risk of condensing room air humidity, which can subsequently freeze up the air channel and block the removal of stale air. To prevent freezing, an electric defroster can be installed at the cold end of the air supply tract, warming up the ambient air at the intake to slightly above 0°C. This, of course, needs electrical energy. It is always a trade-off whether a system with moderate thermal efficiency and almost no risk of freezing is better than a system with high thermal efficiency, but also requiring occasional electrical defrosting. Herein lies the appeal of a ground heat exchanger to ensure that incoming air is always above 0°C. The combined efficiency $\epsilon_{HR + EHX}$ depends on the individual efficiencies ϵ_{HR} and ϵ_{EHX} as follows:

$$\epsilon_{HR+EHX} = \epsilon_{HR} + \epsilon_{EHX}(1 - \epsilon_{HR})\frac{T_{GROUND} - T_{AMB}}{T_{ROOM} - T_{AMB}} \qquad [10.20]$$

Here, the subscripts 'GROUND', 'AMB' and 'ROOM' designate the sub-surface soil temperature, as well as the outdoor and indoor air temperatures. The better ϵ_{HR} is, the lower the achievable improvement of efficiency by an EHX. Since an EHX also needs some fan power and causes additional investment, here, again, a careful investigation of the pros and cons is appropriate. As an example: with $T_{GROUND} \approx 10°C$, $T_{AMB} \approx 0°C$ and $T_{ROOM} \approx 20°C$ (typical values for winter conditions), efficiencies of $\epsilon_{HR} = 0.90$ and $\epsilon_{EHX} = 0.50$ result for the combination of both systems in $\epsilon_{HR} + \epsilon_{EHX} \approx 0.90 + 0.50 (1.00–0.90) 0.50 = 0.925$. This is a marginal improvement in thermal efficiency above $\epsilon_{HR} \approx 0.90$ and shows that the EHX mainly serves to avoid freeze-ups of the heat exchanger.

The most sophisticated system combines an earth heat exchanger, a heat exchanger and a heat pump. This provides the best possible heat recovery from ambient sources and waste heat that can be achieved. However, such a system is also the most expensive and uses the most electricity. Detailed investigations with regard to primary energy and cost effectiveness are therefore advised before a decision is made for such a very advanced HR system.

Generally, advanced ventilation systems need (more expensive) electric energy with a high primary energy (PE) factor of 2.4, up to 3.0, in order to recover (cheaper) thermal energy with a PE factor of 1.1 (for oil and gas). This means that the net energy savings (NES) of such systems cannot really be characterized by looking at thermal efficiencies or COP (HP) only. 'Net' means consideration of auxiliary energy and refers to the primary energy level. Therefore, NES has to be calculated from thermal energy gains ¢EH in terms of its inherent primary energy, which have to be diminished by the (PE weighted) needed auxiliary energy ¢EE. In most cases, ¢EE is electrical energy:

$$\text{NES} = \text{PE (thermal)} \cdot \Delta E_H - \text{PE (electrical)} \cdot \Delta E_E \qquad [10.21]$$

In a similar way, the net energy savings can be evaluated on the basis of the different energy costs for thermal and electrical energy. These cost-related figures even seem to be more appropriate for the common practice than mere energy-based considerations are. Instead of NES, net cost savings (NCS) are defined as:

$$NCS = C_{thermal} \cdot \Delta E_H - C_{electrical} \cdot \Delta E_E \qquad\qquad [10.22]$$

with typically $C_{thermal} \approx €0.045/kWh$ and $C_{electrical} \approx €0.160/kWh$.

It is appropriate to evaluate both terms (Equations 10.21 and 10.22) for any time interval (month, season, year). Whenever NES or NCS become zero or less, the operation of a ventilation system with HR should be shut down or by-passed, respectively.

Since $C_{electrical}/C_{thermal} \approx 3.56$ is different from and actually always greater than $PE_{electrical}/PE_{thermal}$, which is in between 2.18 ($\approx 2.4/1.1$) and 2.73 ($\approx 3.0/1.1$) depending on all-European or national German conditions, the value of NCS can be zero or less even if a positive primary energy balance according to Equation 10.21 still does exist.

It is recommended to evaluate the economic value NCS (Equation 10.22) as a criterion instead of the energy-related quantity NES (Equation 10.21). This describes the common practice to make decisions in a more realistic way. NCS can be used to decide on operational conditions for a given ventilation system, as well as for comparisons between different system options.

References

Heidt, F. D. (1994) 'Lüftung', in Maier, K. H. (ed) *Der Energieberater. Kap.*, 5.1.1.6, S. 1-60, Verlag Deutscher Wirtschaftsdienst GmbH, Köln, Germany

Liddament, M. (1996) *A Guide to Energy Efficient Ventilation: The Air Infiltration and Ventilation Centre*, University of Warwick Science Park, UK

11

Heat Delivery

11.1 Heating by ventilation

Anne Haas

11.1.1 Concept

The low heating power needed by high-performance housing can be covered by using the supply air of a balanced mechanical ventilation system to deliver needed heat. This dual function – delivering fresh air and heat with the same system – is economical. Eliminating a separate heat distribution system is a big saving.

    This does require some careful engineering. The air flow rates of the mechanical ventilation system are specified to ensure good indoor air quality. At the same time, the air flow rate must be adequate to deliver the needed heating power for design conditions. Ventilation losses occur between the heat exchanger (HE) and the room air outlet. Therefore, the heating power supplied by the air must exceed the demand of the rooms (see Figure 11.1.1). Some of the heat lost from the ducts may be 'lost' into rooms along the duct path, as well as in the room being heated.

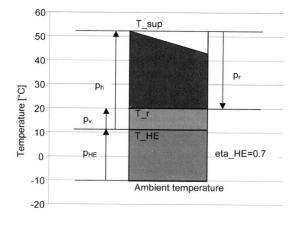

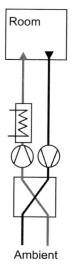

Notes:

p_{HE}, T_{HE}: heat transfer of heat exchanger (HE) (including ground heat exchanger, if present) and supply air temperature after HE (and fan).

p_h, T_{sup}: heating power of air heater and supply air temperature.

p_v: part of heating power ph needed to compensate ventilation losses.

p_r, T_r: heat released in room to compensate for transmission and infiltration losses, $p_r = p_h - p_v$, and room air temperature.

Source: Anne Haas, EMPA 175, Duebendorf, www.empa.ch/abt175

Figure 11.1.1 *Heat delivery and heating power*

Prerequisites for air heating

- *A high-performance balanced ventilation system with heat recovery.* General prerequisites for balanced mechanical ventilation also apply to ventilation with heating.
- *Low heating power demand.* The heating available for a room is limited by the volume of air supplied to the room and the allowable maximum supply air temperature. Assuming a nominal air change rate of 0.3 to 0.5 room volumes/h (about 1 m³/m²h) and a maximum supply air temperature after the air heater of about 50°C, the maximum heat delivery to rooms is approximately 10 W/m² living area. Figure 11.1.2 shows the heating power available for different air flow rates and temperature differences between air supply (T_sup) and return (T_r). This is the basis for the guidelines for Passivhaus design and the requirement of the Swiss Minergie standard.
- *A very well-insulated building envelope.* This is essential if the limited heating power of the ventilation system is to provide comfort. Surface temperatures of walls and windows must be close to the room air temperature. Delivering heat under a window or at an exterior wall is no longer necessary with such insulation levels and window quality.
- *No prolonged and low temperature setbacks.* When the room temperature is set back for a prolonged absence (for example, a week), rooms will take a long time to heat back up, given the limited heating power of the ventilation system. When bedrooms are left to cool down at night, the very good insulation of such houses will minimize the temperature drop – for instance, to less than 2K. Reheating to day temperatures can be quickly achieved by the ventilation heating; but the energy benefit of such a small temperature decrease is negligible.

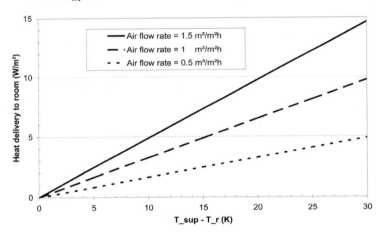

Source: Anne Haas, EMPA 175, Duebendorf, www.empa.ch/abt175

Figure 11.1.2 *Temperature difference, flow rate and heat delivery to room*

11.1.2 Heating technique

The supply air can be heated by:

- hot water coil-supplied heat from a heat storage or a heat source – many different energy sources can be used;
- the condenser of an exhaust air heat pump – in this case, not only the power of the heat delivery, but also the power of heat production, may be limited; and
- direct electric heating – in this case, there is great flexibility concerning the position and subdivision of the air heater.

In single family houses, ventilation and heating equipment are usually in the same room. The air heater is a part of the ventilation unit and is located after the heat exchanger and the fan.

In multi-family houses, it is usually necessary that the room temperature and the air flow rate can be regulated independently and individually by dwelling.

Several configurations of the heating and ventilation equipment are possible:

- individual heating and ventilation systems for each dwelling (as in single family houses);
- an individual air heater connected to a central heating system with an individual ventilation system for each dwelling; and
- an individual air heater connected to a central heating system with a central ventilation system and individual flow rate control for each dwelling.

Individual air heaters for each room are not recommended. If the client demands it, however, direct electric heating is the most common solution. Providing a heat exchanger for each room is expensive and reduces the advantages of combining heating and ventilation.

Solar and ambient energy systems as heat sources perform better when the heat they supply can be at a lower temperature. Air heating requires a relatively high supply temperature. Hot water supplied to an air heat exchanger may need to be 50°C to 60°C to achieve the needed maximum heating power. Domestic hot water heating also requires this temperature range. The amount of energy required for room heating and for DHW is comparable in high-performance houses. Accordingly, if an active solar system meets this demand for supplying water at these temperatures, the collectors should be the high-efficiency type (selective coated absorber with solar glazing or, still better, vacuum tube collectors).

11.1.3 Configurations

Outdoor air supply heating (without recirculation)

Air flow rates that are too high are to be avoided in this configuration because the room air can become too dry. The heating power demand of the building should not exceed 10 W/m² to be able to supply the required heat to the rooms via the supply air. Figure 11.1.3 shows that for typical winter conditions and for an hourly air flow rate of 30m³/person, the indoor air will have approximately 40 per cent relative humidity. Depending on the living area per person, this corresponds to 0.4 to 0.2 room air changes hourly. Assumed in this calculation are mean outdoor humidities for Zurich as follows:

- xa = 5 g/m³ (October–March in Zurich);
- xa = 4 g/m³ (February in Zurich); and
- a moderate internal humidity production: dx/dt = 78 g/(h.P).

In Figure 11.1.3, the left curve assumes a ventilation rate of 30 m³/P , the right curve 60 m³/P.

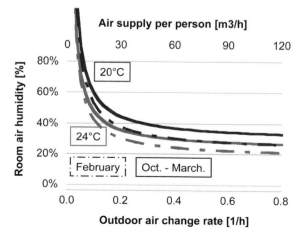

Source: Anne Haas, EMPA 175, Duebendorf, www.empa.ch/abt175

Figure 11.1.3 *Room air humidity (steady state) as a function of outdoor air change rate for two indoor temperatures and two typical outdoor humidity values*

Outdoor air supply heating (with recirculation)

If the heating power demand exceeds 10 W/m², one solution could be to mix some re-circulated air extracted from rooms with low pollution loads (if permitted). This system is more complex and expensive than the outdoor air supply heating. It is not recommended for high-performance housing because odour and pollutants are likely to be (re)distributed within the dwelling.

Air heating combined with a wood stove

If the wood stove is located in the basement, there is no significant difference from other heat supply systems with regard to ventilation air heating. However, there are special concerns if the oven is in one of the living spaces:

- Ideally, the room should be a central open space with thermal mass.
- The peak heating power from the stove radiated and convected to the room should be below 2 kW to 3 kW, and, even so, room temperatures exceeding 25°C for some hours during the firing should be acceptable.
- The stove must be tightly sealed and the ventilation system correctly balanced to avoid the case of an under-pressure in the room drawing out flue gases.
- The wood stove must have a separate air supply.
- Heat should be extracted from the stove via a heat exchanger and transported to other rooms or to the domestic water tank. Tile stoves can deliver heat over an extended period.

11.1.4 Heat distribution

The quantity of supply air for individual rooms is set according to indoor air quality requirements; the supply temperature is usually not set for individual rooms. Furthermore, not all rooms have supply air outlets. Internal and solar gains may result in the heat supply exceeding the heating demand in a specific room. The ventilation supply can only respond to the overall heating demand of the entire zone. This is less problematic than might be expected because high-performance houses tend to have homogenous room temperatures since the thermal resistances between rooms are much smaller than between the rooms and the ambient.

Air distribution system

Ventilation air heating results in rooms where the air that is supplied is warmer than the rooms where the air is extracted. Internal and solar gains can further increase the temperature in these heated rooms. On the other hand, natural convection through open doors can, to a large extent, equalize temperature differences between rooms.

Unintentional and uncontrolled heat losses from the supply air ducting should be minimized. Supply air ducts from the air heater to the supply terminal should always run within the heated house volume, not through attics or crawl spaces.

Although duct losses within the heated volume are not lost, the heat distribution is uncontrolled. Rooms needing heat may not be satisfied, while rooms with duct heat losses may overheat. The heat flow from ducts embedded in walls, floors or ceilings is delayed, making control all the more difficult. When ducts are openly hung in a room, the total amount of heat delivered is the same, but the temperature of the supply air at the outlet is lower. This can improve comfort.

Temperature zoning

It's often desirable that bedrooms are cooler and bathrooms warmer. Such special requirements for specific rooms may be met by running an exposed air duct through a room that should be warmer to supply a room that can be cooler. The intentional heat loss of the duct adds heat to the room that should be warmer, and the room that can be cooler will be supplied less warm air.

By reducing the thermostat set point at night somewhat below room air temperature, occupants have the feeling of 'fresh air' being supplied.

A radiator or wall/floor heating element or hot towel rack is a welcome amenity for quickly warming up or drying clothes, towels, etc and for improved comfort in bathrooms.

11.1.5 Room air flow characteristics

When heating is achieved with the ventilation system, the temperature of the supply air will vary widely over the heating season. The maximum heat air temperatures should not exceed 50°C at the supply air diffuser. At the other extreme, the supply air temperature can be below room temperature during sunny hours in winter, when the heat demand can be completely covered by solar and internal gains. Even so, the room temperature can easily rise – for example, to 24°C – and exceed the set-point temperature. In this case, the air heater will shut off and the temperature of the supply air may drop to as low as 16°C ($T_a = -10°C$; $T_r = 25°C$; $\eta_{HE} = 0.75$) Thus, at the lower end, the supply air temperature difference between room air and supply air can be up to about −8K. Figure 11.1.4 presents simulation results for a high-performance house in Davos and Zurich. Note that heat exchangers with low efficiencies should not be used.

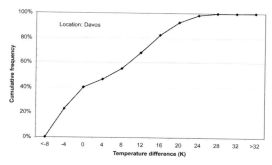
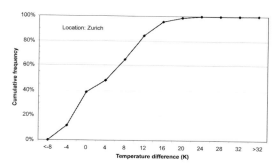

Source: Dorer and Haas (2003)

Figure 11.1.4 *Cumulative frequency of temperature differences between supply air and living room in a high-performance house for the period of October–March: (left) for the cold and sunny climate (Davos); (right) for the moderate climate (Zurich)*

Since the difference between supply air temperature and room air temperature varies considerably, air movement within the room can vary greatly. Experience with existing houses and laboratory measurements indicate that thermal comfort and ventilation efficiency are well within acceptable limits. An overview is given in the following section. For strategy B, the critical point is not the air flow characteristic produced by the ventilation/heating system. Rather, the radiation asymmetry and the risk of cold air down draught at the windows and external walls are the limiting factors for air heating.

Room air flow characteristics for different configurations

The supply air temperature and position of the supply air terminal determine the general room air flow pattern. Supply air that is warmer than the room air and that enters the room horizontally, close to the ceiling, tends to remain in a layer close to the ceiling, even after having reached the opposite side of the room. If the supply air is cooler than the room air, it tends to detach from the ceiling and to form a downward plume. Once arrived at the floor, it spreads over the floor. Heat sources such as occupants, floor heated or sun-warmed surfaces then cause the air to rise. The throw and spread of the supply air terminal have only a minor influence, at least in relatively small rooms.

'Warm' or 'cool' air entering the room horizontally close to the floor shows the opposite behaviour.

If the supply air enters the room with a vertical impulse, mixing is enhanced in cases of 'warm' air entering at ceiling level or 'cool' air entering from floor level.

Where air is extracted, it is of secondary importance. The forming of two air flow regimes is somewhat enhanced when air is extracted at approximately the same height as air is supplied, especially if each occurs on an opposite wall.

Thermal comfort characteristics in the occupant zone

- Vertical temperature gradient. Values above 3 K/m between 0.1 m and 1.1 m are regarded as critical according to EN ISO 7730 (1994).
- Draft risk according to EN ISO 7730 (1994) gives the percentage of dissatisfied persons as a function of room air temperature, air speed and turbulence. Values above 15 per cent are regarded as critical. A draft risk resulting primarily from the air heating is only expected if 'cool' air enters close to the ceiling. The grid shows higher values than the supply air valve (see Figure 11.1.5).

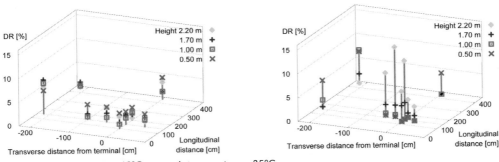

Notes: Supply air temperature = 16°C; room air temperature = 25°C.
Source: Dorer and Haas (2003)

Figure 11.1.5 *Draft risk characteristics: (left) supply air valve, adjustable; (right) simple grid, not adjustable*

Air exchange efficiency

The ideal case for air change efficiency can be described as 'piston flow'. In this case, the air exchange efficiency is equal to one, and the air change time is equal to the nominal time constant. For complete mixing of incoming air and room air, the air exchange efficiency is 0.5 and the air change time is twice the nominal time constant. With displacement ventilation, air exchange efficiencies of 0.6 to 0.7 can be reached.

Measurements at the EMPA as well as in one of the houses of the CEPHEUS project (Schnieders, 2001) show air exchange efficiencies of around 0.5. As expected, the configuration where the room air is extracted via a gap above the door shows the lowest efficiencies in case of heating. There are no significant differences whether the air is supplied via a valve (nozzle) or grid (see Table 11.1.1).

Table 11.1.1 *Air exchange efficiency*

	Supply air valve		Supply air grid	
Supply air temperature (°C)	40	16	40	16
Air exchange efficiency				
Gap below door, with internal heat source	0.52		0.51	
Gap above door, with internal heat source	0.49	0.51	0.45	0.52
Gap above door, no internal heat source	0.51		0.54	

Source: Dorer and Haas (2003)

11.1.6 Conclusions

Sophisticated as well as simple supply air terminals are suitable for heating by ventilation. No specific type or position is required to fulfil usual comfort and indoor air quality criteria. More important are general design criteria for ventilation systems, such as minimizing pressure losses. If possible, extract air transfer devices should not be positioned at the same level as the supply air terminal, especially if they are placed on opposite sides of the room.

For large rooms, differences between supply air terminals with large throw and simple devices are expected to become more distinct. Simple grids require an extra device to adjust the volume flow.

References

Dorer, V. and Haas, A. (2003) 'Aspects of air and heat distribution in low energy residential buildings', *AIVC BETEC 2003 Conference Proceedings Ventilation, Humidity Control and Energy*, Washington, DC, AIVC, c/o FaberMaunsell Ltd, Beaufort House, 94–96 Newhall Street, Birmingham UK, B3 1PB, www.aivc.org

EN ISO 7730 (1994) *Moderate Thermal Environments –– Determination of the PMV and PPD Indices and Specification of the Conditions for Thermal Comfort*, EN ISO, International Organization for Standardization (ISO), Geneva, Switzerland

PHI (Passivhaus Institut) (1999) 'Dimensionierung von Lüftungsanlagen in Passivhäusern', *Arbeitskreis kostengünstige Passivhäuser*, Protokollband no 17, Passivhaus Institut, Darmstadt, Germany, passivhaus@t-online.de

Schnieders, J. et al (2001) *CEPHEUS Wissenschaftliche Begleitung und Auswertung*, Endbericht, CEPHEUS-Projektinformation no 22, Passivhaus Institut, Darmstadt, Germany passivhaus@t-online.de

Websites

Passivhaus Institut: www.passivehouse.com
Air Infiltration and Ventilation Centre: www.aivc.org
Swiss Federal Laboratories for Materials Testing and Research, Laboratory for Energy Systems/Building Equipment (EMPA): www.empa.ch/abt175en

Tools

PHLuft tool to calculate heat transfer from ducts and in heat exchangers: www.passivehouse.com
PHPP Passive House Development Package, Excel – based on the calculation of energy ratings: www.passivehouse.com
COMIS software package for multi-zone airflow simulation: www.software.cstb.fr
TRNSYS/TRNFLOW software package for transient system simulation with multi-zone thermal/airflow building model: www.transsolar.com

11.2 Radiant heating

Joachim Morhenne

11.2.1 Concept

By heating spaces with large surfaces – that is, a wall or a floor – large quantities of heat can be transferred by radiation at comfortable low temperatures. Houses with very small heat demand are ideal candidates for such heat delivery. To ensure that the heat is primarily transferred by radiation, the heating surface temperature has to be close to the room air temperature, otherwise convection quickly becomes the main path of heat transfer for normal room temperatures. Because the radiant heat flux of surfaces, with a temperature of 22°C to 32°C, is low, the surface area has to be large to cover the heat demand. In this case, the part of the energy transferred by radiation is up to 60 per cent.

Warm surfaces increase indoor comfort. Human beings are very sensitive to infrared radiation because they emit heat in this way, mainly by their uncovered skin. The heat loss of the body then depends on the radiation exchange with colder surfaces. In winter, warm room surfaces prevent such discomfort.

Increased surface temperature can save energy by making it possible to provide the same comfort at lower temperatures than possible for houses with cold surfaces. The low operating temperatures of radiating surfaces increase the efficiency and annual useful output of active solar combi-systems (combined water heating and space heating). The low supply temperature allows the solar system to operate at cooler temperatures, increasing system efficiency and extending the hours of solar coverage. Condensing gas furnaces and heat pumps are also able to operate more efficiently when coupled to surface heating.

The most commonly used surface for such heating is the floor, although radiant walls provide better comfort. The latter is used less because it limits freedom in furnishing a space. Systems differ by mass (light or heavy constructions) and by building integration (being inside the wall or installed as a separate surface, such as radiators).

The heating power of radiant surfaces depends on the surface temperature; up to 80 W/m^2 can be achieved. In the case of solar heated systems, 30 W/m^2 to 50 W/m^2 are realistic due to the reduced temperature level.

In high-performance houses heated by ventilation air, the surface temperature of the walls is quite uniform. As an alternative, a radiant heating system with its higher temperatures has the advantage of being able to compensate for the lower surface temperature of windows. A second advantage is the opportunity to tie in an additional heat source. This allows the creation of different indoor temperature zones and provides more power to heat up the building more quickly – that is, after an unoccupied period.

An additional benefit of building integrated radiant heating is that it allows the capacity of the house to be activated as a thermal storage. However, when the mass is used as storage, the risk of overheating increases because of the lag in the heat release.

Heavy radiant heating systems therefore require accurate planning. Houses with minimal passive solar gains and high-performance houses with active solar heating are ideal. In the summer, the thermal mass of a house helps to keep indoor temperatures low and enhances nocturnal cooling in the northern or mid European climate.

11.2.2 Radiant heating system based on water

Floor and wall heating is usually done with tubes embedded in the plaster. This increases the required thickness of the finish slightly. In addition, 1 cm to 2 cm of insulation is necessary. The details are well known and proven. New materials for the tubes (compounds of aluminium and polyethylene) allow endless runs without joints inside the construction. Oxygen diffusion as well as potential leakage is no longer a problem. Metal tubes are still common, too, but have the disadvantage of requiring joints inside the construction.

The design parameters are tube distances, the tube diameter, resistance of the embedding material and inlet water temperature. The achieved heating power varies typically from 40 to 80 W/m^2 for floor heating systems (>0.05 K/W (35 mm screed, 10 mm parquet), tube separation ranging between 33 cm and 5.5 cm, with a tube diameter of 14 mm). Wall heating systems can reach higher values because the tubes are right behind the surface and have a higher heat transfer; up to 150 W/m^2 can be achieved (temperature difference between wall and room air temperature: 15K).

Wall and floor heating systems, in most cases, have an adjacent massive construction. The system needs time to heat up and time to cool down when no more heat is required, making control more difficult. In rooms with high passive solar gains, only a fraction of the heat demand should be covered by wall or floor heating systems to avoid overheating.

Dos and don'ts

- In high-performance houses, wall heating systems should not be installed in exterior walls to avoid higher transmission losses. In case of floor heating, the floor should not be an exterior surface – that is, an overhang.
- Rooms with high passive gains need fast responding heat delivery, best achieved by air or small radiators.
- For solar heated systems using the thermal mass of the building as storage, see the following section on air-heated systems.

11.2.3 Radiant heating systems based on air

The advantage of air is that air does not drip or freeze, so no antifreeze is needed and tightness is not a serious problem. Disadvantages are the poor heat capacity and the low density of air; therefore, large volumes of air are needed to transfer heat. In this section, wall, floor or ceiling heating systems operating in a temperature range of below 35°C are described. This is an ideal condition for solar air collectors. Such systems are also well suited for high-performance houses because such houses need very low heating power (< 4.2 W/m^2).

11.2.4 Solar-supplied radiant heating systems

Direct supply of solar air heat to the rooms of a high-performance house is not advisable. The heat demand is low or non-existent during sunshine hours because windows' solar gains can cover most or all of the heating demand. As a result, solar air heat can only lead to overheating. Thermal storage is therefore essential to delay the radiant heat release into the evening. This can be achieved with either hypocaust (floor heating) or murocaust (wall heating) systems. Such systems can serve many functions: transporting heat, storing heat, radiating heat and acting as a structural part of the building. Furthermore, these systems are partially self-regulating. As the room temperature rises, the temperature difference between the radiating surface and other room surfaces and the room air decreases, so less heat is released (see Figure 11.2.1).

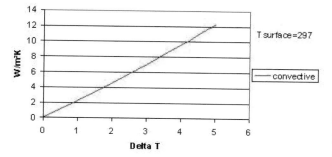

Energy flow by convection

Source: Morhenne Ingenieure GbR, Wuppertal

Figure 11.2.1 *The self-regulation effect of a radiant heating system*

The time delay (τ) between solar heat input and heat release to the room can be engineered by changing the amount of available thermal mass and the dimension of the tubing or air channels (see Figure 11.2.2).

If passive gains are minimal (due to an unfavourable orientation or site shading), active solar gains can compensate the missing passive gains. Figure 11.2.3 illustrates such a configuration.

The dimensions and maximum solar air coverage of the heating demand are limited by the risk of overheating. Due to the time shift, the heat is stored when it is not known whether there will be a future demand for it. To reduce this risk and to increase the storage capacity for solar heat, it is advis-

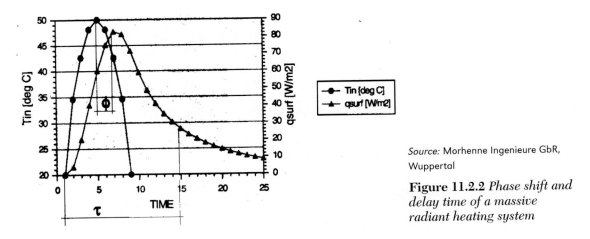

Source: Morhenne Ingenieure GbR, Wuppertal

Figure 11.2.2 *Phase shift and delay time of a massive radiant heating system*

able to provide separate storage areas for solar heat and for the backup heat. Indeed, in high-performance houses, during most of the heating season the backup heating can be delivered using the ventilation air without the need for storage. Thus, radiant storage for the backup heat is economically questionable.

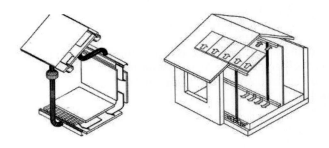

Source: Morhenne Ingenieure GbR, Wuppertal

Figure 11.2.3 *A building scheme with hypocaust and murocaust heated from a solar air collector*

11.2.5 Description of typical solutions

Hypocaust

A hypocaust consists of a massive structure with air channels to heat or cool the element, as shown in Figure 11.2.4.

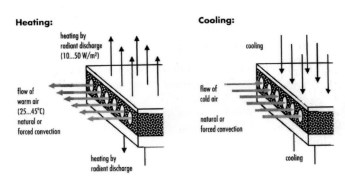

Source: Morhenne Ingenieure GbR, Wuppertal

Figure 11.2.4 *Scheme of a hypocaust*

The material and its thickness affect the heating delay or time shift. The core, through which the warm or hot air is blown, can be built in different ways: prefabricated hollow core floor elements (see Figure 11.2.5) or metal or plastic tubes embedded in cast concrete (see Figure 11.2.6). Systems working by gravity based on the differences in density between cool and warm air have been used in Sicily, but are not known in Central Europe.

 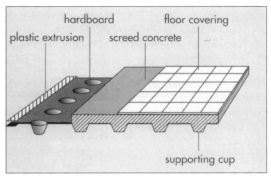

Source: Morhenne Ingenieure GbR, Wuppertal

Figure 11.2.5 *Examples of hypocaust systems: (a) prefabricated; (b) poured in place*

Source: Morhenne Ingenieure GbR, Wuppertal

Figure 11.2.6 *Example for a site-built hypocaust with embedded tubes*

To avoid increased heat losses, exterior facing surfaces should not be used. For construction details, see Hastings and Mork (2000, Chapter IV.6) and Morhenne (1995).

Hypocaust or murocaust heating systems for summer cooling

High-performance houses with hypocaust or murocaust systems can be more comfortable in summer due to their heavier construction. The effect of the mass can be increased by fan-forcing cool air through the channels in the evening, when temperatures can be K to 4.2K cooler than the structure during clear weather periods. When air for the channels in the mass is cooled in an earth heat exchanger, a temperature reduction of at least 5K of the ambient air can be achieved.

11.2.6 Energy savings and system performance

Radiant heating with reduced indoor temperature

In a room with radiant heating, the same comfort is perceived at a lower temperature than in a room with convective heating. Due to the smaller temperature difference between inside and outside, each degree lower room air temperature decreases the heating demand by approximately 6 per cent (assuming that the radiant heating surfaces are not located on exterior walls). However, the savings decrease the more efficient the heat recovery in the ventilation system.

Savings by the energy supply

Heat pumps and condensing gas furnaces perform with a higher efficiency if low temperature radiant surfaces are used to distribute the heat. The COP of an earth-coupled heat pump increases about 30 per cent if the temperature of the heating system is reduced from 45°C to 35°C. The efficiency of a condensing gas furnace increases approximately 3 per cent to 5 per cent.

Savings from solar air-heated hypocaust or murocaust systems

Because high-performance houses require so little heat, it is essential to offset the investment costs of a solar air system by also using it to produce DHW. This is easily accomplished by installing a bypass to shunt the solar hot air away from the heating circuit, past an air-to-water heat exchanger. A reduction of up to 60 per cent of the energy demand for hot water heating is typical.

11.2.7 Conclusions

A solar air radiant heating system for a high-performance house must have thermal storage so that the heat release is delayed to the night hours. This is best provided as an integral part of the massive bearing construction of the house to minimize added costs. Typical solutions are to incorporate air channels in the floor (hypocaust) or masonry walls (murocaust). Good performance depends on a careful match between the collector size, storage capacity and rate of heat release, and heat demand of the house. The latter is especially true for high-performance houses. Over-dimensioning the system can result in overheating and low efficiency. In middle Europe, the useful heat contribution over the heating season of a well-designed system can lie between 50 and 300 kWh/m²/collector. Finally, and importantly, such a system must be coupled to the DHW production in order to be economical. A reduction of up to 60 per cent in the energy for hot water production is then possible. The economics are still further improved if the hypocaust or murocaust system is designed in this way and is used to provide the further benefit of summer cooling.

References

Fort, K. and Gygli, W. (2000) *TRNSYS Model Type 160 for Hypocaust Thermal Storage and Floor Heating*, KF Engineering Services, karel.fort@bluewin.ch, and TRANSSOLAR Energietechnik GmbH, Stuttgart, Germany, info@transsolar.com

Hastings, S. R. and Mork, O. (eds) (2000) *Solar Air Systems: A Design Handbook*, James and James (Science Publishers) Ltd, London, www.jxj.com

Morhenne, J. and Langensiepen, B. (1995) *Planungsgrundlagen für solarbeheizte Hypokausten*, Abschlußbericht AG Solar NRW, Wuppertal, available from Ing.Büro Morhenne GbR, Schülkestr, 4.2, D-42277 Wuppertal, info@morhenne.com

12

Heat Production

12.1 Active solar heating: Air collectors

Joachim Morhenne

12.1.1 Concept

Active solar air systems can effectively cover part of the heating demand for space heating, ventilation air and DHW of high-performance houses. Such systems have important advantages: solar air systems do not drip or freeze, and are simple, efficient and proven systems. Solar air collectors perform comparably to water-based flat-plate collectors; but the collector inlet temperature is, most of the time, lower than is the case with a water collector. This results in higher thermal efficiency. Furthermore, air as the heat transport medium allows for a simple collector construction; but the low density and heat capacity of air require a much higher volume flow to transport the absorbed energy. A disadvantage is the higher electric consumption of the fans compared to that of a pump in a water-based system. To achieve small pressure losses and electric consumption, the hydraulic design of the whole solar air circuit must be optimized. Generously sized air ducts, minimal duct lengths and no sharp bends help in this regard.

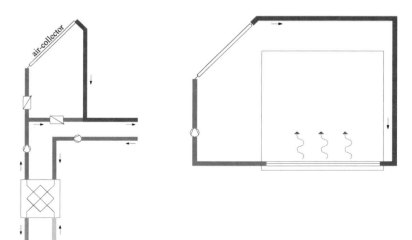

Source: Morhenne Ingenieure GbR, Wuppertal

Figure 12.1.1 *Scheme of (left) solar-assisted ventilation and (right) solar radiant heating*

There are two types of solar air systems:

1   In solar radiant heating, the solar heated air is circulated in a closed loop (see Figure 12.1.1(b)) from the collector through the floor (hypocaust systems) or the walls (murocaust systems), providing radiant space heating (see Chapter 11, Section 11.2).
2   In solar-assisted ventilation systems (open loop), the solar collector preheats intake air after it has passed the heat recovery (see Figure 12.1.1(a)). This installation decreases the collector performance compared to an installation of the collector in front of the heat recovery, but the performance of the whole system is higher. It is an open-loop system in that collector air circulates directly through the occupied space.

To increase the solar contribution, a combination of both systems is possible. The heating of DHW allows for all-year use of the solar resource and, hence, better economy and a much greater reduction in primary energy demand. For a high-performance house, the thermal mass of the solar radiant heating is preferred.

12.1.2 Solar radiant heating

This system uses the load-bearing structure of the house to channel the solar heated air, store the heat and radiate the heat into the room. Radiant heating provides excellent comfort and the storage delays the delivery of the heat to when it is more likely needed.

12.1.3 Solar-assisted ventilation

To integrate an open-loop solar air system with a ventilation system, the only added costs are the collector, connecting air ducts and a controller. If the ventilation unit is close to the collector, these expenditures can be small. Some manufacturers of compact ventilation systems with integrated heat recovery already have prefabricated boxes to connect air collectors. Here, also, the installation and control are easy. A disadvantage of solar-assisted ventilation systems is that the air flow rate required for the house ventilation may not match the optimal air flow for efficient collector performance. Furthermore, on sunny days, there may be little or no need for ventilation heating because passive solar gains cover the load of the well-insulated house.

As described earlier, the solar air collector and control devices are the only components to be added to a high-performance ventilation system. The collector is activated when it gains solar radiation and the temperature inside the collector exceeds the temperature of the fresh air having left the heat recovery. By an automatic control, a flap then opens and the air is blown through the collector, heats up and enters the air distribution inside the building.

One of the main parameters for the system design is the air flow rate and the specific flow rate per m^2 of collector. Dividing the flow rate by the specific flow rate of the collector, the result is the collector area. The specific flow rate is given by the collector producer; typical values are 25 to 50 m^3/h m^2. In high-performance houses, this leads to a resulting collector area with a maximum of 4 m^2 to 8 m^2.

To keep the air inlet temperature to the room comfortable (a range of 20°C to 50°C), using a variable flow rate when the collectors gain solar radiation is recommended. By working with the lowest possible flow rate (given by the minimum ventilation rate) when the solar insolation is low and increasing the air flow up to the maximum flow rate to keep the collector outlet temperature within the given range, the solar gains can be maximized. Possible savings of energy depend on the energy demand of the house, its passive gains and ventilation air flow rate. A reduction of 10 per cent to 15 per cent of the heating demand can be achieved.

However, the maximum flow rate is limited by the installed fan and distribution system because the pressure drop increases with increased air speed. An increase of the collector area and a higher volume flow is furthermore limited by the usability of the surplus hot air inside the building, which has to be proved by dynamic simulation. The usable solar gains are influenced strongly by passive solar gains and the building construction. Only heavyweight constructions allow for storing some of the solar gains and avoid overheating problems. In case of high passive gains, solar-assisted ventilation cannot be recommended. In this case, a solar-heated hypocaust system is the better alternative.

To achieve a higher solar fraction, a parallel installation of both system types is an opportunity, which at the same time increases indoor comfort due to the radiant heating of the hypocaust.

12.1.4 Solar air systems for domestic hot water (summer mode)

High-performance houses in most climates will not have a heating demand until late autumn, and then only through very early spring. Making use of the solar energy during the most sunshine hours in this extended summer season is important. By installing a bypass between the inlet and outlet of the collector, and placing an air-to-water heat exchanger at this location, it is possible to use the solar air system to heat domestic hot water. In most cases, the solar gains in this mode exceed the gains for space and ventilation heating because high-performance houses need so little heating.

Configurations

Two system types for the installation of the heat exchanger are common:

1   a closed loop (bypass); and
2   an open loop.

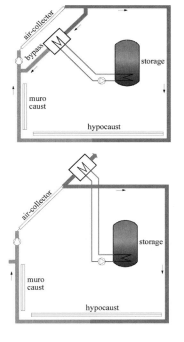
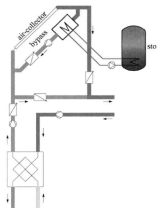

Source: Morhenne Ingenieure GbR, Wuppertal

Figure 12.1.2 *Solar-assisted ventilation system with integrated domestic hot water (DHW): Schemes of closed- and open-loop hypocaust systems and solar-assisted ventilation systems*

Open-loop systems have the advantage of an installation with only a few additional components; unfavourably, the performance is lower (–50 per cent). As a result, open-loop systems are only recommended for large collector areas (> 15 m^2) that are oversized for the purpose of DHW.

Construction details

The main additional components for summer operation of the collector to produce hot water are an air-to-water heat exchanger, a pump, a boiler and a controller. The installation and the design of most of these components are similar to that of 'normal' water collector systems:

- boiler size: 300 litres (for a single family);
- pump with lowest electric consumption;
- differential temperature controller; and
- additional component: air-to-water heat exchanger with efficiency >80 per cent.

The air-to-water heat exchanger can either be integrated within the hot water circuit directly or can be installed into a secondary water loop. The main issues to be solved for the different solutions are freeze protection and hygiene (see Section 12.2 and Chapter 13, Section 13.1 for information on the Legionella problem).

12.1.5 The collectors

Site-built solar air collectors

Due to their simplicity, air collectors are often built onsite using semi-finished products. In most cases, these systems have a low efficiency because of:

- leakage;
- flow distribution inside the collector; and
- poor design of the heat transfer coefficients.

Therefore, site-built collectors are not recommended for high-performance housing.

Factory-built solar air collectors

Over the years, collectors have been engineered to improve their performance. The heat transfer can be improved by increasing the absorber surface area in contact with the air stream. This is done by:

- channelling the air flow first over the absorber surface, then beneath it;
- using an absorber with fins on the underside where the air flows; and
- using a black textile absorber through which the air flows.

The heat transfer between the absorber and the air stream can be increased by:

- creating obstructions in the air flow to cause turbulence and to destroy the insulating boundary layer of air at the absorber surface; and
- making a porous absorber.

To improve winter performance, selective absorber coatings are recommended for high-performance houses. The given figures of performance assume selective surfaces.

Typical technical data as a guide for selecting a collector product:

- glazing 4 mm; $\tau = 0.92$;
- absorber: $\propto > 0.92$, $\varepsilon < 0.1$;
- back losses: $u < 0.6$ W/m^{2}K;
- specific flow rate: 25–80 m^3/m^{2}h; and
- pressure drop: 1–3 Pa/m.

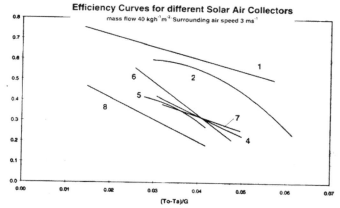

Collectors with:
1   underflow, finned absorber, selective surface;
2   black textile absorber;
4   plane black absorber, underflow;
5   rippled absorber flow on both sides;
6   black painted façade element flow on both sides;
7   site built, trapezoid absorber underflow;
8   black façade element underflow.

Source: Morhenne Ingenieure GbR, Wuppertal

Figure 12.1.3 *Efficiency curves of different air collector types*

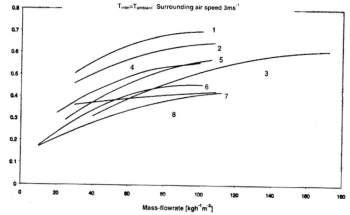

Collectors with:
1   underflow, finned absorber, selective surface;
2   black textile absorber;
4   plane black absorber, underflow;
5   rippled absorber flow on both sides;
6   black painted façade element flow on both sides;
7   site built, trapezoid absorber underflow;
8   black façade element underflow.

Source: Morhenne Ingenieure GbR, Wuppertal

Figure 12.1.4 *Efficiency versus mass flow rate*

Different collector types perform in different ways. For example, plane absorbers transfer less heat to the air stream. Collectors where air flows between the glazing and absorber have higher heat losses. The choice of collector depends on the desired air outlet temperature and the volume flow. Figure 12.1.3 shows the efficiency curves of different collector types. For a detailed examination, see Hastings and Mork (2000).

Due to the high sensitivity of the heat transfer, the flow rate of the collector strongly affects the efficiency, as seen in Figure 12.1.4.

The flow rate of an air collector influences not only the flow resistance and the heat transfer, but also the air outlet temperature. These, in turn, affect collector efficiency. A high flow rate increases the efficiency, but also the pressure drop, so more electricity is consumed to supply the needed fan power. Therefore, a compromise between high thermal efficiency and high electricity demand for the fan has to be found. Figure 12.1.5 gives an impression of the total efficiency.

To reduce the problem of high pressure losses or high flow rates inside the collector, individual collectors should be connected in parallel. The parallel collector array, however, increases the cost for manifolds and air ducts. Therefore, a mix of parallel and serial-connected collectors is needed.

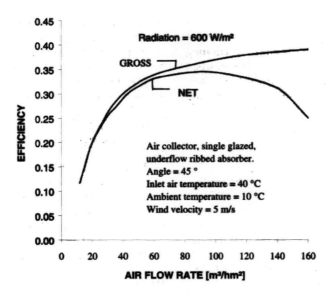

Air collector, single glazed,
underflow ribbed absorber.
Angle = 45 °
Inlet air temperature = 40 °C
Ambient temperature = 10 °C
Wind velocity = 5 m/s

Source: Morhenne Ingenieure GbR,
Wuppertal

Figure 12.1.5 *Collector efficiency: A comparison between thermal efficiency and efficiency considering fan electricity*

Air collectors suitable for high-performance houses are characterized by a high efficiency and low pressure losses. In solar-assisted ventilation systems, the pressure loss is crucial if the existing fans of the ventilation system serve the solar collector. The collector configuration, in this case, should accept a wide range of flow rates.

Building integration

Collectors can be built into the roof or façade, providing the weather skin and part of the insulation of the building envelope. This helps to reduce costs, in theory; but the detailing must be carefully done to ensure rain and wind tightness. Moisture dissipation from the building into the collector is, in most cases, not critical because the collector is vented during operation. In addition, high-performance housing has to have a tight membrane in the wall or roof construction. Systems solutions are available for roof and façade integration.

Source: Andreas Gütermann, AMENA,
Winterthur

Figure 12.1.6 *A Swiss apartment building with integrated solar air collectors*

12.1.6 Construction details: Dos and don'ts

The collectors can be integrated within the roof or the façade. In high-performance houses, hot water heating offers the greatest potential to save energy using solar energy. Therefore, integrating a bypass with an air-to-water heat exchanger is recommended. The collector area and performance should be determined by the space heating or ventilation heating demand. Accordingly, the system may even be over-dimensioned for summer water heating. The optimum collector tilt, in this case, is the latitude of the location when facing south. This is, however, a flat optimum. More important for the system performance is a short distance and a direct duct from to the collector to the heat exchanger, hypocausts or ventilation system. Air ducts have a large surface area to lose heat, so duct runs should be as short as possible.

Dos and don'ts

- Insulate air ducts facing to the ambient (still better, avoid having them).
- Avoid changes of air velocity inside the air system.
- The air velocity should not exceed 2 m/s to 3 m/s.
- Use air-tight dampers and test them to be sure that they are air tight.
- Ensure that ducts and junction boxes are air tight (leaks reduce performance).
- Use special sealing, collars, etc where air ducts penetrate the vapour and wind barriers of the building (this is especially critical in high-performance housing).

References

Fechner, H. and Bucek, O. (1999) 'Vergleichende Untersuchungen an Serien-Luftkollektoren im Rahmen des IEA Tasks 19', 9. *OTTI-Symposium Thermische Solarenergie*, S.91-95 OTTI Energie Kolleg, Wernerwerkstr. 4, D-93049 Regensburg, www.otti.de

Hastings, S. R. and Mork, O. (eds) (2000) *Solar Air Systems: A Design Handbook*, James and James (Science Publishers) Ltd, London, www.jxj.com

Morhenne, J. (2002) *Solare Luftsysteme: Themeninfo II/02*, Bine Informationsdienst Fachinformationszentrum Karlsruhe, www.bine.info

12.2 Active solar heating: Water

Gerhard Faninger

12.2.1 Concept

Heating DHW with solar energy in a high-performance house is sensible. In such houses, the energy needed to heat domestic water can equal or even exceed the energy needed for space heating since the latter has been so far reduced by insulation and heat recovery. Furthermore, demand for heating domestic water is a 12-month energy demand, including the high insolation summer months. Using a solar system is therefore an effective way of reducing the total primary energy demand. Increasingly, the market for solar water systems also includes systems that provide, in addition to water heating, space heating in winter.

12.2.2 Components

Collectors

For a high-performance house, a high-performance collector is a good choice, particularly if the collector should provide both water and space heating. A high-performance collector is able to produce more heat during the shortened mid-winter heating season of such houses.

Flat-plate collectors. A high-performance flat-plate collector is characterized by a superior absorber and glazing. The absorber should have a coating with a high solar absorption, black paint (>95 per cent) and low heat emissivity selective coating (<5 per cent). The glazing should be anti-reflection treated and consist of a low iron glass type to maximize solar radiation transmitted to the absorber. Such flat-plate collectors can easily achieve outlet temperatures of 80°C with a conversion efficiency of about 50 per cent to 60 per cent.

Evacuated tube collectors. This type of collector achieves superior performance because the vacuum surrounding the absorber drastically cuts heat losses to the ambient. Outlet temperatures above 100°C are easily achieved with a higher conversion efficiency compared with a flat-plate collector. The inside-facing underside of the glass pipe has a reflective coating to irradiate the absorber from beneath. Thus, vacuum collectors have the further advantage of not requiring any given slope for optimal performance. The glass pipes can simply be rotated to the optimal incident angle for the application. For this reason, they can be mounted on a south façade or roof.

Properties of collectors. Collectors can be characterized by means of two experimentally determined constants:

1   *Conversion factor*: the collector efficiency when the ambient air temperature equals the collector temperature.
2   *Heat loss coefficient*: the mean heat loss of the collector per aperture area for a measured temperature difference between the collector and the ambient air temperature in W/m^2K.

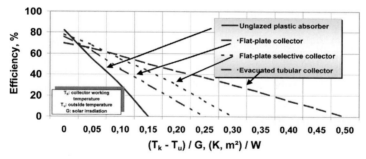

Source: G. Faninger, University of Klagenfurt

Figure 12.2.1 *Efficiencies of different collector types under different conditions and appropriate uses, where* T_k = *collector working temperature (°C);* T_u = *ambient temperature (°C); and* G = *solar irradiation (W/m²)*

These collector constants are determined under exactly defined conditions (global radiation intensity, angle of incidence, air temperature, wind velocity, etc). The performance of different collector types and applications are shown in Figure 12.2.1. The efficiencies are given for the temperature difference between the collector and ambient divided by the solar radiation. Logically, as the collector gets hotter, the efficiency falls off. For heating of high-performance houses, selective coated collectors or vacuum pipe collectors are a good choice.

It is beneficial to integrate solar collectors within the building envelope for aesthetic and economical reasons. For roof installations, where the systems deliver heat over the whole year, the optimal tilt angle (northern hemisphere) is between 30° and 75°. The orientation can be between 30° east and 45° west. Figures 12.2.2(a) and 12.2.2(b) show calculated results for Stockholm, Zurich and Milan. As can be seen, a 90° tilt, or façade-integrated collector, is far from optimum in all locations. However, it

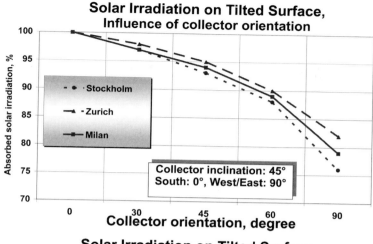

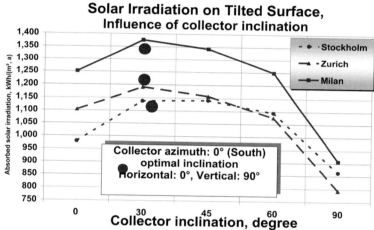

Source: G. Faninger, University of Klagenfurt

Figure 12.2.2 (above) *Solar radiation for different orientations in the reference climates (south = 0°, north = 180°); (below) solar radiation for different tilt angles in the reference climates for a south-facing collector*

performs better in winter with low sun angles. When there is snow cover on the ground, it receives an extra portion of ground-reflected solar radiation. Roof collectors with too little slope, by contrast, will have zero output when covered by snow. A big limitation of façade collectors is, however, that by low sun angles, neighbouring buildings and trees will cast shadows on the collector surface. Façade collectors perform worse in Zurich than in either Milan or Stockholm. This is possibly explained by the higher frequency of overcast weather in Zurich.

Storage

Surprisingly, within a large range, the size of the tank relative to the collector area is not a major factor affecting system performance. This is evident in the example of an apartment block shown in Figure 12.2.3. Doubling the tank size increases the solar share by less than 15 per cent. More important is avoiding the mixing of the hot water at the top of the tank with cooler water at the bottom, the insulation of the tank and the avoidance of thermal bridges (for example, the feet of the tank). The size of the tank should not be oversized because that would increase heat losses and investment costs. For economy and energy efficiency, the tank should be from 1.5 to 2.0 times greater than the daily hot water demand, and the collector area between 1 and 2 m^2/occupant. Typically, designs for solar hot water systems in households are 3 m^2/300 litres for up to 3 persons, and 8 m^2/500 litres for 4 to 5 individuals. Performance for these two variations is shown in Figure 12.2.4.

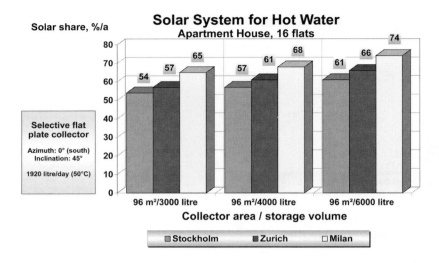

Source: G. Faninger, University of Klagenfurt

Figure 12.2.3 *Influence of storage size on system output for 96 m² of collectors serving an apartment block*

For solar-combined space heating and domestic water heating systems, the storage can be combined with the heat distribution subsystem – for instance, floor heating, which further increases the heat storage capacity. In this case, heat can be extracted from the lower section of the tank for the radiant floor heating and the upper part of the tank for DHW. The water supplied to the collector can come from a heat exchanger at the bottom of the tank where the coolest temperatures occur. This maximizes the collector efficiency. The location of the hot return from the collector to the tank depends upon the flow rate. For high-flow collectors, this connection can be quite low. On the other hand, this connection should be a higher or even better variable (stratified) for low-flow collectors.

For solar combi-systems where hot water is supplied to a water-to-air heat exchanger in the air supply duct or to a water-to-water heat exchanger in a water heat distribution system, the connection should be at the top of the tank, where the highest temperatures occur. For radiant floor heating, the connection can be in mid tank, since the required temperature supply is much lower.

12.2.3 Solar hot water preparation

The annual system efficiency of solar hot water systems ranges from 30 per cent to 70 per cent in a cold climate and can be even higher for milder climate types. Systems should be designed to cover nearly 100 per cent of the summer demand, as shown in Figure 12.2.5 for three climates. In temper-

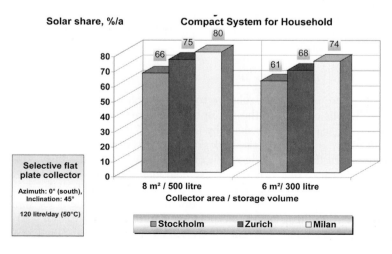

Source: G. Faninger, University of Klagenfurt

Figure 12.2.4 *Two schemes for sizing the storage-to-collector area for the three reference climates*

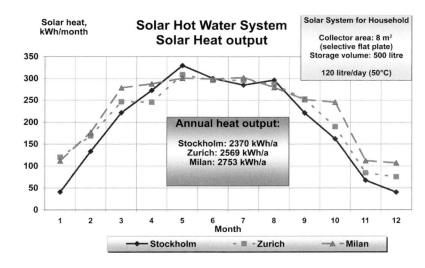

Source: G. Faninger, University of Klagenfurt

Figure 12.2.5 *Monthly solar heat output of a household solar DHW system with 45° tilt and 8 m² of collectors supplying a 500 litre storage tank in three climates (demand 120 litres/day at 50°C)*

ate climates, the annual coverage should reach 70 per cent for a single family house and 40 per cent for an apartment block. Coverage for the latter is generally lower because of lack of roof space for the stack of apartments below. Summer coverage in the temperate and mild climates should be designed to be under 100 per cent to reduce system overheating.

Solar hot water systems in an apartment house, although the coverage may be smaller, generally costs less per residential unit compared to systems for single family houses. Indeed, as the collector

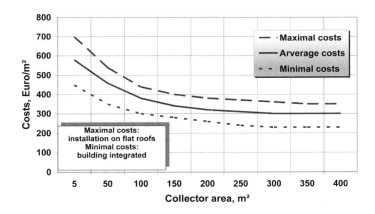

Source: G. Faninger, University of Klagenfurt

Figure 12.2.6 *Collector costs in relation to collector area*

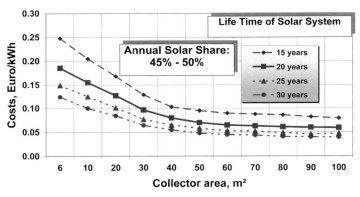

Source: G. Faninger, University of Klagenfurt

Figure 12.2.7 *Solar heating kWh costs in relation to collector area*

area for a single installation increases, the unit costs decrease sharply up to approximately 100 m², as can be seen in Figure 12.2.6. This translates to lower kWh costs for the solar heat, as illustrated in the example for Vienna in Figure 12.2.7.

Hygienic aspects of solar water heating. In some solar active system configurations the storage tank contains drinking water. There is then the risk of the so-called Legionnaire's disease, *Pneumonia Legionella*. It is caused by Legionella, or rod-shaped, mobile, aerobic bacteria that occur naturally in surface water and groundwater. They begin to propagate at temperatures between 20°C and 50°C, with optimum growth occurring between 30°C and 40°C. Above 60°C, they die off quickly. A long residence time in water at favourable temperatures may result in high concentrations of Legionella. Stagnant water in pipes or parts of an installation that have not been flushed are breeding grounds for these bacteria.

To prevent Legionella, the water temperature should either be below 25°C or above 50°C. Disinfecting a contaminated system can be done by flushing it, then heating the water to 60°C for 20 minutes. In general, solar thermal systems for hot water preparation are backed up by an auxiliary heating system to achieve temperatures above 50°C. In this manner the risk of Legionella contaminated water can be minimized.

A distinction is made between small and large systems:

- Small systems are considered to have a very low risk and do not need special attention. Small systems are installations in one or two family houses, or installation with a volume less than 400 litres and with less than 3 litres in pipes between the heater outlet and draw-off point.
- Large systems should be designed so that they can be heated up to 60°C to a frequency prescribed by the building/sanitary code.

12.2.4 Solar combined heating and hot water systems

Many configurations of solar combi-systems and backup systems have been tried. From 1975 to 1985, these systems were custom engineered. Through a cooperation of the International Energy Agency (IEA) Solar Heating and Cooling Programme (SHC) Task 26: Solar Combi-systems (see www.iea-shc.org/task26/index.html), existing designs have been analysed and optimized and a valuable design handbook produced (Weiss, 2003). Today, solar companies offering simple and economical systems frequently offer system design as part of their service. Components of solar combi-systems are factory assembled in compact units, making the onsite work of the installer easier and ensuring better reliability.

Currently, installed systems demonstrate that solar space heating is possible even in northern locations. In high latitudes, it would seem that such systems make little sense, given the minimal to zero solar radiation in mid winter. However, solar irradiation from September to October and March to May can make a useful contribution during the beginning and end of the heating season. Especially in northern countries, as well as in alpine areas, some heating during the summer period will increase living comfort.

In summer, the solar radiation is double that of winter, ensuring a high coverage of DHW demand. To achieve maximum overall system efficiency, priority is given to the load (DHW or space heating) with the lowest temperature level so that the solar collector works with the highest efficiency. Figure 12.2.8 shows the computed monthly performance of a combi-system in the Zurich reference temperate climate.

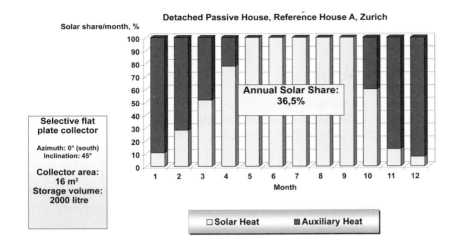

Source: G. Faninger, University of Klagenfurt

Figure 12.2.8 *Solar share from a combi-system in Zurich for a detached house with 16 m² of collector tilted at 45° and supplying a 2000 litre storage tank*

12.2.5 Centralized solar heating systems

In centralized concepts, a central storage tank is supplied heat from collectors located through the housing project. The major advantage of a centralized system is the reduced unit costs due to the scale of the project, when all houses have collectors. A further advantage is the small tank heat loss because its large volume results in a very beneficial surface-to-volume ratio. This benefit is offset, however, by the serious heat loss from all the pipe runs. This is especially critical in summer when the losses are the same but the demand for heat is small. It is also serious in winter, given the small space heating demand of very low energy housing.

References:

Faninger, G. (2004s) *Solar Thermal Systems with Water Collector*, available at www.energytech.at
Faninger, G. (2004b) *Market Deployment of Solar Housing in Austria*, available at www.energytech.at
Faninger, G. (2004c) *Solar Supported District Heating for Housing Estates*, available at www.energytech.at
Weiss, W. (2003) *Solar Heating Systems for Houses: A Design Handbook for Solar Combi-systems*, James and James Ltd, London

Solar system planning tools

Meteonorm: METEOTEST, Fabrikstrasse 14, CH 3012 Bern, Switzerland, office@meteotest.ch, http://www.meteotest.ch
Polysun: Institut für Solartechnik SPF, Hochschule für Technik Rapperswil (HSR), Oberseestrasse 10, CH 8640 Rapperswil, Switzerland, spf@solarenergy.ch, www.solarenergy.ch
SHWwin: *Zur Auslegung von Brauchwasseranlagen, Teilsolare Raumheizung, Nahwärmenetze*, Institut für Wärmetechnik, TU Graz (only German version available), www.wt.tu-graz.ac.at
TSOL: Dr. Valentin EnergieSoftware GmbH, Stralauer Platz 33-34, D 10243 Berlin, Germany, info@valentin.de, www.valentin.de

Websites

International Energy Agency (IEA): www.iea.org
International Energy Agency (IEA) Solar Heating and Cooling Programme (SHC): www.iea-shc.org
IEA SHC Task 26 homepages: www.solenergi.dk/task26/downloads.html

12.3 Fossil fuels

Carsten Petersdorff

12.3.1 Concept

In high-performance houses, while the heat demand is reduced to a very low level and occurs during only a few months of the year, it does not decrease to zero. Certainly, a significant part of the space heating and major part of the hot water demand can be covered by solar energy. However, to cover 100 per cent of the demand would be economic nonsense. Such a system would be grossly over-dimensioned most of the year, having to dispose of heat. A backup heating system to cover the peaks is essential. Burning a fossil fuel is a proven means of providing this backup. Due to the small absolute quantities of fuel consumed, the environmental impact is negligible. Especially in high-performance houses, the following should be considered:

- *Connection costs*: because the absolute amount of heat required is so small, the fixed costs must be kept minimal, including the investment cost, the connection to networks, fuel storage, and maintenance, operational and administrative costs.
- *Low peak demand*: the peak demand capacity for high-performance homes decreases with lower heating energy demand to levels of a few kW. 10 W/m^2 is typical for space heating peak demand in a high-performance house. Even this, though very small, only occurs during the coldest, sunless hours of the year. The majority of space heating systems on the market are oversized for such small demands. For domestic water heating, the peak can be kept small according to the size of the storage tank.
- *Losses in heating and auxiliary systems*: with lower total energy consumption, energy losses in heating systems and auxiliary systems become increasingly important. Thermal storage and heating devices should be installed within the heated space of the building as far as possible so that energy losses contribute to the heating. Pumps and control systems need to have no or low standby losses and must show good part-load efficiency.
- *Hot water*: energy demand for DHW remains at the same level (approximately 700 kWh/a per person), while space heating demand is cut to a fraction in high-performance buildings. Accordingly, the proportion of energy required for DHW becomes important.

12.3.2 Fossil fuels

The term fossil fuel applies to energy carriers that were formed from plant and animal organisms some millions of years ago. During their lifetime, these life forms absorbed carbon dioxide (CO_2) from their environment and now store carbon in underground reservoirs in the form of natural gas, crude oil and coal. Burning fossil fuels releases the stored chemical energy, while emitting CO_2 again.

The reserves of fossil fuels are, by definition, limited. Estimates suggest that all economic reserves of oil will last approximately 40 years under the current consumption rate. For gas, the reserves are estimated to last some 60 years, while the coal resources are predicted to last for some 170 years, as seen in Table 12.3.1. With increasing demand – for example, from developing countries – these times will be proportionally shorter.

Table 12.3.1 *Fossil fuels, reserves and projected availability (reach)*

2001	Resources	Identified reserves	Reach (years)
Oil	236 Gt	152 Gt	43
Natural gas	378 Tm^2	161 Tm^2	67
Coal	4594 Gt	661 Gt	210

Note: G = 10^9; T = 10^{12}
Source: BMWA (2003)

Commonly used fossil fuels for space heating can be divided into fuels that can be stored on site (for example, coals, oil and propane) and fuels delivered by a network (such as natural gas). The characteristics of the different fossil fuels are given in Table 12.3.2.

Table 12.3.2 *Characteristics of common fossil fuels*

	Natural gas		Propane		Light fuel oil		Hard coal		Lignite	
Composition (per cent)	CH$_4$	70–90	C3H8	>98	C	86	C	81–91	C	45–65
	VOC	5–15			H	12	H	4.1–5.5	H	4.8–6.1
	CO$_2$	0–10			O	0.8	O	3–10	O	18–30
	N$_2$	0–15			S	1.2	N	1–2	N	0.4–2.8
	H$_2$S	0–2					S	0.5–6	S	0.3–3.4
Lower calorific value	8.8–11.1 kWh/m^3		12.9 kWh/kg		11.8 kWh/kg		7.9–8.7 kWh/kg		2.6–8.3 kWh/kg	
Household price	€0.40/m^3		€0.38/litre		€0.38/litre					
Specific CO$_2$ emissions	229 g/kWh$_{fin}$				293g/kWh$_{fin}$		396g/kWh$_{fin}$		377g/kWh$_{fin}$	

Source: BMWA (2003)

Each fossil fuel has inherent environmental disadvantages, both in transport and storage. Coal emits dust when transported and needs a voluminous dry space for storage. Oil emits fumes in case of temperature increase and must be stored in tanks that require periodic checkups for tightness. Propane needs to be stored in pressurized tanks, making it unsuitable for inside or underground storage because of explosion danger. Considering these aspects, natural gas and propane are the most favourable fossil fuels with respect to environmental aspects, whereas oil and coal rank behind gas and propane on the same environmental level.

12.3.3 Types of systems

Atmospheric boilers

In atmospheric boilers, fuel (oil or gas) is burned under atmospheric pressure. For oil, this results in an inhomogeneous fuel–air mix, varying flame temperatures and the formation of carbon monoxide (CO) and volatile organic compounds (VOCs) harmful to man and the environment. Unburned fuel adds to this. Atmospheric burning gas boilers, however, have very low emissions. They are still common because of their technical simplicity, high reliability and good fuel utilization ratios up to 90 per cent to 93 per cent. Capacities range down to as low as 5 kW. Oil-fuelled atmospheric boilers are not installed in state-of-the-art heating systems because of their high emissions of volatile organic compounds and CO.

Charged boilers

A fan's supply of combustion air makes the system more flexible for part-load operation and operation under different meteorological pressures. The fan is typically installed at the air intake before the furnace. Installation in the flue gas is unusual because of material problems. The fan may be positioned on the exhaust air side if the chimney does not draw sufficiently to overcome the pressure drop of a large heat exchanger (condensing boilers), catalysts, etc. Charged oil and gas-fuelled boilers have standardized fuel utilization ratios of 92 per cent to 95 per cent and are manufactured in capacities as low as 5 kW.

Condensing boilers

Such boilers recover energy from condensing water vapour in the flue gas as one of the combustion products. This necessitates low temperatures in the heating system and larger heat exchanger surfaces. The latter increase the pressure drop over the heat exchanger, possibly making a repositioning of the fan necessary. The condensed water from a gas burner is slightly acid, but can be disposed of via the normal sewage system. In the case of oil boilers, sulphur dioxide (SO_2) in the flue gas forms sulphurous acid (H_2SO_3), which needs to be neutralized before being discharged into the sewage system. Condensing boilers are more expensive than equivalent atmospheric boilers but are up to 10 per cent more efficient. This results from the highly standardized fuel utilization ratio of up to 109 per cent and 104 per cent (relative to the lower calorific value) for gas and oil boilers, respectively. System capacities are equivalent to atmospheric and charged boilers. Because high-performance houses can operate at low heat supply temperatures, condensing boilers are a good match.

Booster for ventilation system

Ventilation systems with an efficient exhaust air heat recovery only need a small booster heater to provide sufficient heating power. Several solutions are available: heat pumps that extract heat from the exhaust air after the heat exchanger or solar thermal systems backed up by electric or fossil-fuelled furnaces. Natural and propane gas-fired condensing heaters can supply this backup today. Small and highly efficient oil boilers with low emissions are still under development. Several systems developed for fossil fuels have been adapted to burn renewable fuels, such as oil from sunflower seed.

Combined systems

Combined systems that produce both heat and electrical power (combined heat and power, or CHP) are attractive, given the high primary energy value of electricity. Because of their high investment costs they are not interesting for high-performance single family houses because their demand for heat is too small. Where buildings and loads can be aggregated, over a micro heating network to create a greater heating demand, such systems become plausible. Example systems include small natural gas engines or Stirling engines coupled to a heat pump and electrical generator. The fuel cells technology for residential applications, which is now in a pilot phase, is promising.

Centralized systems: due to the small heating demand and small peak capacity requirements, a small central heating plant supplying several rows of houses or blocks of apartments may be sensible. At this aggregated scale, higher investment cost systems, such as geothermal heat supply, may become feasible.

12.3.4 Outlook to the future

Systems for high-performance housing have to be carefully sized, with care given to avoiding over-dimensioned systems. The very low amounts of heat required constrain how much can be justified in capital costs to buy and maintain the system. Fossil fuel combustion requires periodic emission check-ups of the burner and flue. Meter reading and billing charges take on a disproportionate magnitude in high-performance houses. Producing the heat centrally and distributing it seems sensible; but the pipe network must also be amortized and the heat losses of the grid are large when compared to the small supply demand. For all of these reasons, heat pumps have been more popular for houses, which are highly insulated and have minimal heating demand, to date, than fossil fuel combustion systems as a backup heat source.

References

BMWA (Bundesministerium für Wirtschaft und Arbeit) (2003) 'Nationale und internationale Entwicklung', *Energiedaten 2003*, BMWA, Berlin, www.bmwa.bund.de

12.4 Direct electric resistance heating

Berthold Kaufmann

12.4.1 Electrical space and water heating

Electricity is a high-level energy form (100 per cent exergy) that can provide almost all energy services, from supplying electric light, the mechanical drive of electric tools and modern information technology. For all of these activities, there is no substitute for electricity.

On the other hand, there are many possible substitutes for the task of space and water heating – for example, the needed heat can be produced directly from burning fuels. From a technical point of view, combustion technology is highly advanced and cost effective.

When combustion has the task of producing electricity, the heat must first be converted by a thermodynamic process – for instance, by a steam engine or turbine. This conversion results in substantial losses of energy. The thermodynamic efficiency of such machines is only about 0.3, or 30 per cent. Only the best combined gas and steam turbines that combine the two functions in subsequent steps reach a thermodynamic conversion efficiency, in total, of about 56 per cent. These highly efficient systems are, up to now, very rare so that the average end-to-primary energy conversion factor in Europe is, at present, about 38 per cent (CEPHEUS-GEMIS, 2004).

The conversion factor will hopefully improve in the near future as conventional sources of primary energy are increasingly replaced by renewable sources. The growth rate of all renewable energy sources together has been anticipated to increase to about 25 per cent of the total energy production by 2020. Yet, even if this ambitious goal is reached, the amount of renewable energy available will still be limited and prices for electricity can be expected to rise. So there is a strong argument that electricity is and will continue to be too valuable to be 'burned' merely to produce low temperature heat!

12.4.2 Alternative technologies for heat production

Small heat pumps using exhaust heat from a ventilation system with heat recovery can provide seasonal performance factors (SPFs) higher than 3, making heat production by this method more efficient than direct electric heating. The investment costs for these combined systems are higher than for an ordinary resistance heater, but the energy savings during the system lifetime can offset this.

12.4.3 Peak power supply and freeze protection by direct electric heating

There are some applications where direct electric heating to cover peak heating demand may be sensible and cost effective.

When domestic water is heated by a low power heat pump coupled to a 150 litre to 200 litre boiler, there may be hot water shortage for short periods during the year. To economically solve this problem, a flow-through water heater is a reasonable alternative. This heater should be arranged after the heat pump so that direct electric heating is only called for when the heat pump is unable to deliver the needed heating power. If the system is properly dimensioned, such occurrences should be rare. Accordingly, the absolute amount of electricity consumed for this purpose should be minimal over the year.

By the same reasoning, a reserve radiator in a living room can be sensible. It can be regulated to only switch on when the system control recognizes that the heat pump cannot deliver enough heat. If this occurs too frequently, an error message can be generated to inform the occupant or building manager.

A third plausible application is heating air. A pre-heater in the outside air duct can be activated to ensure that the supply air is always above –5°C. This prevents humid room exhaust air from freezing up and shutting down the ventilation heat exchanger. The duct thermostat should be set so that incoming air is not heated above +2°C in order not to waste heat (Kaufmann et al, 2004). The air heater can be a simple unit comprised of an inexpensive electric resistance grid positioned in the air flow. When the regulator is properly adjusted, heating time will be kept minimal in Central European climates.

References

CEPHEUS-GEMIS (2004) *Global Emission Model for Integrated Systems*, available at www.oeko.de/service/gemis/de/material.htm#infos

Feist, W. (2005) *Zur Wirtschaftlichkeit der Wärmedämmung bei Dächern*, Protokollband no 29, Arbeitskreis Kostengünstige Passivhäuser (AKKP), 1, Auflage, Darmstadt, Germany

IEA (International Energy Agency) (2001) *World Energy Outlook 2000 Highlights*, OECD, Paris

Kaufmann, B., Feist, W., Pfluger, R., John, M. and Nagel, M. (2004) *Passivhäuser erfolgreich planen und bauen: Ein Leitfaden zur Qualitätssicherung im Passivhaus*, Erstellt im Auftrag des Instituts für Stadtentwicklungsforschung und Bauwesen (ILS), Aachen, Germany

Reiß, J. (2003) *Messtechnische Validierung des Energiekonzeptes einer großtechnisch umgesetzten Passivhausentwicklung in Stuttgart-Feuerbach*, Fraunhofer IBP, Stuttgart, Ergebnisse des Forschungsvorhabens Passivhaustagung, Hamburg, Germany

12.5 Biomass

Gerhard Faninger

12.5.1 Forms of biomass for heating housing

Biomass is a very broad term; this section addresses one form of biomass: wood products. These can be in the form of firewood, bark and wood chips from the forests, and as remnants of the wood processing industry compressed into pellets. Modern wood-fired boilers offer a high degree of automation, operational safety, and low noise and dust production. The environmental advantage of biomass is clearly that it is simply completing the natural cycle, from vegetation growth through decay and returning to the growth cycle. Burning biomass simply accelerates this degradation process, producing no more CO_2 than would occur by decomposition. One issue can be raised: whether the ash after combustion finds its way back to the forest floor.

Source: G. Faninger, University of Klagenfurt

Figure 12.5.1
Automated wood pellet central heating

12.5.2 Wood stoves

Firewood is an ancient and sustainable fuel source for keeping a shelter warm. During the last decade, remarkable improvements have been made in wood stove performance regarding both efficiency and emissions. Such stoves typically include a heat exchanger coupled to buffer storage. Unfortunately, there is only a small choice of products with the small heating capacity (< 5 kW) needed by high-performance housing. Figure 12.5.1 shows one example system that can operate at very low heating power because the firewood is placed vertically in the oven. Subsidies for woodstoves are rare to non-existent compared to other biomass solutions. The living quality that a wood fire brings to a home is, however, often decisive.

1 *Loading tube for thermal stratification*
2 *Tube heat exchanger*
3 *Low-Flow heat exchanger*
4 *Hot water heat exchanger, high-grade steel*
5 *Heat insulation, 90 mm, with Alu-surface*
6 *Heating inlet*
7 *Heating outlet*
8 *Solar-High-Flow-heat exchanger*

Load: 3,9 kW – 14 kW
Storage volume: 800 litre + 60 litre

SOLARFOCUS, Austria
www.solarfocus.at

Storage for combined solar-pellets boiler

Source: Solarfocus, www.solarfocus.at

Figure 12.5.2 *Combined water storage, pellet burner and integrated pellet storage system*

12.5.3 Pellet ovens

Pellet ovens can be room units or central units located, for example, in the basement. Figure 12.5.2a illustrates a central heating system using a pellet-fired boiler and variations of pellet storage. A combined water storage, pellet burner and integrated pellet storage is shown in Figure 12.5.2b. A high efficiency with minimized emissions is achieved even when the heat demand of the building is 30 per cent below the peak demand when a 'stop and go' operation occurs. The frequencies of start-ups can be minimized by a buffer store. Ideally, in summer, heat demand for DHW should be almost entirely provided by a solar thermal system. This is an ideal system for high-performance housing striving for sustainability. The life-cycle costs of pellet heating are comparable with those of an oil burner system today.

The use of wood in the form of pellets instead of firewood facilitates the automation of the fuel supply to the boiler. The wood in this form burns more efficiently and cleanly. Mass production of pellet boilers has reduced their costs. The pellets are produced from sawdust under high pressure and without input of chemical products (binder). The 100 per cent natural wood pellets are transported in a tank lorry and pumped dust free into a storage bin link with a feeder to the boiler (see Figure 12.5.3). New on the market are storage-integrated pellet burners.

Such systems are already cost competitive in regions where pellets or chips from forest residues are available. Nevertheless, these systems have an economically limited radius from wood-fuel distributors; in Austria, the maximum radius is considered to be about 80 km.

12.5.4 Wood-fired district heating systems

Because high-performance houses need so little heat, a community wood-fired system can improve the economics of wood-fired heat production by sharing the overhead costs (see Figure 12.5.4). There are practical problems, however. During the non-heating season, the demand for heating DHW from the district heating is very small relative to the pumping power and distribution energy losses. The boilers are also oversized for only hot water production and are therefore operated inefficiently. This problem can be alleviated if the domestic water heating demand is primarily covered by a solar thermal system.

A critical planning aspect is the hydraulic design of the pipe network. Four-pipe networks and two-pipe networks are used. Experimental data clearly show that two-pipe networks perform better than four-pipe networks with regard to plant efficiency and solar utilization. Two-pipe-networks reveal the lowest need for auxiliary energy for all building geometries and energy densities. Two-pipe networks can be combined with decentralized heat exchangers or with decentralized tanks. With

Source: AEE-INTEC, Gleisdorf, www.aee.at

Figure 12.5.3 *Wood pellet transport*

individual tanks it is possible to operate the network at a lower temperature for space heating (< 40°C) and a higher temperature for hot water preparation (about 65°C to 70°C). Network heat losses are thus smaller than is the case with networks with heat exchangers that must operate at maximum temperature all of the time. On the other hand, multiple decentralized storage tanks cost collectively more than just decentralized heat exchangers.

The seasonal performance of a solar-supported wood-fired district heating system in Tschantschendorf, Austria, is illustrated in Figure 12.5.5. Outside the heating season, solar collectors supply sufficient heat to the storage tank to cover the demand for three to five days. Although the annual solar coverage for space heating and hot water preparation is only about 14 per cent, during the non-heating season the solar system covers more than 80 per cent of the demand!

In summary, wood-fired district heating plants are most efficient when the system is shared by many users (high demand density). The distribution heat losses can be minimized by rational housing estate plans, highest quality pipe insulation and lowest possible return temperatures (< 40°C during non-heating months). The recharging strategy of the boiler should optimize the contribution of solar collectors.

Source: AEE-INTEC, Gleisdorf, www.aee.at

Figure 12.5.4 *Wood chip district heating plant*

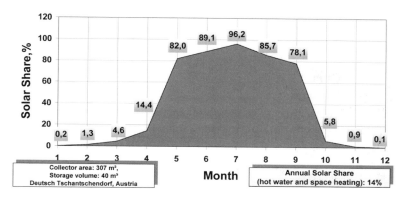

Source: G. Faninger, University of Klagenfurt

Figure 12.5.5 *Combined solar-biomass district heating: Monthly share of solar heat*

References

Faninger, G. (2000) *Combined Solar-Biomass District Heating in Austria.* Solar Energy Vol. 69, No. 6, pp. 425 - 435, 2000.

Websites

International Energy Agency: www.iea-bioenergy-task29.hr; www.iea-bioenergy.com

12.6 Fuel cells

Karsten Voss, Benoit Sicre and Andreas Bühring

12.6.1 Concept

Fuel cells, like batteries, are electrochemical power sources. Whereas batteries store energy, fuel cells transform energy. A fuel cell steadily supplied with fuel generates electricity. The fuel can be virtually any chemical substance containing hydrogen. When hydrogen alone is not readily available as a fuel, it can be produced from substances such as natural gas, oil or methanol by a process called 'reforming'. Reforming, however, consumes energy, produces waste heat and is generally not emission free. Ideally, hydrogen is produced from water by electrolysis, where the electricity is generated by solar power (solar hydrogen).

Within a fuel cell, hydrogen reacts with oxygen – pure or extracted from the air – and induces an ion flux through the electrolyte (usually an ion-porous membrane). Electrical power is generated while water is produced as a main reaction product (see Figure 12.6.1). This high-exothermic electrochemical reaction can be carried out at various temperature levels, depending on the type of cell (see Table 12.6.1). The temperatures together with the waste heat from the reformer have to be considered for applications with combined heat and power use (CHP). The electrochemical reaction under real conditions induces a voltage ranging from 0.6 V to 0.9 V DC per cell. Therefore, cells are stacked (connected in series) to reach a useful voltage. In a high-performance house, the DC current is converted to AC by an inverter, comparable to those developed for PV applications. With the exception of autonomous houses, the systems are grid connected.

The main advantage of fuel cells is their potentially greater ratio of power to heat generation (power factor) compared to CHP generators driven by combustion engines. The smallest commercial CHP unit currently available features a power output of 1 kW. Thus, such systems are well suited for single family high-performance houses.

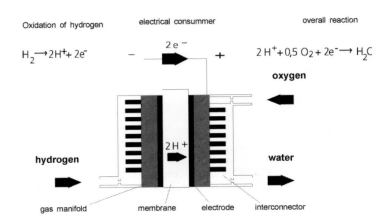

Oxidation of hydrogen   electrical consumer   overall reaction

$H_2 \rightarrow 2H^+ + 2e^-$ $2e^-$ $2H^+ + 0.5\ O_2 + 2e^- \rightarrow H_2O$

oxygen

hydrogen   water

gas manifold   membrane   electrode   interconnector

Source: K. Voss, Wuppertal University

Figure 12.6.1 *The basic electrochemical fuel cell process: Oxidation of hydrogen by means of oxygen*

Today, the most promising fuel cell technologies for high-performance single family houses are the PEM-FC (polymer electrolyte membrane fuel cell) and the SO-FC (solid oxide fuel cell). SO-FC systems are still being tested in large-scale field tests (Ballhausen, 2003). The PEM technology primarily profits from the enormous development efforts within the automobile industry. The main weakness for applications in the housing sector is the need for the complex reforming of natural gas to produce pure hydrogen with a minimal content of CO and at a high energy efficiency. The 1000°C needed temperature level of the SO-FC technology results in high thermal stress for cell materials made largely of ceramics. At such high temperatures a more or less continuous operation or hot standby mode is necessary. To improve economy, efforts are under way to decrease the operating temperature down to 800°C. The strength of the SO-FC is the possible internal reforming of natural gas to hydrogen with sufficient purity. This has the added benefit of reducing the overall system complexity.

Table 12.6.1 *Characteristic data of the principal fuel cell systems*

	Polymer electrolyte membrane fuel cell (PEM-FC)	AFC	PAFC	MCFC	Solid oxide fuel cell (SO-FC)
Electrolyte	Ion exchange membranes	Mobilized or immobilized potassium oxide	Immobilized liquid phosphoric acid	Immobilized liquid molten carbonate	Ceramic
Operating temperature (°C)	80	65–220	205	650	600–1000
Charge carrier	H+	OH–	H+	CO_{3-}	O–
External reformer for CH_4	Yes	Yes	Yes	No	No
Prime cell components	Carbon based	Carbon based	Graphite based	Stainless based	Ceramic
Catalyst	Platinum	Platinum	Platinum	Nickel	Perovskites
Product water management	Evaporative	Evaporative	Evaporative	Gaseous product	Gaseous product
Product heat management	Process gas + independent cooling medium	Process gas + electrolyte calculation	Process gas + independent cooling medium	Internal reforming + process gas	Internal reforming + process gas

Source: DOE (2000)

12.6.2 Environmental impact

To fairly judge the overall environmental impact of fuel cells, the reforming process, as well as the material flow from production to recycling, down-cycling or disposal, must be considered. Low emissions of the fuel cell process itself are only one part of the story. In addition, conflicting situations where a fuel cell is used have to be taken into account – for example, the usefulness of 'free' waste heat by fuel cells in a house with a solar thermal DHW system.

A detailed life-cycle assessment of fuel cell systems, currently under development, will provide quantified data on key energy and material flows associated with the manufacturing and operation of fuel cells (Krewitt, 2003). Ecological and economic effects resulting from the introduction of stationary fuel cells into the German energy system are investigated in detail. Long-term scenarios enable the quantification of environmental impacts (for example, changes in greenhouse gas emissions and material flows), and the benefits and burdens on the national economy, as well as the employment effects resulting from a reinforced introduction of decentralized stationary fuel cells in Germany. The study also identifies barriers and appropriate market instruments.

12.6.3 Economics: Status and trends

Fuel cell systems are still very expensive, but the hope is to bring costs down in the not too distant future. Whereas power costs for automobiles are targeted by the US Department of Energy (DOE) at €45/kW (OAAT, 2002), specific costs of approximately €1500 would be acceptable for combined heat and power units in housing (Bornemann, 2002). This favours the assumption that housing is a promising application of this technology. On the other hand, such units must run 40,000 hours, whereas applications for automobiles must only last one tenth of this duration. A disadvantage of the use of fuel cells, compared to heat pumps, is the need for an additional fuel supply. This might be solved by supplying high-performance houses with stored liquid gas, methanol or future special fuel cell 'gasoline' in canisters. It would be worth considering types of fuels appropriate for automobile fuel cells in order to benefit from synergetic effects.

12.6.4 Integration of fuel cells in high-performance houses

Several unique aspects of high-performance housing make applications of fuel cells interesting. While, in high-performance housing, the heating requirement is small, the electrical demand is not necessarily proportionally small. This means that a fuel cell sized to meet the heating demand will not likely generate more electricity than is needed. This shifts the focus from pure electricity generation for the grid to trying to cover the electrical demand of the house itself.

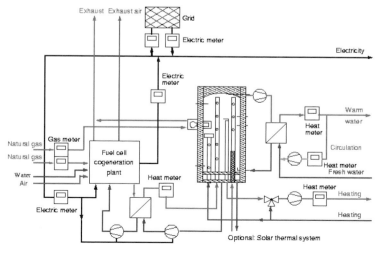

Source: Vetter and Wittwer (2002)

Figure 12.6.2 *Basic layout of a fuel cell as the house energy supply system with grid connection*

In order to limit system complexity, the demand for space heating and domestic hot water must be high enough to serve as the sole heat sink for the fuel cell. This low and seasonally relatively constant heat demand makes it possible to not have to have a second heat source for peak power management. A prerequisite for the continuous operation of a low power fuel cell is a high-efficiency, properly dimensioned thermal storage tank.

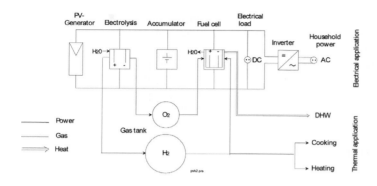

Source: K. Voss, Wuppertal University

Figure 12.6.3 *Energy supply system of the 'self-sufficient solar house'*

If the fuel cell is dimensioned for its electrical output, the availability of plentiful 'waste heat' may diminish the motivation for the thermal qualities of the house. This shifts the concern from design driven by conserving heat to total performance design where the concern is minimizing CO_2 emissions for all the energy needs of the household.

12.6.5 Early examples

The so-called 'self-sufficient solar house' in Freiburg, Germany, demonstrated how a house could be heated and powered by fuel cell back in 1991. A 0.5 kW PEM-type fuel cell unit was operated with solar hydrogen. Power was supplied to the off-grid house and waste heat was used as winter backup of the solar DHW system. Heat for space heating was produced by direct burning of hydrogen in the ventilation system of the house. Fuel cell operation was triggered by the electricity need of the house, when the battery charge was down. Economics were not considered in this original scientific experience. The whole system achieved an electrical efficiency of 45 per cent (Voss, 1996).

Field tests of fuel cells were initiated by several European utilities in 2002. The pre-market series of solid oxide fuel cell (SO-FC) units of the Swiss manufacturer Sulzer Hexis were used in one of these test series. Identical units were installed and monitored in buildings of various types and energy demand levels. Considering the need for continuous operation and the requirement that an identical unit serve various house types, it was decided to integrate a gas burner of typical household sizes as part of the unit. The gas burner meets the peak heat demand, whereas the fuel cell covers the base heating load.

Table 12.6.2 *Key system data of Sulzer Hexis HXS 1000 Premiere*

Power capacity, fuel cell	1 kW
Heat capacity, fuel cell	3 kW
Backup burner capacity	12/16/22 kW
Electric efficiency	25–30 per cent
Total efficiency	Approximately 85 per cent
Boiler volume	200
Fuel	Natural gas
Dimensions	1080 mm x 720 mm x 1800 mm
Weight	350 kg

Source: www.hexis.com

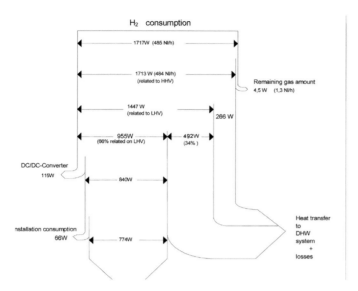

Note: Where natural gas is used, additional energy flows and losses would have to be considered for the reforming process.

Source: K. Voss, Wuppertal University

Figure 12.6.4 *Measured energy flow diagram of the polymer electrolyte membrane (PEM) fuel cell operated with hydrogen*

12.6.6 Conclusions

Natural gas-fed fuel cell systems have achieved an end prototype phase adequate for large-scale field testing. However, substantial technical improvements are still needed before market entry will be possible.

Durability, reliability and the lifetime of the components need to be improved, especially for the high temperature systems. Currently, cell degradation (primarily corrosion or malfunction of components) limits the practical operating life fuel cells. Moreover, the energy consumption of the parasitic components (typically, fans and pumps) must be reduced. When these challenges are overcome, fuel cells will be an attrac-

Source: Hexis AG, Winterthur, www.hexis.com

Figure 12.6.5 *The Sulzer Hexis system*

tive means of producing electricity and heat in the context of housing (Vetter and Sicre, 2003).

Although natural gas-supplied fuel cells have a lower environmental impact than some competing technologies, decisive emission reductions are unlikely as long as fuel cells must be supplied by a fossil fuel. A transition, making use of biogas, would improve the environmental impact of fuel cells substantially. The construction of nation-wide grids supplying solar hydrogen seems totally unrealistic at current costs; but unrealistic today may look different in 25 years.

The potential of fuel cell applications in high-performance housing is promising since the power-to-heat ratio of such buildings better matches that of fuel cell CHP systems. Simulation results show clearly that no additional gas heater is required since the heating peaks can be easily covered by an electrical heater without jeopardizing the primary energy balance of the house.

References

Ausschuss (2001) *Brennstoffzellen-Technologie*, Bericht des Ausschusses für Bildung, Forschung und Technikfolgenabschätzung, Drucksache 15/5054, Berlin, Germany

Ballhausen, A. (2003) *Energiedienstleistuung mit Brennstoffzellen – Contracting-Lösung für Privatkunden*, Proceedings of the Conference *Brennstoffzellen-Heizgeräte zur Energieversorgung im Haushalt*, Haus der Technik, Essen, Germany

Bornemann, H. J. (2002) *Hybrid Power: A European Perspective*, Second DOE/UN Workshop and International Conference on Hybrid Power Systems, www.netl.doe.gov/publications/proceedings/02/Hybrid/Hybrid2Bornemann.pdf

Britz, P. (2002) *Das Viessmann Projekt Brennstoffzellen-Heizgerät zur Hausenergieversorgung*; Proceeding of the Fuel Cell Conference Haus der Wirtschaft, Stuttgart, Germany

DOE (US Department of Energy) (2000) *Fuel Cell Handbook*, fifth edition, Science Applications International Corporation, US Department of Energy, Office of Fossil Energy, National Energy Technology Laboratory, Morgantown, West Virginia, US

Krewitt, W. et al (2003) *Policy Context, Environmental Impacts and Market Potential of the Application of Decentralised, Stationary Fuel Cells*, Proceedings of the Hannover Messe, Hannover, Germany

OAAT (Office of Advanced Automotive Technologies) (2002) *Office of Advanced Automotive Technologies Cost Model Identifies Market Barriers to PEM Fuel-Cell Use in Automobiles*; DOE, www.cartech.doe.gov/research/fuelcells/cost-model.html

Vetter, M. and Wittwer, C. (2002) *Model-based Development of Control Strategies for Domestic Fuel Cell Cogeneration Plants: Proceedings of the French–German Fuel Cell Conference 2002*, Forbach-Saarbrücken

Vetter, M. and Sicre, B. (2003) *Sind Mini-KWK-Anlagen für das Passivhaus geeignet? Anforderungen und Potenziale, Beitrag zur Passivhaus-Tagung 2003*, Tagungsband, Hamburg, Germany

Voss, K. (1996) *Experimentelle und Theoretische Analyse des Thermischen Gebäudeverhaltens für das Energieautarke Solarhaus Freiburg*, Thesis, Ecole Polytechnique Federale de Lausanne, Switzerland

Website

Hexis Ltd: www.hexis.com

12.7 District heating

Carsten Petersdorff

12.7.1 Concept

District heating is a collective heating system supplying several buildings. High-performance housing can also benefit from this shared approach. Given the very small heat demand of individual high-performance houses, the capital costs for the backup heating become very expensive. When one heating plant can serve many houses, the economics improve and there is a greater selection among types of systems. Examples include solar seasonal storage, waste incineration plants and gas engine heat pumps. An added advantage of such a large central facility is that they can be more easily adapted to future developments than exchanging the heating system in each individual building. The idea of such micro-heating networks derives from urban district heating, but design modifications are essential.

In the US as well as in some European cities, steam systems up to 175°C are common. In Europe, systems operating with hot water at temperatures of 90°C to 130°C are more common. Some systems even operate at temperatures below 90°C. Such lower temperature systems are well suited for local district heating, solar seasonal storage or heat pumps. Requirements for operation, distribution and onsite installation are more flexible and costs per unit of heat can be significantly lower than for high temperature systems. For all of these reasons, such systems are the best suited to serve high-performance housing.

A typical district heating system has two subsystems:

1   *Heat generation*: for district heating plants to produce hot water (or steam) may be relatively simple – for example, a single, large gas-fired boiler. To improve efficiency, however, multiple boilers are often built to cover base, intermediate and peak loads. A co-generation or renewable system can meet the base loads and a separate peak load system can provide standby capacity, as needed. This also increases system reliability.
2   *Heat distribution*: two concepts are common: two- and four-pipe systems.

Two-pipe systems are most common in residential areas. They supply heat for both space heating and domestic water heating via hot water (or steam). The cooled distribution medium returns to the central boiler via the return pipe. The heat supply must be at least 65°C to ensure safety for DHW from Legionella bacteria. A two-pipe system may also be used for space heating only; but this requires homeowners to have their own DHW heating systems.

Four-pipe systems, although more expensive, provide the greatest flexibility because space heating energy and DHW heating are served separately. As a result, the space heating supply circuit can operate at lower temperatures. Circulation losses are correspondingly smaller and the whole circuit can be switched off outside the heating season, which is a large part of the year for high-performance houses.

12.7.2 Designing district heating

Design of heat production by annual duration

Figure 12.7.1 illustrates a typical annual duration curve. The key design parameters are total system peak demand, average load requirements and load variations from day to day and season to season.

Many heating plants have a highly efficient or renewable energy system for the base load. This system typically covers 25 per cent to 40 per cent of the load and supplies 70 per cent to 90 per cent of the consumed heat on a yearly basis. Example plant types include:

*   biomass (wood, energy from waste);
*   geothermal energy;
*   solar collectors for space heating;
*   combined heat and power generation (for example, fuel cells, motor engines, micro-turbines); and
*   electrical or gas-driven heat pumps.

The peaks may be covered by a gas-fired boiler.

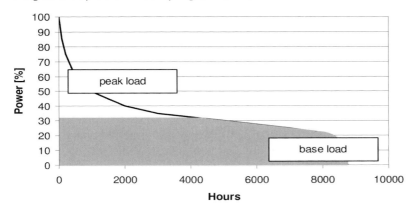

Source: Carsten Petersdorff, Ecofys GmbH, Köln

Figure 12.7.1 *An annual duration curve*

Peak shaving

To increase the share of the base load system, thermal storage is useful. The principle is to produce surplus heat and store it during low demand periods. As a result, the system can operate closer to its optimal efficiency throughout the day. When peak demand occurs, the stored heat can be drawn on. Because district heating systems service multiple users with varying peak load requirements, the load curve tends to be smoother than each individual load curve. The result is that both the heat supply and storage capacity can be proportionately lower than would be the case for heating plants and storage for each individual building.

Seasonal storage

Extrapolating the storage principle to a seasonal basis is very advantageous for solar use. With large seasonal storage systems, solar energy can be collected during summer and stored until needed in the heating season. Given the shortening of the heating season of high-performance houses to the sun-poor mid winter, this is a big advantage. The annual solar contribution can be as high as 70 per cent, even in a northern climate. Indeed, the first large solar heating plants were built during the late 1970s, with Sweden as the main pioneer. Other facilities followed in Denmark, The Netherlands and Finland, as well as Sweden. More recently, Germany has constructed several large demonstration systems.

12.7.3 Heat distribution for high-performance housing

Due to the low space heating demand of high-performance houses, heat production must be simple and with low capital costs. Producing heat collectively for many houses saves having to buy and maintain a system in each individual house. The extremely low energy demand leads to special requirements for such a district heating system.

Independence of distribution costs

The investment costs of heat distribution piping are nearly independent of the heat demand. Therefore, the specific distribution costs increase with the sharply decreased heat demand of high-performance houses. This is, however, equally true for competing decentralized oil and gas systems. Studies have shown the cost differences between central and decentral systems is minimal or even favours decentralized systems if the pipe running between houses are short. This is already the case for terraced houses with a comparatively low density of 25 houses per hectare (Nast, 1996).

Heat losses and auxiliary energy

The heat losses of conventional district heating systems range between 5 per cent and 17 per cent, depending on the heat density in the area and the length of the piping. The lower heat demand of high-performance housing makes circulation heat losses more pronounced. These losses depend mainly on the length and the layout of the piping and only secondarily on the heat demand of the houses. Energy consumed by auxiliary systems (such as pumps) also gains significance. Pump energy depends on the flow rate (m^3/h), the diameters of the pipes and the rotational speed of the pump. The average pump energy for a district heating system serving conventional houses can be estimated as 1 per cent of the transported heat. This percentage would be higher for high-performance housing estates. For all of these reasons, the circulation system has to be optimized to the special demands of such housing.

Circulation losses are primarily determined by the temperature difference between the pipe interior and surrounding (ground) temperature. Given this temperature difference, the specific heat loss (W/mK) depends on the thickness and the material of the insulation and on the diameter of the piping. Figure 12.7.2 shows typical heat losses of piping for different configurations.

			average operating temperature TB [°C]									
DN	K-Value [W/mK]	**40°**	**50°**	**60°**	**70°**	**80°**	**90°**	**100°**	**110°**	**120°**	**130°**	
20	0.161	4.8	6.4	8.0	9.7	11.3	12.9	14.5	16.1	17.7	19.3	
25	0.178	5.3	7.1	8.9	10.7	12.5	14.2	16.0	17.8	19.6	21.4	
25	0.154	4.6	6.2	7.7	9.2	10.8	12.3	13.9	15.4	16.9	18.5	
32	0.192	5.8	7.7	9.6	11.5	13.5	15.4	17.3	19.2	21.1	23.0	
32	0.172	5.2	6.7	8.6	10.3	12.0	13.8	15.5	17.2	18.9	20.6	
40	0.242	7.3	9.7	12.1	14.5	16.9	19.4	21.8	24.2	26.6	29.0	
40	0.210	6.3	8.4	10.5	12.6	14.7	16.8	18.9	21.0	23.1	25.2	
50	0.268	8.0	10.7	13.4	16.0	18.8	21.5	24.1	26.8	29.5	32.2	
50	0.234	7.0	9.4	11.7	14.0	16.4	18.7	21.0	23.4	25.7	28.1	

Heat loss during operation:
$q = K \cdot (TB - TE)$ [W/m]

K = Specific heat losses [W/mK]
TB = Average operating temperature [°C]
TE = Average earth temperature [°C]

Heat loss q [W/m] for single-line pipe by parallel laying

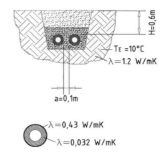

Source: Carsten Petersdorff, Ecofys GmbH, Köln

Figure 12.7.2 *Typical heat losses of piping*

In the case of good insulation, the mass flow in the piping has a minor influence on the heat losses that results in approximately constant heat losses independent of the amount of heat transported. Consequently, heat losses can amount to up to 30 per cent of the heat production in summer when only small amounts of heat are needed for DHW and there is no space heating demand.

Cost-efficient network construction

In traditional district heating, insulated steel pipes in fixed lengths are welded together to form a larger network. To be profitable, such a distribution technique requires a relatively high heat density. Highly efficient houses do not provide such a density; other constructions of the network are therefore necessary.

Plastic pipes. The operating conditions of smaller district heating systems, involving a maximum temperature of 90°C and a pressure of 6 bar, allow the use of plastic pipes. Two models of plastic pipe systems are available:

1   sectional pipes in fixed lengths (for example, 12 m); and
2   flexible plastic pipe in lengths up to about 200 m for smaller diameters.

Plastic pipe technology shows the biggest economic advantage with small pipe diameters. A 30 per cent to 40 per cent cost reduction can be obtained with such a system, compared to conventional systems.

Reduced earthworks. Further cost reductions are possible when both the supply and return pipes are integrated in one twin pipe (see Figure 12.7.3). A benefit of this system is the improved insulation. An alternative is 'piggy-back laying'. This reduces the excavation costs. Pipes are not arranged side by side, but rather on top of each other. The overall costs for both techniques are about 85 per cent of those of standard steel pipe systems.

Methods of laying. Figure 12.7.4 shows different methods of laying pipes. Flexible plastic pipes can efficiently avoid obstacles such as trees. Further cost-effective techniques are the looping-in method and the laying from building to building. Both methods avoid branch connections.

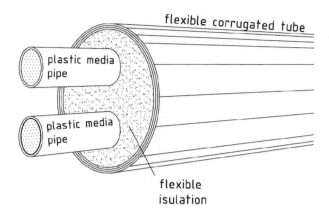

flexible corrugated tube

plastic media pipe

plastic media pipe

flexible isulation

Source: Carsten Petersdorff, Ecofys GmbH, Köln

Figure 12.7.3 *A flexible integrated plastic pipe system with two media*

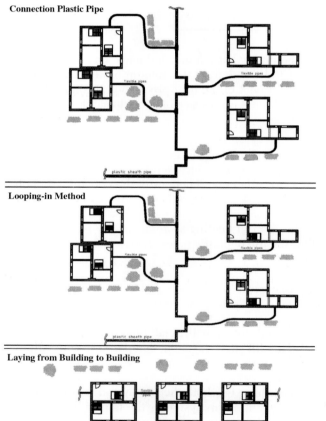

Connection Plastic Pipe

Looping-in Method

Laying from Building to Building

Source: Carsten Petersdorff, Ecofys GmbH, Köln

Figure 12.7.4 *Methods of pipe laying*

Costs of the piping. Table 12.7.1 compares the average costs of traditional piping systems with the minimal costs of a project in Odense, Denmark. Total investment costs of the district heating network could be reduced to about 30 per cent of traditional piping systems.

Table 12.7.1 *Costs of district heating piping*

Cost comparison	Diameter (mm)	25	50	80	100	150
Piping costs (conventional laying)	(€/m)	250	300	360	400	510
Minimal piping costs (Odense, Denmark)	(€/m)	70	90	105	120	160
Cost savings		72 per cent	70 per cent	71 per cent	70 per cent	69 per cent

Cost-efficient supply stations

The end user can either be supplied with thermal energy indirectly or directly.

Indirect systems incorporate heat exchangers at the energy production location and at the user's location. This allows freedom of pressure ratios among different networks. Furthermore, the networks can survive leaks at the consumer side. For these reasons, indirect connection is often preferred. Such systems are also the most economical for high-performance houses.

Direct systems do not have isolated subsystems. Hot water is fed directly into the customer's heating system. Domestic hot water is either distributed by a separate hygienic piping system, heated via a heat exchanger or heated decentrally at the individual houses. The direct connection is usually the more economical solution.

Table 12.7.2 *Costs of sub-stations*

Costs of sub-stations	Direct system (€)	Indirect system (€)
Single family house	1500–2500	2000–3500
Multi-family house (30 kW)	1700–3500	2200–5500

Connection of several houses to a sub-station and then 'sub-distribution' is especially interesting for high-performance housing. Cost savings of up to 50 per cent compared to the direct system are possible.

Example distribution costs

Table 12.7.3 summarizes the main parameters for typical small district heating areas. The heat losses of the networks are between 5 and 10 kWh/a per m^2 living space; the district heating system, excluding the heat production, costs between €1000 and €2500.

Table 12.7.3 *Design parameters for a small distribution system*

		Detached house	Row houses	Multi-family houses
Living space per dwelling	(m^2)	140	120	70
Average piping length per dwelling	(m)	14	7	3
Specific heat losses	(W/m)	10	12	14
Operation time	(h/a)	8760	8760	8760
Heat losses network	(kWh/m^2a)	8.8	6.1	5.3
Spec. costs network	(€/m)	120	140	160
Investment costs network	(€)	1680	980	480
Investment costs substation	(€)	800	800	500
Total investment costs per dwelling	(€)	2480	1780	980

An example project

A good example of a small semi-central system is the solar housing estate in Gelsenkirchen (North Rhine-Westphalia, Germany). The 48 single family houses in the southern tract have a semi-central heating system for each row of houses. Solar heat and electricity generated within the houses is transported to each row's central unit. Heat is then distributed back to the individual houses as demand requires. Sixty per cent of the DHW demand is covered by solar energy. These central units are managed by the local utility.

12.7.4 Conclusions

Houses that are highly insulated and have minimal heating demand require a low cost energy supply to cover the limited remaining heat demand. An existing district heating system might be a good solution, but only if low connection costs can be negotiated.

For new housing estates with high-performance housing where the goal is a large coverage of demand by renewable energy, a district heating system offers important advantages. Central solar systems offer economic economies of scale and make seasonal heat storage plausible. Alternatives such as large fuel cell systems, biomass plant and co-generation units are also possible.

The biggest challenge that district heating must address is keeping the costs down, given the low absolute of heat demand level, and minimizing the distribution heat losses. Proven engineering solutions addressing these issues are available if the housing density justifies such a system.

References

Dötsch, C., Taschenberger, J. and Schönberg, I. (1998) *Leitfaden Nahwärme*, Fraunhofer-Institut für Umwelt-, Sicherheits- und Energietechnik (UMSICHT), Oberhausen, Germany

Fisch, N., Möws, B. and Zieger, J. (2001) *Solarstadt. Konzepte*, Technologien Projekte, Stuttgart, Germany

Nast, P. M. (1996) *The Competitiveness of Group Heating in Modern Estates*, Euroheat and Power, Fernwärme International, Brussels, Belgium, and German District Heating Association (AGFW), Frankfurt (Main), Germany

Witt, J. (1995) *Nahwärme in Neubaugebieten – Neue Wege zu kostengünstigen Lösungen*, Öko-Institut e.V., Freiburg, Germany

12.8 Heat pumps

Andreas Bühring

12.8.1 Concept

Heat pumps transform heat from a lower temperature to a higher temperature, using energy with a high exergy level. Exergy is the ability of energy to perform work. Typically, the energy supply for heat pumps is electricity. The most known applications are household refrigerators.

In the low pressure part of the heat pump, liquid working fluid is heated and changes to a vapour (evaporation). The evaporator obtains the needed heat from ambient air, earth, water or exhaust air. A compressor raises the pressure of the working fluid and, at the same time, the temperature. Most common small capacity compressors are piston machines or scroll compressors, normally driven by an electric engine.

On the hot side of the heat pump, the heat is transferred from the working fluid to another fluid in a heat exchanger (condenser). In this way, the working fluid condenses to a liquid. The extracted heat can be used for space heating (by supply air or radiators) or DHW heating. The useful heat is approximately equal to the sum of the heat gains in the evaporator plus the driving power for the compressor. The return of the working fluid to the evaporator is controlled by an expansion valve. In normal situations, no working fluid leaves the heat pump since it is a closed circuit.

The performance of a heat pump is characterized by the term coefficient of performance (COP). This is the ratio of useful heat output and energy input for the compressor plus auxiliary units. The yearly COP of a heat pump is given by Equation 12.1:

$$\beta_{a,hp} = \frac{\int_{a} \dot{Q}_{useful} \times dt}{\int_{a} (P_{el,cm} + P_{el,aux}) \times dt}$$
   [12.1]

12.8.2 Environmental impact

The environmental impact of heat pump heating systems is dominated by the source of the electrical power. If the power production is dominated by regenerative energy (that is, water power), the negative environmental impact is much lower than is the case where power comes from coal-fired or nuclear power plants.

   If the refrigerant leaks, this also has a negative environmental impact. The global warming potential (GWP) gives the atmospheric thermal impact in relation to CO_2. The direct ozone depleting potential (ODP) gives the impact against atmospheric ozone. Most common refrigerants are fluorinated hydrocarbons as R134a or mixtures as R407c and R410a. They have a high GWP and no ODP. Older heat pumps used chlorinated hydrocarbons such as R22 or R12 with a high ODP. These are no longer allowed. New heat pumps also use pure hydrocarbons as R290 (propane) or CO_2 without ODP and with a small GWP. But their use is more difficult because they are flammable (R290) or must operate under significantly higher pressures.

12.8.3 Heat pumps in high-performance housing

Heat pumps used in low energy houses often use the ground as a heat source. In effect, the ground stores solar energy from summer to winter. At depths of 2 m and more the ground temperature begins to even out to the annual average temperature. A mixture of water and glycol are circulated through the pipes to extract this heat. Examples also exist where the refrigerant is circulated through the buried pipes (direct evaporating systems). The most common configuration is horizontal pipes, buried 1.5 m below ground with a horizontal separation of 50 cm. The resulting heat extraction from the ground is in the range of 15 W/m to 30 W/m. As an alternative, the pipes may be vertical, normally with a maximum depth of 100 m and a heat extraction from the ground in the range of 30 W/m to 60 W/m.

   If the heat pump only provides space heating, systems without a storage tank are possible in high-performance houses (Afjei et al, 2000). For example, the thermal mass of a floor heating system can serve as storage. This is feasible because highly insulated houses cool down very slowly. If, however, the same heat pump also heats DHW, a storage tank is needed. This tank could also be the storage for a solar collector. Figure 12.8.1 illustrates a typical heat pump system with earth-buried pipes. The heat is distributed by radiators or by supply air via a heat exchanger in the supply air stream. The ventilation system with heat recovery is separate from the heat pump system (see Figure 12.8.2).

   A compact heating and ventilation unit was developed by industry with support from Fraunhofer ISE for application in solar passive buildings (Bühring, 1999). These ventilation units not only have an air-to-air heat exchanger for passive heat recovery, but also include an additional exhaust air heat pump. This removes the residual heat from the exhaust air and uses it for space heating and domestic hot water (Bühring, 2001). The units can also be connected via a storage tank to a thermal solar system, which is designed to meet the hot water demand fully in summer (see Figure 12.8.3).

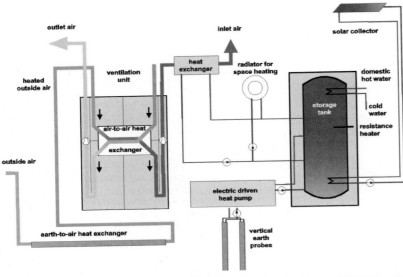

Source: Andreas Bühring

Figure 12.8.1 *Principle of using earth-coupled heat pumps in low energy houses*

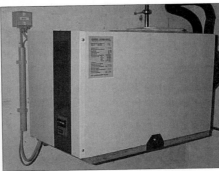

Source: Andreas Bühring

Figure 12.8.2 *Separate components in a modular system with an earth-coupled heat pump in a monitoring project; the ventilation system is on the left side, the heat pump on the right side*

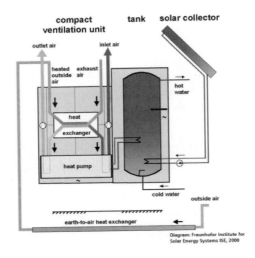

Source: Andreas Bühring

Figure 12.8.3 *Principle of compact heating and ventilation units for solar passive houses (compact HV unit)*

Compact heating and ventilation (HV) units already command 30 per cent of the market for energy supply systems serving German 'passive buildings' (Feist, 2001). A large proportion of the 78 houses monitored by the Freiburg ISE also used such a system (see Figure 12.8.4).

12.8.4 Testing and experience

Energie Baden-Württemberg (EnBW), the regional power supplier, sponsored the Fraunhofer ISE to monitor 78 solar passive houses in Baden-Württemberg. Monitoring results of a demonstration house in Büchenau are shown in Figure 12.8.5. A compact ventilation unit with an integrated exhaust air heat pump, earth-to-air heat exchanger and solar collector serve this house with 120 m² living area. The measured annual space heating load of 22 kWh/m²a, the domestic water heating load of 15 kWh/m²a and the ventilation and control electricity are covered by 13 kWh/m²a of electricity total for all the technical systems of the house. The annual COP of the heat pump reaches 3.2.

In Figure 12.8.6, the measurement results in the EnBW monitoring programme are summarized. On the left side is the group with modular earth-coupled heat pumps and on the right side, the group with compact HV units. In the first year the modular group has a significantly higher electrical demand because of problems with some control parameters. In the second year, the modular systems performed better, but were still less efficient than the compact systems.

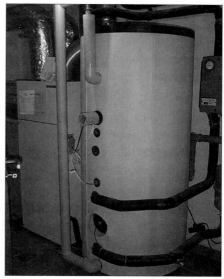

Source: Andreas Bühring

Figure 12.8.4 *Example of a compact heating and ventilation unit*

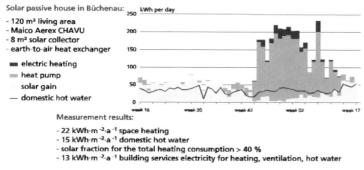

Source: Andreas Bühring

Figure 12.8.5
Measurement results from the solar passive house in Büchenau/Bruchsal

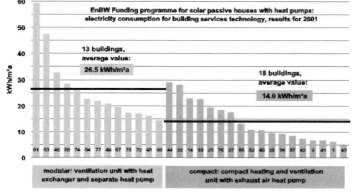

Source: Andreas Bühring

Figure 12.8.6
Comparison of the electricity needed for building services in solar passive houses when individual components are combined (left) and compact heating and ventilation units (right) are used; each column represents the monitored building services system in a single passive house

12.8.5 Conclusions

Electrical-driven heat pumps can be a highly efficient and economical solution to supply heat to high-performance houses. Integrated systems are more reliable than systems assembled from components that require onsite adjusting.

References

Afjei, T., Betschart, W., Bühring, A., Shafai, E., Huber, A. and Zweifel, G. (2000) *Kostengünstige Niedrigtemperaturheizung mit Wärmepumpe – Technisches Handbuch*, Bundesamt für Energie, Switzerland

Bühring, A. and da Silva, P. (1999) *Heat Supply in Passive Houses with a Compact Ventilation Device and Integrated Exhaust Air Heat Pump*, Proceedings of the sixth International Energy Agency Heat Pump Conference, Berlin, Germany

Bühring, A. (2001) *Theoretische und experimentelle Untersuchungen zum Einsatz von Lüftungs-Kompaktgeräten mit integrierter Kompressionswärmepumpe [Theoretical and Experimental Investigations on the Application of Compact Heating and Ventilation Units with Integrated Compression Heat Pumps]*, PhD thesis at the Technical University, Hamburg-Harburg, Fraunhofer IRB-Verlag, Stuttgart, Germany

Feist, W. (ed) (2001) *Das Passivhaus 2001: Fakten, Entwicklungen, Tendenzen [The Passive House 2001: Facts, Developments, Trends]*, Conference Proceedings of the Fifth Passivhaustagung, Böblingen, Germany

12.9 Earth-to-air heat exchangers

Karsten Voss

12.9.1 Concept

An earth-to-air heat exchanger (eta-hx) consists of one or more air ducts buried in the ground. Ambient air is drawn through the ducts by free or forced ventilation, allowing the ground to temper the incoming air flow. At increasing depths, the ground temperature becomes nearly constant over the year, assuming the average annual ambient temperature. Accordingly, the air passing through a pipe buried 2 m deep will be warmed in the winter and cooled in the summer. An eta-hx as part of a building ventilation system is a simple construction and therefore reliable. The energy savings from an eta-hx are relatively small so that the construction must be inexpensive.

12.9.2 Eta-hx in high-performance housing

An eta-hx in high-performance housing is part of a strategy to increase the use of ambient energy. It can serve three possible functions:

1   Preheat intake ventilation air in winter.
2   Prevent freeze-ups of the heat recovery unit of the ventilation system.
3   Cool intake ventilation air in summer.

Function 1: Preheat intake ventilation air in winter

In a high-performance house with a highly efficient air-to-air heat recovery ventilation system, the benefit of preheating intake air with an eta-hx is small. The air temperature increase by the eta-hx reduces the temperature difference across the air-to-air heat exchanger of the ventilation system, reducing its heat recovery. The more efficient the air-to-air heat exchange, the lower the benefit of the eta-hx (see Table 12.9.1). Were the heat exchanger 100 per cent efficient, there would be no benefit from the eta-hx. Modern heat exchangers can operate with an overall efficiency of 80 per cent

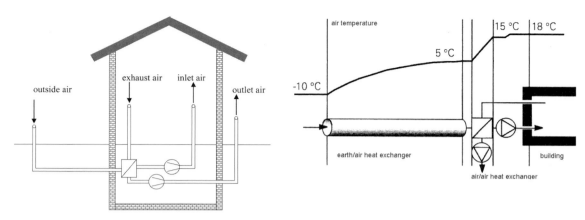

Source: K. Voss, Wuppertal University

Figure 12.9.1 *Basic system layout* (left) *and temperature profile* (right) *for a high-performance house application, winter mode*

to 85 per cent. Practice suggests that it is more sensible to invest in a high-performance air-to-air heat exchanger, rather than in a less efficient heat exchanger combined with an eta-hx.

A slight improvement in comfort can occur, however. Comfort in winter is strongly affected by the temperature difference between the room air and entering ventilation air. The temperature increase shown in Table 12.9.1, though small, is nevertheless still a benefit. The importance of this benefit is greatest in the case of supply air heating.

Figure 12.9.2(a) shows an example of an eta-hx during construction for a terrace house in Neuenburg, Germany. The system consists of three plastic pipes (PPs) in parallel, each 20 m long, 110 mm internal in diameter at 1.5 m depth. The average air flow is 140 m³/h.

Figure 12.9.2(b) presents annual performance as monthly sums. Due to the simple operating strategy, there is a minor heat gain in summer, as well as cooling in winter. Nevertheless, the main yields occur during the appropriate season.

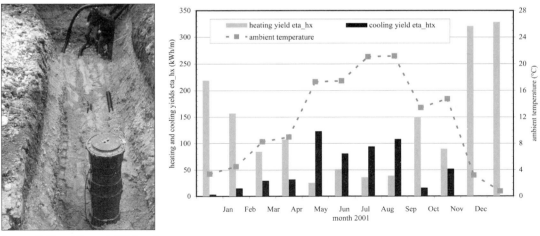

Source: K. Voss, Wuppertal University

Figure 12.9.2 *An earth-to-air heat exchanger (eta-hx) during construction for a terrace house in Neuenburg, Germany* (left); *annual performance of the terrace houses* (right)

Ventilation heat demand and supply air temperatures for combinations of an air-to-air heat recovery system with an eta-hx are presented in Table 12.9.1. The example is for the following conditions: –10°C ambient temperature, 20°C indoor temperature and 10°C undisturbed ground temperature. The efficiency of the eta-hx is assumed to be 90 per cent with a balanced mass flow in the heat recovery system. The marked line emphasizes a typical heat recovery system for high-performance housing using conservation strategy.

Table 12.9.1 *Performance of an air-to-air heat recovery system with an earth-to-air heat exchanger (eta-hx)*

Efficiency of heat recovery by the air-to-air heat exchanger	Heat recovery without eta-hx		Heat recovery with eta-hx (90 per cent efficiency)	
	Effective ventilation losses	Supply air temperature	Effective ventilation losses	Supply air temperature
per cent	per cent	°C	per cent	°C
50	50	5.0	18	14.0
60	40	8.0	16	15.2
70	30	11.0	12	16.4
80	20	14.0	8	17.6
90	10	17.0	4	18.8
100	0	20.0	0	20.0

Function 2: Prevent freeze-ups of the heat recovery unit of the ventilation system

Due to the moisture sources in buildings, the extracted air frequently has higher water content than the ambient air. During typical winter indoor conditions with a room temperature of 20°C and a relative humidity of 40 per cent, water vapour will condense when the dew point of 6°C is reached. This can occur when the extracted room air passes through the heat recovery unit. Freezing of this condensed water can be expected when ambient air entering the heat exchanger is below –2°C. The higher the efficiency of the heat recovery, the more often freezing conditions will occur. Adding an eta-hx to keep the supply air above circa – 2°C is a simple, reliable and well-proven freeze-protection measure. This concept competes with other methods such as:

- heating the extract air; or
- adjusting the air flow to a defined misbalance for critical periods.

An eta-hx might be the right choice in cases where other benefits are valuable – that is, heating energy savings or thermal comfort in summer (functions 1 and 3).

Function 3: Cool intake ventilation air in summer

During summer, high-performance housing can be just as comfortable as conventional housing. An eta-hx can help to achieve summer comfort by 'cooling' the supply air. This application is illustrated in Figure 12.9.2. The air flow of 120 m^3/h is cooled by 8K, yielding a cooling capacity of 317 W (specific heat $c_{p,air}$ = 0.33 Wh/m^3K). For comparison, 1 m^2 of highly insulating triple glazing (total energy transmittance g = 42 per cent) fully irradiated by the sun (500 W/m^2) produces solar heat gains of 210 W. This relation demonstrates that summer cooling by an eta-hx cannot compensate for large unshaded glass areas! On the other hand, this cooling power can lower indoor temperatures effectively if windows are shaded and closed during the hot part of the day.

12.9.3 Ground temperatures

The temperature of the ground is the result of:

- heat exchange at the surface via convection and shortwave and long-wave radiation;
- cooling through evaporation (dependent upon the vegetation); and
- heat conduction within the earth and groundwater flows.

A simplified but well-validated approach to estimate ground temperatures is to use air temperature data from typical meteorological data files (that is, test reference years, MeteoNorm data) to generate a time series of ground temperatures. Figure 12.9.3 shows results for an eta-hx in Freiburg, Germany, with an annual average ambient temperature of 10.4°C, amplitude 9.2°C and clay soil. This calculation requires the input of the soil properties, which are seldom known. Therefore, most calculation programs use a classification of general soil types. The most favourable conditions for heat transfer from the ground occur where there is groundwater. Unfortunately, excavation costs and sealing problems make the construction prohibitive, in most cases. As soil properties can influence the thermal system performance by up to 30 per cent, a careful determination of soil type and backfill around the pipes is necessary for accurate predictions. Of greater importance, however, is the layout of the eta-hx. Over-dimensioning can easily compensate for misjudgement of the soil properties.

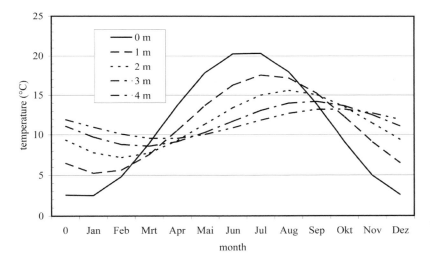

Source: K. Voss, Wuppertal University

Figure 12.9.3 *Calculated ground temperature as a function of depth of clay soil type in Freiburg, Germany*

12.9.4 System configurations and sizing

The aim of system sizing is to minimize the costs of reaching a certain temperature level or energy gain under given circumstances of climate, available space, interaction with the building, etc. In the theoretical case of 100 per cent thermal efficiency (h), an eta-hx always supplies air at the soil temperature:

$$\eta = (T_{out} - T_{in})/(T_{ground} - T_{in}) \qquad [12.2]$$

Due to the asymptotic decrease in the temperature difference between the soil and the air passing through the pipe, the first metre is the most effective and the last metre is the least effective. If the objective is to achieve high energy gain, a register of short pipes is a good solution and lengthy low yield segments should be avoided. If the objective is merely freeze protection of the heat recovery unit, then a long single pipe is adequate.

To fairly assess the benefit of an eta-hx, the electricity consumed by the fan motor to pull the air through the earth pipes must be considered in relation to the heat gain:

$$COP = \text{heat gain/electricity consumption.}$$ [12.3]

Typical observed coefficients of performance are, indeed, impressive, in the range of 20 to 60. The COP strongly depends on the air velocity within the eta-hx and its length. Typical pressure drops should be below 2 Pa per metre length. In total, an eta-hx may produce up to 10 per cent of the pressure drop of the whole ventilation system.

The following are a few design guidelines for engineering a system:

* *Pipe profiles.* In most application ducts, circular cross-sections are used. They are most economical and strongest in resisting earth pressure.
* *Pipe materials.* Most small systems use plastic pipes with smooth internal surfaces. Such piping is available in long, lightweight single segments (5 m) or in diameters up to 110 mm as flexible tubing from a roll. Such pipes or tubes are economical to lay, have low risk of leakage at joints and resist damage from inhomogeneous soil settlement. Ducts made of concrete are more economical for diameters greater than 150 mm. Due to higher installation costs, they are common only in large-scale applications. Such piping with their frequent joints has a higher risk of groundwater leakage. Concrete is also not tight against radon infiltration.
* *Depth.* Excavation costs typically limit laying depths to between 1.5 m and 3 m.
* *Location.* Pipes located below a building generate higher heat gains than pipes laid in open areas. This is partly the result of building heat loss down into the ground, which is then recovered by the eta-hx. On the other hand, the heated volume of high-performance housing is often insulated from the basement, minimizing this effect. Lastly, pipes buried under the basement can be difficult to access if leakage is problematic.
* *Pipe or pipe register.* In the case of small systems, single pipes are more economical than a register of parallel pipes. This is explained by the high investment costs (that is, plastic form parts) to connect the air inlets and outlets.
* *Pipe distances.* Parallel pipes perform worse than a single pipe due to the thermal interaction between the pipes. This interaction is small (less than 10 per cent difference to a single duct) if the pipes are separated by at least 2 m.
* *Bypass.* A bypass provides an alternative path for the air when the eta-hx is not needed. This reduces the fan electricity consumption of the ventilation system. As a result, the COP improves. Experiences from high-performance housing suggest that due to control complexity and investment costs, a bypass is not favourable in small applications.

12.9.5 Hygiene

During summer operation, the air may be cooled in the eta-hx below the dew point (30° air temperature, 80 per cent humidity, dew point 26.2°C). As a result, condensation will occur and then, with time, disappear as it evaporates. The question arises whether humid and warm conditions within the pipes promote bacterial or fungal growth. Hygienic investigations of 15 different systems in Switzerland have shown that, in general, the concentration of bacteria and fungal spores, in fact, decrease due to the use of the buried pipes since the source of mould is mainly external and the inlet air carries few organisms. Results have been underlined by further studies on demonstration housing projects of this International Energy Agency (IEA) activity. In the case of increased hygienic demands, fine filters can further reduce the concentration of bacteria and spores. It is good practice to locate the air inlet well above the ground (>2 m) and away from sources of contamination (such as compost, plants, car parking or sewage vents).

Cleaning can be done by flushing the pipes with water after some years. To accommodate the water runoff, the pipes should be sloped to a drain outlet of some kind (but not connected to the sanitary system). Generally, the air filter is the most critical part of the system. It must be protected from penetration by rainwater, snow, high humidity and condensation. Easy access is important so that regular changing or cleaning of the filter is possible at least once a year.

12.9.6 Examples

Table 12.9.2 lists the configurations of the eta-hx systems found in the demonstration houses of this IEA activity. These data and comments offer an initial overview on system types and relevant considerations for high-performance housing.

Table 12.9.2 *Typical eta-hx configurations applied in the International Energy Agency (IEA) task demonstration buildings*

Location	Function	Air flow	Earth-to-air heat exchanger				Material	Bypass
			d	l	Ø	A		
		m³/h	m	m	mm	m²		
Neuenburg, Germany	1,2,3	120	1.0/2.0	60	110	20.7	PE	no
Büchenau, Germany	1,2,3	150	1.5	30	150	14.1	PVC	no
Stuttgart, Germany	1,2,3	100	2.0	30	200	18.8	PE	no
Rottweil, Germany	1,2,3	88	1.0	34	200	21.4	PVC	yes
Wenden-Hilmicke, Germany	1,2	255	1.2	99	126	39.2	PVC	no
Horn, Austria	1,2	150	1.7	50	160	25.1	PE	no
Klagenfurt, Austria	1,2	200	2.0	60	150	28.3	PVC	no
Dornbirn, Austria	1,2	200	2.0	60	150	28.3	PVC	no
Nebikon, Switzerland	1,2,3	127	1.6	30	200	18.8	PVC	no
Wallisen, Switzerland	1,2,3	450	0.8	25	150	11.8	PE	no
Winterthur, Switzerland	1,2,3	800	2.0	180	170	96.1	PE	no

Notes: d: laying depth; l: single duct length; Ø: internal diameter; A: total surface area.

12.9.7 Conclusions

An earth-to-air heat exchanger in high-performance housing is part of a strategy to increase the use of ambient or renewable energy. However, the eta-hx competes with the air-to-air heat exchanger of the ventilation system. With the prewarming of inlet air by the eta-hx, there is less temperature difference in the air-to-air heat exchanger to drive the heat recovery. The main arguments for an eta-hx are preventing freezing in the air-to-air heat exchanger and providing modest cooling of the supply air in summer.

Table 12.9.3 *Simulation tools*

Name	Source	Website	Comments
GAEA	Universität Siegen, Germany	www.nesa1.uni-siegen.de	Time-step simulation of eta-hx using an analytical form factor model.
PHLuft	Passivhaus Institut, Germany	www.passiv.de	Time-step simulation of eta-hx using a capacity model (without consideration of interaction of earth-register tubes).
WKM	Huber Energietechnik, Switzerland	www.igjzh.com	Time-step simulation of eta-hx using a capacity model. The user interface of WKM is based on MS-Excel and therefore requires this software. WKM is capable of variable air flow rates, and calculates sensible and latent heat flows and the spell of condense water.

References

Blümel, E., Fink, A. and Reise, C. (2001) *Luftdurchströmte Erdreichwärmetauscher – Handbuch zur Planung und Ausführung*, AEE-INTEC, Gleisdorf, Austria, and Freiburg, Germany

Dibowsky, G. and Wortmann, R. (2003) *Luft-Erdwärmetauscher, Teil 1 – Systeme für Wohngebäude, Luft*, Ministerium für Schule, Wissenschaft und Forschung des Landes Nordrhein-Westfalen, Düsseldorf, www.ag-solar.de/de/service/downloads.asp

Flückinger, B., Wanner, H. P. and Lüthy, P. (1997) *Mikrobielle Untersuchungen von Luft-Ansaugregistern*, ETH, Zürich

Gieseler, U. D. J., Bier, W. and Heidt, F. D. (2002) *Cost Efficiency of Ventilation Systems for Low-energy Buildings with Earth-to-Air Heat Exchange and Heat Recovery*, Proceedings of the International Conference on Passive and Low Energy Architecture (PLEA), Toulouse, France, pp577–583

Hollmuller, P. and Lachal, B. (2001) 'Cooling and preheating with buried pipe systems – monitoring, simulation and economic aspects', *Energy and Buildings*, vol 33, issue 5, pp509–518

Pfafferott, J., Gerber, A. and Herkel, S. (1998) 'Erdwärmetauscher zur Luftkonditionierung', *Gesundheitsingenieur*, vol 119, no 4, pp201–213

Sedlbauer, K., Lindauer, E. and Werner, H. (1994) 'Erdreich/Luft-Wärmetauscher zur Wohnungslüftung', *Bauphysik*, vol 16, no 2, pp33–34

Zimmermann, M. (ed) (1999) 'Luftansaug-Erdregister', in *Handbuch der Passiven Kühlung*, EMPA, Dubendorf

12.10 Ground-coupled and geothermal heat

Hans Erhorn and Johann Reiss

12.10.1 Concept

Geothermal heat can be used to generate electricity and heat; but the geology of Central Europe limits its application for heating purposes. In spite of its huge energy potential, this environmentally friendly technology is currently only rarely used. In comparison to solar energy that reaches the Earth (5.4×10^{15} MJ/a), the terrestrial heat flux through the Earth's crust is nearly 6000 times smaller (10^{12} MJ/a). This is, however, still three times greater than the total worldwide energy consumption.

How it is used

In Central Europe, geothermal heat can primarily be used in the following ways (depending on the respective geological situation and appearance):

- petrophysical systems (use of the heat embedded in rocks – for example, magna or hot dry rock);
- geothermal systems with a high enthalpy of > 600 J/kg (high pressure water lenses, steam systems);
- hydro-geothermal systems with a low enthalpy of < 600 J/kg (aquifer or thermal springs);
- surface-near geothermal systems with temperatures below 25°C (geothermal heat probes/ground loops, absorber piles, geothermal heat collectors, groundwater wells); and
- deep geothermal ground loops (below a depth of 400 m).

The different heat densities and temperature levels lead to the following applications:

- electrical power generation (petrophysical and geothermal systems with high entropy);
- direct use (hydro-geothermal systems with low enthalpy and near surface geothermal systems for preheating of air); and
- near-surface direct use enhanced by using a heat pump to extract additional heat before the water is returned (see Figure 12.10.1).

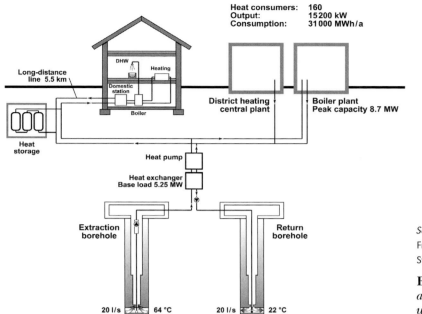

Heat consumers: 160
Output: 15 200 kW
Consumption: 31 000 MWh/a

Source: H. Erhorn and J. Reiss,
Fraunhofer Institut für Bauphysik,
Stuttgart

Figure 12.10.1 *Scheme of a heating distribution net using geothermal heat for a large community*

There are also systems that simply store heat (surplus heat or cool air from solar or heat pump systems), such as aquifers or caverns.

12.10.2 Applications

The high investment costs limit electrical power generation to only a few specific geological regions with near-surface steam storages. Otherwise, the normal temperature gradient of 3.5K per 100 m of depth requires too deep borings (for example, 5000 m) to get the required temperatures to produce electricity.

Using lower temperature heat is, however, often very plausible for heating buildings – ideally, groups of buildings or large buildings. For a single family home, the costs are usually prohibitive. Groups of buildings can be supplied with geothermal heat via a grid distribution system, as is done in Paris. The required deep drilling and the necessary appliances (primary circle system for aquifer and a secondary system for users) are expensive, so can only be justified if shared by a network of users. High-performance housing is not an ideal target group because the investment/gain ratio is rather poor, given the very small demand.

Near-surface geothermal systems, in which a heat pump can achieve nearly constant heat fluxes throughout the year, are a much more promising approach. Such systems can also be used for preheating/cooling outside air before it enters the air heating unit (AHU), and may thus significantly reduce the heat losses of the ventilation system. Such a configuration also avoids the freeze-up problem of high-efficiency ventilation air-to-air heat exchangers, as shown in Figure 12.10.2.

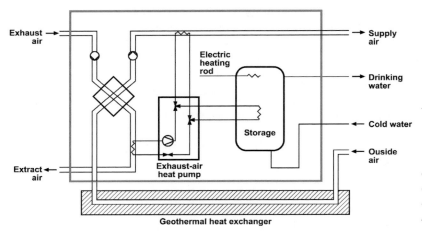

Source: H. Erhorn and J. Reiss, Fraunhofer Institut für Bauphysik, Stuttgart

Figure 12.10.2 *Ground-coupled air heat exchanger for preheating air in high-performance houses*

12.10.3 Design insights

Heating

Heat from near-surface layers can be taken from groundwater directly by using a fountain technology. Heat can also be extracted from near-surface earth layers by means of horizontally or vertically installed heat exchangers (see Figure 12.10.3). The extracted heat will be transformed by heat pumps to a higher temperature level. The lower the temperature of the heating system, the higher the efficiency of the heat pump. The heat pumps normally run in a monovalent mode, using buffer storage to harmonize the in-stationary demand of the heating during the day and the different seasons. Typical load values for heat pumps are 5 kW to 100 kW.

Investment costs required for adapting the heat source from the earth to the heat pump are in the range of €500 to €800 per kW. Systems with low outputs between 2 kW and 3 kW, for instance, are in the region of approximately €3500. The highest costs are caused by horizontally installed earth heat exchangers because extensive excavation work is required. A garden area measuring approximately 1.5 to 2.0 times the heated area of the house is needed to bury the heat exchanger. The use of

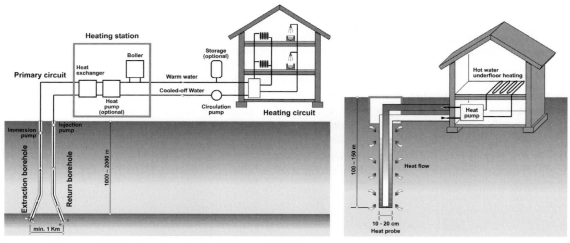

Source: H. Erhorn and J. Reiss, Fraunhofer Institut für Bauphysik, Stuttgart

Figure 12.10.3 *Comparison of: (a) a direct-use system with (b) a vertical geothermal heat exchanger coupled to a heat pump system*

groundwater via fountains leads to approximately 35 per cent higher annual costs due to the intensive maintenance costs required for these appliances. Investment expenditures for a heat pump and buffer storage with a range of performance between 5 kW and 100 kW amount to €500 and €800 per kW. Costs for a small heat pump with an output of between 2 kW and 5 kW (including buffer storage, piping and installation) are about €8000 to €10000.

The heating energy-related costs for the whole system in conventional houses amount to 5 cents per kWh (assuming electrical power costs for the heat pump of 5.5 cents per kWh). Because of the high standard costs for the installations, costs may easily increase to factor 2 and more in high-performance houses. Normally, however, costs are 25 per cent to 40 per cent lower than for solar-assisted heating systems. Only fossil and biomass-fired systems are usually a little more economical than earth-coupled heat pumps.

Preheating fresh air

Channelling the fresh air through earth channels before entering the AHU leads to a highly efficient use of geothermal heat. The installation is usually very cost efficient because the construction hole can be used without any extra costs for moving the earth. The extra costs for a single family home are usually less than €200, and a saving potential of approximately 1000 kWh can be used. This leads to heating energy-related costs of approximately 5 cents per kWh. Because homeowners may elect to install the heat exchanger themselves to save money, special care should be taken regarding the following points: the tubes should be generously dimensioned to minimize pressure losses and thereby minimize the needed fan power; they should also be sloped to drainage so they can be flushed for cleaning, and protected from dirt and debris by a filter for incoming air.

References

BMU (Federal Minister for the Environment, Nature Conservation and Nuclear Safety) (2004) *Geothermie – Energie für die Zukunft*, BMU, Berlin

FIZ (Fachinformationszentrum Karlsruhe) (ed) (2004a) *Geothermie, CD-ROM Energie, CD-ROM Datenbanken über erneuerbare und konventionelle Energien*, Eggenstein-Leopoldshafen

FIZ (Fachinformationszentrum Karlsruhe) (ed) (2004b) *Geothermie: Basic Energies 8*, Stuttgart

IRB (Fraunhofer-Informationszentrum Raum und Bau) (ed) (no date) *Erdwärmenutzung*, IRB-Literaturdokumentation, no 7046, Stuttgart, Germany

Sanner, B. and Bussmann, W. (eds) (2004) *Erdwärme zum Heizen und Kühlen [Geothermal Heat for Heating and Cooling Purposes]: Potentiale, Möglichkeiten und Techniken der Oberflächennahen Geothermie*, Geothermische Vereinigung e.V., Kleines Handbuch der Geothermie, vol 1, Geothermische Vereinigung e.V., Geeste

Websites

Bundesministerium für Umwelt, Naturschutz und Reaktorsicherheit (BMU): www.erneuerbare-energien.de

Geothermische Vereinigung e.V. (GtV): www.geothermie.de

International Geothermal Association (IGA): www.iga.igg.cnr.it

Schweizerische Vereinigung für Geothermie (SVG): www.geothermal-energy.ch

13

Sensible Heat Storage

13.1 Thermal storage

Gerhard Faninger

13.1.1 The basics of heat storage in heating systems

A heating system may need thermal storage when:

- there is a mismatch between thermal energy supply and energy demand;
- intermittent energy sources are utilized; or
- solar fluctuations in solar heating systems must be evened out.

In highly efficient houses, the need for thermal storage is often short term. In such instances, water is a very efficient storage medium for both space heating and hot water production.

Heat can be stored in three ways:

1 *Sensible heat storage.* The storage is based on the temperature change in the material. The unit storage capacity (J/g) is equal to heat capacitance × temperature change. Possible 'sensible heat' storage media are liquids (typically water) and solid materials (typically soil and stone).
2 *Phase-change storage.* If the material changes its phase at a certain temperature while heating the substance, then heat is stored in the phase change process. Reversing the process, heat is released when, at the phase-change temperature, the material cools back to the original state. The classic material used in phase-change storage is Glauber salt (sodium sulphate).
3 *Reversible chemical reaction storage.* Heat can be stored through sorption or thermo-chemical reactions. Systems based on this principle have negligible heat losses. The storage capacity is the heat of reaction or free energy of the reaction. Thermo-chemical storage materials have the highest storage capacity of all storage media. Some of the materials may even approach the storage density of biomass. Solid silica gel has a storage capacity that is up to about four times that of water. Prototypes of sorption storage are in the design and testing phase. One approach is to use metal hydrides.

Table 13.2.1 illustrates some of the materials that can be used for thermal storage. The storage capacity and desired temperature range are the two key parameters to select and size the storage.

Table 13.1.1 *A sample of storage materials and key properties*

Medium	Temperature (°C)	Capacity (kWh/m³)
Water	Temperature difference = 50°C	60
Rock		40
$Na_2SO_4 x 10H_2O$	24	70
$CaCl_2 x 6H_2O$	30	47
Paraffin	20–60	56
Lauric acid	46	50
Stearic acid	58	45
Pentaglycerine	81	59
Butyl stearate	19	39
Propyl palmiate	19	52
Silica gel $N+H_2O$	60–80	250
Zeolite 13 X + H_2O	100–180	180
Zeolite + methanol	100	300
$CaCl_2$ + ammonia	100	1000
$MeHx + H_2$	50–400	200–1500
$Na_2S + H_2O$	50–100	500

13.1.2 Water storage technology

Storing heat in water serves to bridge sunless periods in the case of solar hot water and combined heating systems, to increase the system efficiency in combination with cogeneration systems, and to shave the peak in electricity demand and improve the efficiency of electricity supply in the case of an electrically heated hot water tank.

Water tank storage technology is mature and reliable. Sensible heat storage in water is still unbeaten in terms of simplicity and cost. In refined systems, the inlet/outlet heights in the tank can vary according to supply and storage temperatures. Thermally stratified water tanks can improve the annual system efficiency by 20 per cent or more. Figure 13.1.1 illustrates variations of preserving the stratification effect to maximize storage efficiency. For combined space and water heating, multiple tanks are a good solution. There could, for example, be a short-term, mid-term and long-term tank.

The storage need in a solar system is often determined by the ratio of the maximum to minimum monthly solar radiation. Figure 13.1.2 gives this data for different latitudes. When the maximum–minimum ratio is less than 5, even wintertime solar energy may be enough to provide the heat load, whereas values higher than 10 mean such a large fluctuation that a seasonal storage or

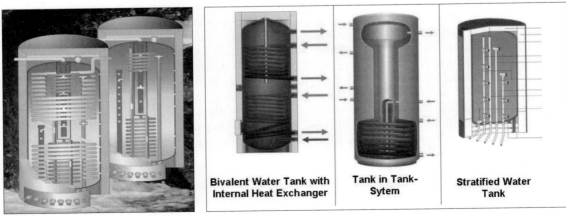

Bivalent Water Tank with Internal Heat Exchanger Tank in Tank-Sytem Stratified Water Tank

Source: Gerhard Faninger, University of Klagenfurt

Figure 13.1.1 *Types of water storage systems to achieve stratification*

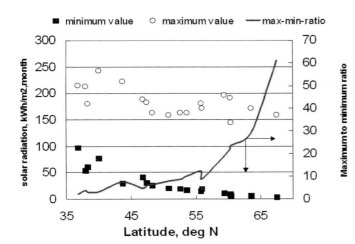

Source: Gerhard Faninger, University of Klagenfurt

Figure 13.1.2 *Solar radiation by latitude, including minima, maxima and their ratios*

backup system is necessary. In high latitude Northern Europe, the winter solar radiation falls under the utilization limit.

Water heat storage can be categorized by the duration of the storage.

Short-term storage for solar hot water systems typically has a storage capacity between 1.5 and 2.0 times the daily hot water demand. Even with short-term storage, generous insulation of the tank is essential (see Chapter 12, 12.2 'Active solar heating: Water').

Mid-term storage for solar-combined heating systems and solar-supported district heating should cover the heat demand for three to five days. For detached and row single family low-energy houses, a storage volume of about 800 to 1500 litres will be suitable.

Seasonal storage is one means of achieving a high annual share of solar heat in northern latitudes. A realistic target is to provide a heat capacity of six months in existing housing or four months in high-performance housing (which have a shorter heating season).

Solar heating plants with seasonal storage may take a decentralized and a centralized approach. In a decentralized approach, the storage and collectors are placed within the individual houses as in an ordinary active solar heating system but of a larger size. In the centralized concepts, solar heat is collected in one storage unit from which the heat is distributed to many houses, as illustrated in Figure 13.1.3. The advantage of scale is that the relative heat losses and tank costs decrease with the decreasing tank surface-to-storage volume ratio of ever larger tanks. The relative heat losses are proportional to the surface/volume, or, $V^{2/3}/V = V^{-1/3}$. Therefore, as $V \rightarrow \infty$, the relative losses $\rightarrow 0$. Such a system may be considered for low energy housing. For high-performance housing at the level of the Passivhaus standard, the costs and heat losses of the pipe network are proportionately very high for the absolute amount of heat required. A further advantage of a centralized system is the reduced unit costs when large numbers of collectors are purchased.

Figure 13.1.4 illustrates different large-scale sensible heat storage concepts. Concepts such as earth pits or rock caverns are large water reservoirs built into the ground. Aquifer storage employs the storage capacity of water-mixed ground. Aquifer storage is very simple and needs only a few wells to operate. Vertical pipes may be laid into the ground, enabling the use of the thermal capacity of the ground. Ground heat storage may also be employed effectively through heat pumps yielding a larger DT. The most frequently used 'seasonal' thermal storage technology, which makes use of the underground, is *aquifer thermal energy storage*. This technology uses a natural underground layer (for

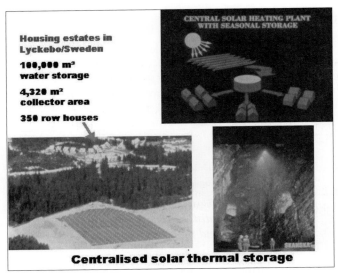

Source: Gerhard Faninger, University of Klagenfurt

Figure 13.1.3 *An example of seasonal thermal storage*

example, sand, sandstone or chalk layer) as a storage medium for the temporary storage of heat or cold. The transfer of thermal energy is realized by extracting groundwater from the layer and by re-injecting it at the modified temperature level at a separate location nearby. A major condition for the application of this technology is the availability of a suitable geological formation.

Other technologies for underground thermal energy storage are borehole storage, cavern storage and pit storage. Pit storages are mainly used for offices and housing estates. Ground heat exchangers are also frequently used in combination with heat pumps, where the ground heat exchanger extracts low temperature heat from the soil. Large underground water storage (for example, cavern storage and pit storage) is technically feasible, but its application is still limited because of the high level of investment required.

Since solar thermal systems with seasonal storage are always site dependent, the design has to account for the local conditions. Detailed simulations and systematic variation of design parameters are necessary for the design and the analysis of the overall performance and economics.

Already, in some special cases, seasonal storage solar heating may be found economically justified; but this conclusion is not yet generally valid for other sites and applications. The practical possibilities for long-term storage would be dramatically improved with higher storage capacities within latent and chemical storage concepts (see Section 13.2 'Latent heat storage').

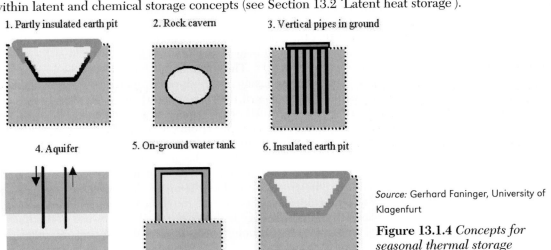

Source: Gerhard Faninger, University of Klagenfurt

Figure 13.1.4 *Concepts for seasonal thermal storage*

13.1.3 Other means of heat storage

Phase-change storage

When more heat should be stored in a small volume than is possible with sensible heat storage, phase-change materials offer one solution. The change of phase can be a melting or a vaporization process. Melting processes have energy densities of 100 kWh/m^2 compared to 25 kWh/m^2 for sensible heat storage. Vaporization processes are combined with a sorption process. Energy has to be withdrawn at a low temperature when charging and be delivered at a high temperature when discharging the storage. Energy densities of 300 kWh/m^2 can be achieved.

Reversible chemical reaction storage

The physical principle of the sorption process is illustrated in Figure 13.1.5. The basic principle is: AB + heat ↔ A + B. Using heat, a compound AB is broken into components A and B, which can be stored separately. Bringing A and B together, AB is formed and heat is released.

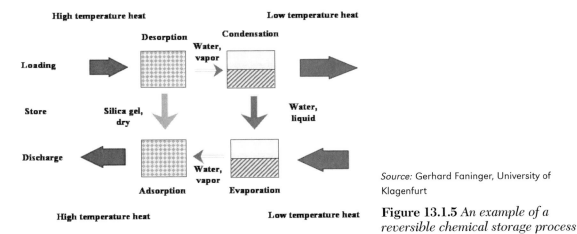

Source: Gerhard Faninger, University of Klagenfurt

Figure 13.1.5 *An example of a reversible chemical storage process*

Non-reversible chemical reaction storage

This means of energy storage is superior to all the above means. The classic example is petroleum. Solar energy has been stored in plant material, which decomposed into oil, and now millions of years later, with no energy loss during the storage, 10,000 kWh/m^3 can be released by simply burning it – an incredible energy density. The only small problem is that the rate of use exceeds the rate of geological production, given the millions of years' time span!

References

Fanninger, G. (ed) (1998) *Proceedings of the Fifth International Summer School Solar Energy*, University of Klagenfurt, July 1998, University of Klagenfurt, Austria

Faninger, G. (2004) *Thermal Energy Storage*, available at www.energytech.at

Lund, P. D. (1998) *Thermal Energy Storage*, Helsinki University of Technology, Advanced Energy Systems, FIN-02150 Espoo, Finland

Websites

International Energy Agency (IEA):
www.iea.org; www.iea-shc.org; www.ecbcs.org/; www.cevre.cu.edu.tr/eces/

13.2 Latent heat storage

Gerhard Faninger

13.2.1 The physical principle of latent storage

Latent heat storage uses the principle of the change of phase of a material to absorb or release heat. When a material is heated and changes its state (between a solid, liquid or gas), it will store much more heat than would occur from just 1 Kelvin temperature increase. When the material cools down and reverses back to the original state, this heat is then released. This heat of fusion is typically 80 to 100 times larger than the heat required for heating a material 1°. The storage capacity is equal to the phase-change enthalpy at the phase-change temperature + sensible heat stored over the whole temperature range of the process. This process is illustrated using the example of water in Figure 13.2.1.

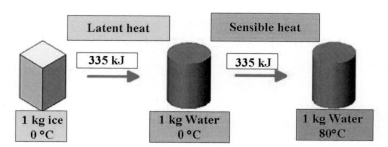

Source: Gerhard Faninger, University of Klagenfurt

Figure 13.2.1 *Heat absorbed and released by phase change*

13.2.2 Materials for storage

As thermal storage media, phase-change materials (PCMs) such as paraffin and eutectic salts offer an order-of-magnitude increase in thermal storage capacity, and a big advantage is that their charge and discharge occurs almost at a constant temperature.

The classic example for phase-change materials are salt hydrates. One common type is Glauber salt ($Na_2SO_4.10H_2O$), discovered during the 17th century by Johann Glauber. Sodium sulphate decahydrate has an ideal melting point of 32°C for building heating applications.

13.2.3 Phase-change materials in building constructions

Phase-change materials can be incorporated within building materials and thus contribute to lower energy consumption and power demand by storing solar energy during the day in winter or storing cold air at night during the warm summer season.

Since the PCM has a sharp change in the heat storage or release rate at the phase-change temperature, it can be used for temperature regulation. For example, mixing PCM into the building material could increase the thermal capacity of a wall board. To illustrate this great capacity, consider a concrete wall, in comparison. When it is heated or cooled 10K to 15K, it can absorb or release approximately 10 kWh/m³. This is about one fifth of the heat storage capacity of paraffin, a classic PCM. Mixing two different PCMs in a suitable proportion theoretically gives the possibility of matching the phase-change temperature exactly with the temperature of the application.

The PCM concept is particularly interesting for lightweight building construction. Figure 13.2.2 shows some examples. Phase-change applications in buildings typically involve liquid/solid transitions. The phase-change material is solidified when cooling sources are available and melted when cooling is needed. PCMs have two important advantages as storage media: they can offer an order-of-magnitude increase in heat capacity and, for pure substances, their discharge is almost isothermal.

Phase-change material implemented in gypsum board, plaster or other wall-covering material would permit the thermal storage to become part of the building structure. PCMs have an important advantage as storage media: they can offer an order-of-magnitude increase in thermal storage capacity. For example, 30 per cent of the recent BASF Micronal PCM mixed with plaster allows a 0.5 inch thick plaster layer to act as a 6 inch thick brick wall in terms of thermal capacity around 26°C. This allows the storage of high amounts of energy without significantly changing the temperature of the room. As heat storage takes place inside the building, where the loads occur, rather than externally, additional transport energy is not required.

Extended storage capacity for night storage of cold air during the summer obtained by using PCM wallboard is able to keep the room temperatures close to the upper comfort limits without using mechanical cooling.

Cooling of residential buildings in milder climates contributes significantly to electrical consumption and peak power demand, largely due to very poor load factors. Thermal mass can be utilized to reduce the peak power demand, to downsize the cooling systems, and/or to switch to low-energy cooling sources.

The use of PCM wallboard coupled with mechanical night ventilation in office buildings offers the opportunity for system downsizing in climates where the outside air temperature drops below 18°C at night. In climates where the outside air temperature remains above 18°C at night, the use of PCM wallboard should be coupled with discharge mechanisms other than mechanical night ventilation with outside air.

So far, few samples of PCM-treated wallboard have existed. There are several approaches to treating wallboard with PCM material. Thanks to the recent technology of micro-encapsulation of PCM, new products were released in 2004. Capsules of Micronal from BASF can be mixed with plaster to enhance the thermal properties of a wallboard.

13.2.4 Phase-change materials in tanks

PCMs can also be included in containers of different shapes. One common container is the plastic capsules or nodules (SLT) that are put into a tank where the heat transfer fluid (usually) water melts or solidifies the PCM. Figure 13.2.3 shows some examples. Several different PCMs with melting points ranging from –21°C up to 120°C are commercially available. Phase-change materials and chemical reactions are also used for heating and cooling purposes in small applications such as hand warmers (sodium acetate trihydrate).

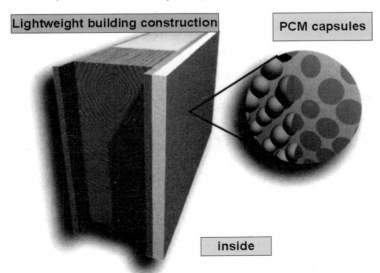

Source: Gerhard Faninger, University of Klagenfurt

Figure 13.2.2 *Phase-change material in building constructions*

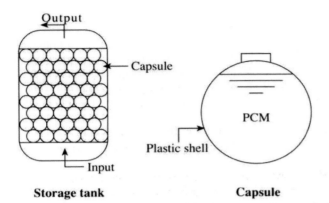

Source: Gerhard Faninger, University of Klagenfurt

Figure 13.2.3 *Phase-change materials in tanks*

Recent research work has tried to incorporate PCM into a solar tank in order to increase stratification and/or heat storage capacity. A good candidate is sodium acetate with some additives to increase thermal conductivity and reduce super-cooling. Commercial products could reach the market within three years.

Micro-encapsulation of PCM in a fluid (called a slurry) can increase the ability of the fluid to transport and store heat. Some research work is also heading in this direction to enhance the solar loop of a solar combi-system.

Small PCM storage units have been sold mainly for special applications. PCM storage still requires research and development efforts to be practical. The main goal of a new international research project in the framework of the International Energy Agency Solar Heating and Cooling Programme (IEA-SHC Task 32) is to investigate new or advanced solutions for storing heat in systems, providing heating or cooling for low energy buildings.

References

Faninger, G. (2004) *Thermal Energy Storage*, available at www.energytech.at

Stetiu, C. and Feustel, H. E. (1997) *Phase-Change Wallboard and Mechanical Night Ventilation in Commercial Buildings*, Lawrence Berkeley National Laboratory, Berkeley, CA

Websites

International Energy Agency (IEA): www.iea.org; www.iea-shc.org

14

Electricity

14.1 Photovoltaic systems

Karsten Voss and Christian Reise

14.1.1 Concept

High-performance houses need very little heat, but a considerable amount of electricity, which is all the more significant when considered in primary energy terms. In this chapter, we assume that 1 kWh of heat from natural gas requires 1.14 kWh of primary energy, while 1 kWh of electricity requires 2.35 kWh of primary energy to produce. For this reason, it is highly attractive to consider ways of producing electricity from a renewable source, onsite. A photovoltaic (PV) system is an expensive investment, but promises trouble-free electricity production over a long life time.

It can be useful to compare the cost of PV to the costs of energy saving measures within the framework of least-cost planning. As a result of the high primary energy equivalent of electricity in the majority of European countries, the electricity yield of a PV system has roughly the same value as the heat output from a solar thermal system. This is true both for substituted primary energy and prevented CO_2 emissions (Voss et al, 2002).

As discussed above, the primary energy equivalent of the annual PV yield can offset some to all of the primary energy (fossil fuels and electricity) needed by a house. In the case of an all-electric house (for example, space heating and DHW supplied by a compression heat pump), the PV yield can be directly compared to the electricity consumption by these technical systems. A sophisticated energy-saving concept is a precondition for such a PV application. Figure 14.1.1 shows the relevance of the PV output for different high-performance housing concepts. The light grey arrows indicate primary energy delivered; the dark grey arrows point to the primary energy equivalent of the annual PV yield. The width of each arrow indicates the amount of energy. Except for the stand-alone case, all PV systems are grid connected.

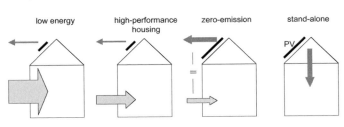

low energy   high-performance   zero-emission   stand-alone
              housing

Source: Karsten Voss and Christian Reise

Figure 14.1.1 *The relevance of the photovoltaic (PV) energy yield in different housing concepts*

While PV panels are expensive, the simplicity of such an all-electric system also has economies. For example, no large thermal storage tank is needed, as would be the case to achieve the same annual solar coverage by a solar thermal system. At the current level of PV building applications, the electricity grid serves as the seasonal 'storage unit'. In limited numbers, such houses have almost no effects on the grid's power quality, line loads or transformers. In large solar housing developments, these aspects must, however, be considered.

14.1.2 The performance of PV systems

Energy

Optimal systems in Central Europe achieve an annual yield between 800 and 900 kWh per kW_p. The unit 'kW_p' is the power output from a PV cell under standardized test conditions: temperature 25°C, solar radiation of 1 kW, and a solar spectrum equivalent to1.5 atmospheres. For the middle European solar radiation levels, a PV system with a design of 1 kW_p will supply between 950 and 1025 kWh of electricity annually. This equates to 2200 to 2400 kWh of primary energy. Depending on the module efficiency, an area of 8 m^2 to 10 m^2 of crystalline silicon is required per kWp. About twice this area is needed for amorphous silicon. Glass/glass or insulating glass modules that allow for the penetration of daylight need still larger areas due to the space between the solar cells.

The yield primarily depends on the incident solar radiation and, thus, on the orientation of the collecting surface. More than 90 per cent of the maximum possible solar radiation can be obtained by a range of tilts and orientations. Vertical building façades, however, receive not more than 70 per cent of the maximum solar radiation, even if they are oriented to the south. In addition, there are also higher reflection losses from the PV panels and a higher probability of shading due to surrounding buildings than on roofs, so that usually only about 60 per cent of the optimal yield can be achieved. An exception is locations with extended periods of snow cover. This can substantially increase the solar irradiation on façades (for example, for mountain huts).

Figures 14.1.2(a), (b) and (c) show the relative annual total for radiation on surfaces for different orientations (180° = south) and tilt angles (0° = horizontal). Distributions were determined for Stockholm (Sweden), Zurich (Switzerland) and Milan (Italy) from top to bottom (see Table 14.1.1), and may be scaled with the global radiation total for the location in question in Central Europe. The isolines are plotted for 97.5 per cent, 95 per cent, 90 per cent, 85 per cent, 80 per cent, 75 per cent, 70 per cent, 60 per cent, and 50 per cent of the maximum irradiation.

Table 14.1.1 *Annual solar irradiation data for three cities*

		Stockholm	Zurich	Milan
Latitude	° N	59.21	47.20	45.43
Longitude	° E	17.57	8.32	9.28
G_{hor}	kWh/m^2a	952	1087	1272
G_{opt}	kWh/m^2a	1199	1240	1437
α_{opt}		45°	35°	35°

Notes: G_{hor} = global radiation on horizontal.

G_{opt} = global radiation for optimum inclination.

α_{opt} = angle of inclination for maximum radiation.

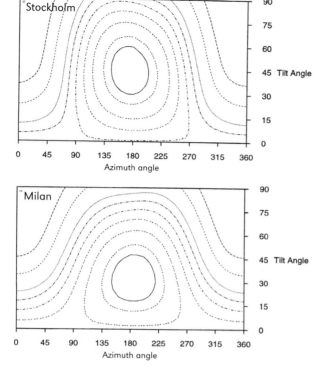

Source: Karsten Voss and Christian Reise (based on TRY data)

Figure 14.1.2 *(a) Relative annual radiation on surfaces with different orientations and tilts: Stockholm, Zurich and Milan*

Economics

The cost of a system decreases with increasing size. For example, in Germany during 2004, a small PV system with standard modules cost about €6500/kW$_p$; the price decreases to about €5000/kW$_p$ for large systems. System costs with PV roofing tiles are 2 per cent to 30 per cent higher. Modules installed as overhead glazing or as a component of functional insulating glass units cost substantially more, but such applications have other values, as well. In the best case of a large system with standard modules, the cost per substituted unit of primary energy is about €0.20/kWh. In the case of a small unit on a house, the equivalent cost is about €0.25/kWh (basis: 25 years' lifetime; 2 per cent maintenance and insurance costs; 4 per cent real interest rate, no subsidies).

Embodied energy

The primary energy needed today to produce a PV system is between 8000 to 11000 kWh/kW$_p$ for standard modules with crystalline silicon solar cells. For an optimally orientated system, this energy is amortized in three to five years (Möller et al, 1998). If amorphous silicon is used, the production energy is about 5000 kWh/kWp, so that amortization times of less than two years can be achieved. In all cases, it should be considered that the embodied energy needed for the production of a component can decrease with improvements of the production processes and the plant utilization.

When life-cycle energy is considered, a PV system with the highest possible yield should be selected. By contrast, as the heating demand of a high-performance house is decreased, producing this heat becomes increasingly expensive and the energy amortization period grows. With increasing PV energy production when the electricity is fed into the grid, the amortization time decreases.

14.1.3 Photovoltaic systems for high-performance housing

Residential PV systems are typically sized between 1 and 3 kW$_p$. Assuming the primary energy consumption of a standard house with a floor area of 150 m² (33,000 kWh/a), this private power supply meets between 8 per cent and 24 per cent of the total primary energy demand for heating, ventilation and DHW. In high-performance housing, it provides a notable 20 per cent to 60 per cent. Combining PV together with extensive conservation measures can easily lead to a 'zero primary energy balance' house.

Figure 14.1.3 shows such a demonstration house by a German manufacturer of prefabricated houses (architecture: Seifert und Stöckmann, Frankfurt; Energy concept and monitoring: Fraunhofer ISE, Freiburg). The PV system on the roof has an area of 27 m² and is rated at 3 kW$_p$. Heat is supplied by a condensing gas boiler combined with 8 m² solar collectors. During the season 2001/2002, energy consumption of the house and the contribution of the PV system were monitored (see Figure 14.1.4). After subtracting the electricity consumption for the technical systems serving the heating, ventilation and DHW systems, 19.8 kWh/m²a were fed to the grid. On a primary energy basis, after the 21 kWh/m²a of natural gas needed for heating and DHW, there is still a surplus of 34 kWh/m²a. This surplus almost completely covers the electricity consumed by the household appliances. Figure 14.1.4 shows electricity consumption for the building services, as well as all household appliances. All energy data refer to primary energy. The energy balance curve results from balancing demand and PV yield. The curve demonstrates the seasonal mismatch of demand and supply and, therefore, the function of the grid as seasonal storage.

Source: Fraunhofer ISE

Figure 14.1.3 *'Zero-energy balance' house in Emmendingen, Germany*

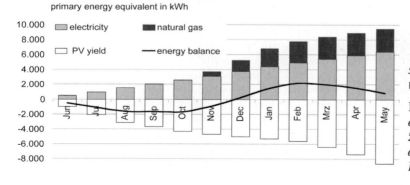

Source: Karsten Voss and Christian Reise

Figure 14.1.4 *Monitored energy consumption in 2001/2002 for the demonstration house in Emmendingen, Germany*

14.1.4 Conclusions

When installed in high-performance houses, PV systems can compensate for a significant share of the primary energy consumed for heating, ventilation and DHW at realistic investment costs. The same PV system in a conventional house could not begin to cover even a significant fraction of the energy consumed. In order to be economical and ecological, a high system yield with a favourable orientation and tilt are essential. Not all systems that are attractive to the eye fulfil these criteria. The task is thus to strive for an architecture which succeeds in combining the building and its energy technology within the context of sustainable construction and costs. High-performance houses need high-performance PV systems! PV in high-performance housing has an assured future.

References

Goetzberger, A., Stahl, W., Bopp, G., Heinzel, A. and Voss, K. (1994) 'The self-sufficient solar house Freiburg', *Advances in Solar Energy*, vol 9, pp1–70

Möller, J., Heinemann, D. and Wolters, D. (1998) *Ecological Assessment of PV Technologies*, Proceedings of the Second World Conference and Exhibition on Photovoltaic Solar Energy Conversion, Vienna, pp2279–2282

Voss, K., Kiefer, K., Reise, C. and Meyer, T. (2002) 'Building energy concepts with photovoltaics – concept and examples from Germany', *Advances in Solar Energy*, vol 15, American Solar Energy Society, Boulder, US

Websites

International Energy Agency www.iea-pvps.org

14.2 Photovoltaic-thermal hybrids and concentrating elements

Johan Nilsson, Bengt Perers and Björn Karlsson

14.2.1 Co-generation of electricity and heat

A photovoltaic-thermal (PV/T) hybrid is, in principle, a cooled PV module where electric energy and heat is extracted simultaneously. A typical hybrid is shown in Figure 14.2.1, where polycrystalline silicon cells laminated on a conventional solar absorber with a copper tube are visible. The heat from the hybrid absorber shown in Figure 14.2.1 is collected by water running in the copper tube. Another option is to cool the cells with air and to use the hot air for ventilation or to heat water. Concentrators can be used to increase the irradiation on the hybrid, and this is discussed in more detail in section 14.2.4.

Source: Energy Research Centre of The Netherlands

Figure 14.2.1 *Photovoltaic-thermal (PV/T) module with polycrystalline silicon cells taken apart to show the principal design*

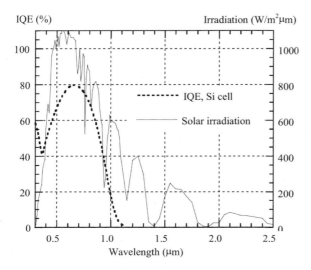

Source: Björn Karlsson

Figure 14.2.2 *Spectral distribution of solar radiation and the internal quantum efficiency for a silicon solar cell*

When the solar radiation impinges on the solar cell it gives a voltage of around 0.6 V between the front side and back side of the cell, and simultaneously heats up the cell and the fin. If the fin is cooled by feeding water through the copper tube, both electric energy and heat can be obtained. The mechanisms for transformation of radiation to heat and electricity in a solar cell are partly explained in Figure 14.2.2, which shows the spectral sensitivity of a solar cell.

A silicon PV cell absorbs all radiation for wavelengths below the band gap (1.1 µm) and converts some of it to potential energy of the electrons, which can be extracted as electric power. Most of the radiation energy is, however, converted to heat. The cell is transparent for wave lengths above the band gap. This means that all of this radiation will be transmitted through the cell and absorbed in the absorber fin. For wavelengths below the band gap, the radiation is converted to electricity with varying efficiency. A commercial solar cell has an efficiency of 10 per cent to 15 per cent for transformation of radiation to electric energy, which means that 85 per cent to 90 per cent of the solar radiation is converted to heat. This heat is lost to the surroundings for a conventional PV module. In a hybrid, part of this heat is, instead, used for heating up the cooling medium, which is normally water or air.

14.2.2 Photovoltaic-thermal (PV/T) hybrids versus separate systems

The performance of a typical solar cell decreases with 0.4 per cent per centigrade of temperature increase. Correspondingly, the efficiency of a single crystalline silicon module decreases from typically 14 per cent at an operating temperature of 25°C to 12 per cent at an operating temperature of 60°C.

The performance of a solar collector also deteriorates with an increasing operating temperature since the losses to surroundings are proportional to the temperature difference between the absorber and the ambient. This means that the production of both heat and electricity is favoured by lowering the operating temperature. A minimum temperature of the heat is, however, generally required by the given application. The minimum temperature for pool heating is typically 25°C, for DHW 55°C, and for solar district heating 75°C. Another issue that complicates the problem is that the temperature of the cells in Figure 14.2.1 during high irradiance is 5°C to 10°C above the temperature of the cooling medium.

Table 14.2.1 shows the thermal performance of a standard flat-plate collector with a selective absorber in comparison with a collector with a hybrid absorber. The hybrid absorber has a high thermal emittance and, therefore, a higher U-value than the standard collector. The optical efficiency is usually also lower since the absorptance of the silicon cell is lower than the absorptance of the thermal absorber. When an electric load is connected to the PV cells, the optical efficiency is further decreased since part of the radiation is converted to electricity.

The cell temperature will be around 65° during operation in a DHW system with a hybrid collector. If a standard PV module is assumed to have an operating temperature of 40°, the annual electric output of the hybrid will be around 10 per cent lower than the output of the standard module. As a heat collector, the hybrid absorber exhibits a relatively high thermal emittance and this results in higher heat losses and, therefore, lower efficiency. The performance deterioration of the thermal output is also in the order of 10 per cent.

Compared to one PV module beside a thermal collector, a hybrid with the same number of cells and the same collector area will deliver approximately 10 per cent less electricity and 10 per cent less heat. The PV/T system will, however, only use half the mounting space of the side-by-side system, and this will balance the performance decrease. The fact that the two components are combined into one will also decrease the cost of installation. Another important benefit of the hybrid system is the uniformity in appearance. Solar collectors and PV modules installed beside each other will have different appearances, while PV/T modules all have the same appearance, and this will give a more uniform impression.

Table 14.2.1 *Typical performance parameters of flat-plate collectors and flat hybrids*

	Optical efficiency η_0	Heat loss factor $F'U$ (W/m²K)
Collector with selective absorber	0.75	4.4
Hybrid collector without electric load	0.72	6.8
Hybrid collector with electric load	0.66	6.8

14.2.3 PV/T hybrid types

Water or air are the common heat collection media in PV/T hybrids (Elazari, 1996; Hollick, 1998). Principal sketches of the two types are shown in Figure 14.2.3.

The hot water can be used for space heating, DHW or pool heating, as was discussed in previous sections. The cold water is pumped into the hybrid collector in the lower part of the figure and is led through the module and out the top, and the heat is collected in a storage tank. Figure 14.2.4 shows a PV/T water hybrid.

For the PV/T air system, the air can flow naturally on the back side of the PV cells, or it can be forced using a fan. Forced circulation makes the heat collection more efficient, but it is at the expense of a higher electricity demand due to the fan. The warm air can be used in ventilation for preheating of the incoming air, in which case the ventilation fan is used to circulate the air.

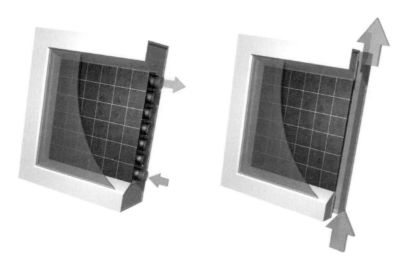

Source: Energy Research Centre of The Netherlands

Figure 14.2.3 *Water cooled PV/T hybrid* (left) *and air-cooled PV/T hybrid* (right)

Source: Energy Research Centre of The Netherlands

Figure 14.2.4 *PV twins: A PV/T water module*

The main problem with an air-cooled PV system is to find a suitable need for the preheated air. The hot air is generally obtained during time periods of relatively high ambient temperatures, when the heating load is low. This effect will be even more pronounced in a well-insulated building with a requirement for heating during low ambient temperatures only, or in mild climates. This means that it is interesting to use the hot air for heating water via an air-to-water heat exchanger. The natural circulation of air that occurs when the PV module is heated during the day can also be used in natural ventilation in mild climates (Tripanagnostopoulos et al, 2002).

14.2.4 Concentrating elements for PV/T

The overall problem with the use of PV systems is the high costs for the modules. This makes it interesting to concentrate irradiation on the PV module, thereby minimizing the required PV area. This will also reduce the energy payback time of the system considerably. This is of interest since the use of PV cells significantly increases the energy payback time of a hybrid compared to a conventional solar collector.

Most conventional concentrating systems track the sun. Tracking systems are, however, not practically or economically suitable for building integration due to the complexity of the tracking system and the moving parts.

Non-tracking concentrators have been developed in the field of solar thermal collectors. One such family of concentrators is called compound parabolic concentrators (CPCs). A standard type CPC is illustrated in Figure 14.2.5. It is a trough system with parabolic mirrors and a flat absorber in the bottom collecting the irradiation.

When such concentrators are used in PV applications, there is a problem of elevated temperatures of the cells due to the high intensity of the irradiation. This problem is solved if the normal PV laminate is substituted by a PV/T absorber, which, in that case, will cool the cells effectively. A concentrator such as the CPC in Figure 14.2.5 will only accept light from a limited angle of incidence interval, indicated by θ_a in the figure. This can be seen in the right part of the figure that shows that all light with an angle of incidence less than θ_a is accepted in a full CPC. The laws of thermodynamics show that the concentration factor (how much the light can be concentrated) is determined by this interval of acceptance according to Equation 14.1. The interval of acceptance has thus to be chosen as an optimum for collecting as much irradiation as possible:

$$C = 1/\sin(\theta_a)$$ [14.1]

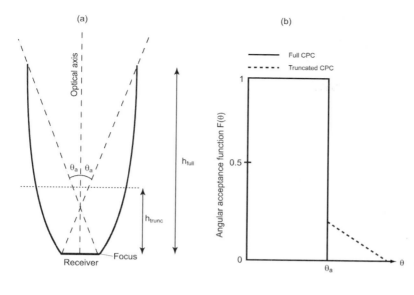

(a)

(b)

Source: Johan Nilsson

Figure 14.2.5 *Geometry of a compound parabolic collector (CPC) (left); the angular acceptance for a full and a truncated CPC (right)*

A CPC with a high concentration ratio will be deep due to the parabolic shape of the mirrors. By truncating the mirrors, as is shown in Figure 14.2.5, the size can be reduced considerably without changing the concentration ratio much. The acceptance function of a truncated CPC is shown in the right part of the figure. As can be seen in the left part of the figure, the aperture of the truncated CPC is smaller, and less light will therefore be collected.

The concentrator in Figure 14.2.6 is required to be tilted around its east–west axes four to six times per year in order to keep the solar radiation within the acceptance angle of the concentrator. This type of concentrator is obviously not very well suited for building integration. It should be installed on the ground or on a flat roof. A roof installation can be seen in Figure 14.2.6.

Source: Björn Karlsson

Figure 14.2.6 *The geometry of a truncated standard CPC concentrator with a concentration factor of C = 4 and an acceptance angle of q = 12°*

14.2.5 Concentrating elements for building integration

Building integrated concentrating elements can be obtained through optical geometries that are strongly related to the geometry in Figure 14.2.5 (Mallick et al, 2004). Figure 14.2.7 shows a parabolic trough concentrator for roof integration. The hybrid absorber in the centre of the trough receives irradiation from both mirrors. The system is stationary and is intended to be installed with the absorber along the east–west axis. Due to the fact that the two parabolic mirrors are tilted at different angles, there is no need to move the trough at all during the year. This system has been designed for cold climates with low solar radiation during the winter. The back mirror reflects most of the light in the winter, spring and fall, and the front reflector reflects most of the light in the summer. The tilt and size of the mirrors have been designed to collect the maximum amount of annual irradiation.

Source: Adsten et al (2005)

Figure 14.2.7 *Stationary asymmetric CPC concentrator (MaReCo) installed on a roof in Stockholm; the acceptance interval is 20° to 65°*

Another building-integrated PV/T hybrid is the solar window. The window is shown in Figure 14.2.8. It consists of adjustable parabolic reflectors and a hybrid absorber. When the reflectors are in the open position shown in the figure, daylight will enter the room. No light is concentrated onto the

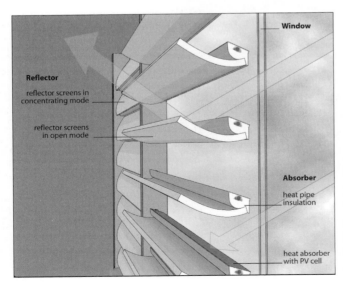

Source: Fieber (2005)

Figure 14.2.8 *The solar window: The window is shown in open position, when daylight will enter the room; when the window is closed (the reflectors are tilted clockwise), the light is concentrated 2.45 times onto the hybrid absorber*

absorber; only light striking the absorber directly will generate heat and electricity. When the reflectors are closed, all of the light will be concentrated onto the absorber. The system has a concentration factor of 2.45.

The reflectors are insulated on the back side and this will lower the U-value of the window when the reflectors are in the closed position. The window is intended to be closed when it is dark outside and when it is not cloudy. It will then reduce the heat losses at night and concentrate the light as much as possible when there is enough sunlight available, while working as a shading device. It is not possible to concentrate the diffuse radiation on cloudy days, and the window will therefore be open to give as much daylight as possible.

The reflector of the solar window is well suited for building integration on a wall due to its dimensions: the depth of the system is small in comparison to its height. This makes it possible to manufacture wall elements that can be easily integrated within the façade. Figure 14.2.9 shows such a system integrated within a building in Aneby, Sweden (Adsten et al, 2005).

Source: Björn Karlsson

Figure 14.2.9 *A façade-integrated concentrating solar collector*

References

Adsten, M., Helgesson, A. and Karlsson, B. (2005) 'Evaluation of CPC-collector designs for stand-alone, roof or wall installation', *Solar Energy*, vol 79, no 6, pp638–647

Elazari, A. (1996) 'Multi-purpose solar energy conversion system', *Solar Energy*, vo. 57, no 3, pIX

Fieber, A. (2005) *Building Integration of Solar Energy – A Multifunctional Approach*, Report EBD-T–05/3), Division of Energy and Building Design, Department of Construction and Architecture, Lund University, Lund, Sweden

Hollick, J. C. (1998) 'Solar cogeneration panels', *Renewable Energy*, vol 15, pp195–200

Mallick, T. K., Eames, P. C., Hyde, T. J. and Norton, B. (2004) 'The design and experimental characterization of an asymmetric compound parabolic photovoltaic concentrator for building façade integration in the UK', *Solar Energy*, vol 77, no 3, pp319–327

Tripanagnostopoulos, Y., Nousia, T., Souliotis, M. and Yianoulis, P. (2002) 'Hybrid photovoltaic/thermal solar systems', *Solar Energy*, vol 72, no 3, pp217–234

Websites

Solarwall: ww.solarwall.com

14.3 Household appliances

Johan Smeds

During the last decades, electricity consumption for household appliances has increased substantially. For example, between 1970 and 1999, the energy use for household appliances in Swedish dwellings doubled from 9.2 to 19.6 TWh (Energimyndigheten, 2000). This fact clearly shows the necessity of taking a closer look at the energy use of household appliances. The different kinds of household appliances discussed in this section can be summarized as follows: washing machines and dryers; dishwashers; refrigerators and freezers; cooking equipment such as ovens and stoves; and, finally, lighting and other equipment – for example, radios, TVs and computers.

14.3.1 Household energy use

Since the amount of energy used for household appliances is almost as big or even bigger than the amount used for heating modern, well-insulated dwellings, there is a clear potential for economic and environmental gains by reducing their energy use. A reduction in energy use for household appliances can be even more important in comparison to other energy uses of a household since the source of energy for household appliances is mostly electricity. The delivery of electricity is combined with losses in the power plant and in the grid. Therefore, even a small reduction can have a rather large effect on the use of cumulative primary energy. For an energy efficient detached house built in 1990, the yearly energy use in Sweden is approximately 15,000 kWh. 5000 kWh are used for heating, another 4500 kWh are used for household appliances, 3500 kWh for DHW and 2250 kWh for fans and pumps (Lövehed, 1995). The shares of energy use are shown in Figure 14.3.1.

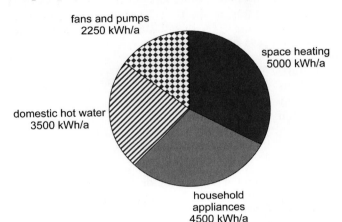

Source: Johan Smeds

Figure 14.3.1 *Shares of energy use in an energy-efficient Swedish detached house in 1990*

14.3.2 Potential reduction of energy use for household appliances

The energy use of 4000–5000 kWh for standard household appliances in 1987 can be reduced by approximately 42 per cent to 2770 kWh per year (Lövehed, 1995) by using best available technology (BAT) of 1995. Compared to the average of 1987, the energy use can be reduced by 54 per cent with BAT of 2002 (Niedrig Energie Institut, 2001). As shown in Table 14.3.1, the yearly energy use would then be 2178 kWh. The efforts made by developing new energy-efficient products are clearly shown by comparing the total energy use for BAT 1995 and BAT 2002. A reduction of 21 per cent for the energy use of BAT is achieved within seven years. Table 14.3.1 shows the energy used yearly in an average household for cooking, washing, drying, dishwashers, refrigerators, freezers, lighting and other electrical appliances, such as radios or television sets. A similar potential of reduced energy use for household appliances is documented in the *Mure* report on best available technologies in housing (Eichhammer, 2000). Despite the massive reduction in the use of electricity for refrigerators and freezers, there is still a potential to lower the electricity use even more. Simulations show that the energy use of an average German refrigerator can be lowered by 93 per cent from 370 kWh/a to only 27.6 kWh/a by using modern technology with vacuum insulation (Feist, 2001). According to Feist (2001), a refrigerator/freezer combination, built with the best technology known from today's research, could, in future, use as little as 100 kWh/a. This is to be compared to 230 kWh/a for the best refrigerator/freezer combination on the market in 2002.

Table 14.3.1 *Yearly energy use of electrical appliances*

Appliance	Standard 1987 (kWh/a)	BAT 1995 (kWh/a)	BAT 2002 (kWh/a)
Cooking	1030	568	568
Washing + drying	750	621	308
Dishwasher	370	250	198
Refrigerator + freezer	1450	457	230
Lighting + other	1180	874	874
Total	4780	2770	2178

14.3.3 Environmental effects

For calculating environmental effects, it is assumed that the electricity is generated according to the European electricity mix (EU-17). The non-renewable primary energy factor will, in this case, be 2.35 and the use of 1 kWh of electricity will cause 0.43 kg of CO_2 equivalent emissions (GEMIS, 2004). For standard appliances from 1987, the yearly energy use of 4780 kWh results in 2055 kg of CO_2 equivalent emissions and a primary energy use of 11,233 kWh. For appliances with the best available technology of 2002 and a yearly energy use of 2178 kWh, the CO_2 equivalent emissions are reduced to 937 kg and the primary energy use is reduced to 5118 kWh.

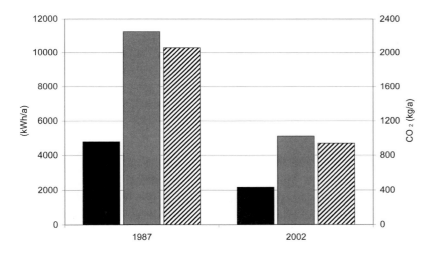

Source: Johan Smeds

Figure 14.3.2 *CO_2 equivalent emissions, non-renewable primary energy demand and electricity end use 1987 (standard) and 2002 (best available technology)*

14.3.4 Internal loads and space heating demand

For a house with a well-insulated building envelope and using effective heat exchangers in the exhaust air, it is absolutely necessary to invest in energy efficient appliances with best available technology in order to avoid overheating. This is not so important for dishwashers or washing machines, since most of the surplus heat from such appliances leaves the house with the wastewater. It is very important, though, for appliances such as tumble dryers, refrigerators, freezers and lighting equipment, where almost 100 per cent of the energy use is a heat gain to the indoor environment. In order to reduce the total energy use of a household, and in order to avoid overheating, the energy use of appliances in high-performance houses has to be kept at a very low level. Even in a cold climate region, the heating period of new high-performance buildings extends over only a few winter months. During the rest of the year the internal load of electrical appliances will either help to keep a comfortable indoor temperature or cause overheating.

Dynamic building simulations with the computer program DEROB-LTH (Kvist, 2005) of a single family house reaching passive house standards, situated in Stockholm, show that the use of standard appliances will reduce the space heating demand by only 257 kWh per year, while the use of electricity for appliances is 1893 kWh higher in comparison to energy efficient appliances. This means that only 13 per cent of the increased energy use due to standard appliances reduces the heating demand of the building. The construction of the simulated single family house corresponds to solution 1a of the high-performance single family house described in Chapter 8, Section 8.2 of Volume 1 in this series. The assumed electricity use of household appliances for four persons (two adults and two children) is shown in Table 14.3.2.

Table 14.3.2 *Electricity use of standard and energy-efficient household appliances*

Appliance	Standard case	Energy efficient case
Refrigerator	350	128
Freezer	550	299
Oven, microwave, coffee maker	212	212
Stove	356	356
Dishwasher	430	218
Washing machine	420	188
Dryer	640	214
Lights	850	300
Other	574	574
Total	**4382**	**2489**

14.3.5 Discussion

Assuming that the energy use could be cut radically by 50 per cent by using only the best available technology, the annual energy use for household appliances in Sweden would decrease from 19.6 TWh to 9.8 TWh. If everyone who had to invest in a new household appliance would choose the most energy efficient product available, this decrease in energy use could be a reality within the next 15 years, assuming that this is the average lifetime of household appliances and that the use of electrical appliances would be the same as today.

Reduction of peak load

Using energy-efficient household appliances also has a positive effect on the electrical grid because it can be dimensioned for a lower peak load. The peaks appear mostly during winter, in the morning hours and in the late afternoons when people are at home using their electrical appliances. The less installed power a household has, the less it influences the total load on the electrical grid. Today there are no limits on how many watts a household is allowed to have installed. A regulation might help to avoid extreme peak situations where fossil fuels have to be used as additional sources of energy. A vision into the future might show solutions where electricity providers are given the possibility of deciding by remote control when water is heated or laundry is dried in order to even out the power load. This way, the electricity provider will be able to optimize their production system. This could result in a new kind of contract between electricity providers and consumers, where the remote control option for the electricity provider gives lower energy costs for the consumer. Similar solutions affecting only the electrical space heating of houses is already in use in Germany.

Alternative energy sources

Using alternative energy sources for household appliances can help to reduce the load on the electrical grid. Under certain circumstances, it will also help to reduce CO_2 emissions and the primary energy use. On the European market for white goods, there are, for example, washing machines with two water connections that can be connected to the domestic hot and cold water (Spargeräte website, 2005). If the DHW is provided by non-electric renewable energy sources, there will be an improvement in environmental performance. The DHW can be heated by either solar collectors, biomass or by environmentally friendly district heating. Some appliances on the market also use natural gas, which can be an alternative to electricity if it is available. The use of natural gas will again help to reduce the load on the electrical grid; but the environmental gains are limited on the Nordic market since the electricity generation is not based on fossil fuels.

A massive reduction of installed power in a household makes the use of standalone solar photo-voltaic systems interesting for covering at least parts of the electricity use of appliances. With a minimized load, the battery backup of a solar PV system can be dimensioned to cover not only the dark period of a night, but also longer periods of darkness during winter months. Many of today's appliances can be run on direct current (DC) so that there are no conversion losses necessary to convert the solar electricity to alternating current (AC). Today, ventilation fans for apartments or single family houses can run on DC (Ziehl-ebm website, 2005) and there are several DC products on the market for lighting, refrigerators and freezers.

Investment costs and payback time

The question is when an investment in energy-efficient household appliances can be justified. From a consumer's perspective, if an old appliance in an existing house is to be replaced with a new appliance, it can generally be justified when the price level of efficient appliances is the same as for standard appliances. Unfortunately, the market situation does not always make best available technology a good choice economically. Due to higher investment costs for developing such a product, the producers tend to offer the product at a price that is higher than a standard appliance. The increase in price largely corresponds to the cost savings due to the lower energy use. The payback time for the most energy efficient appliances on the market can be extremely long though. No customers, except perhaps enthusiasts, would buy a tumble dryer that is three times as expensive as a standard one that costs about €540. A standard tumble dryer, presented on the Swedish Consumer Agency's homepage (www.konsumentverket.se), uses 3.53 kWh for one drying procedure. The most efficient tumble dryer uses 1.75 kWh. If a tumble dryer is used three times a week and if the price for electricity is calculated as €0.11 per kWh, including taxes, the yearly savings will be $(3.53–1.75) \times 3 \times 52 \times 0.11 =$ €30.50 and the resulting payback time is €1080/€30.50/a = 35 years (€1080 is the difference in price between a standard tumble dryer and the most energy efficient one). Unfortunately, this makes the most efficient tumble dryer a very bad investment since its payback time is much longer than its expected lifetime. It has to be emphasized that despite this negative example, there are many energy efficient appliances that are offered at a reasonable price level. So, even for a household with an average or low income there are possibilities of saving energy by choosing products at a low price level. The price of durables does, of course, not only depend on their energy performance, but rather on the quality or the prestige of the brand. The competition among retailers on the national market is limited and a few producers of white goods dominate the market. Mostly, the same products as on the Swedish market, but also many appliances using natural gas or washing machines with two water connections, can be found at a lower price level in neighbouring European Union countries. Alone, the differences in value-added tax could make it interesting for a private consumer to import the product from another European country.

Responsibility for investment

The problem, especially in the Swedish housing market, is that the building contractors of new homes primarily offer turnkey projects with all white goods already included. It is in the builder's interest to simply buy the cheapest products available to increase their margin of profit. The buyer, on the other hand, should be interested in the product with the lowest energy use since this will affect their energy bill for the next decade or even longer. When investing in a new home, it should, therefore, be the buyer and not the builder who decides on which appliances are to be installed. In other European countries, as, for example, Germany, it is common that the buyer of a house is responsible for the appliances since the houses are generally sold without any household appliances at all. In Sweden, a conflict also occurs with rental apartments. The house owner usually lets the apartment with all white goods already installed, having an interest only in investing in the cheapest equipment. The tenant then has to pay the electricity bill without being able to affect energy use.

14.3.6 Conclusions

On a large scale, the use of energy-efficient household appliances together with a general reduction in installed power in dwellings will have a positive impact on our energy system. This change could allow us to either use the available energy and power for other purposes or to close down energy plants that could be harmful to the environment. In addition, energy efficient appliances help to keep a comfortable indoor climate with less overheating in modern, well-insulated buildings.

References

Eichhammer, W. (2000) *Mure Case Study: Best Available Technologies in Housing*, Fraunhofer Institute for Systems and Innovation Research (FhG-ISI), Karlsruhe, Germany

Energimyndigheten (2000) *Energiläget 2000*, Report ET 35: 2000, Statens Energimyndighet, Sweden

Energy + Lists (2002) *Energy + Lists*, database, accessed 28 February, www.energy-plus.org

Eriksson, J. and Wahlström, Å (2001) *Reglerstrategier och beteendets inverkan på energianvändningen i flerbostadshus*, Projektrapport, EFFEKTIV, Sveriges Provnings och Forskningsinstitut, Sweden

Feist, W. (1997) *Stromsparen im Passivhaus*, Passivhaus Institut, Darmstadt, Germany

Feist, W. (1998a) *Sparsames Wäschetrocknen*, Passivhaus Institut, Darmstadt, Germany

Feist, W. (1998b) *Elektrische Geräte für Passivhäuser und Projektierung des Stromverbrauchs*, Passivhaus Institut, Darmstadt, Germany

Feist, W. (2001) *Energieeffizienz*, Passivhaus Institut, Darmstadt, Germany, www.passiv.de

Fung, A. S., Aulenback, A., Ferguson, A. and Ugursal, V. I. (2003) 'Standby power requirements of household appliances in Canada', *Energy and Buildings*, vol 35, pp217–228

GEMIS (2004) *Global Emission Model for Integrated Systems*, Öko-Institut, Germany, www.oeko.de/service/gemis/

Kvist, H. (2005) *DEROB-LTH for MS Windows, User Manual Version 1.0 –20050813*, Energy and Building Design, Lund University, Lund, Sweden

Lövehed, L. (1995) *Villa ´95*, Report TABK–95/3029, Institutionen för byggnadskonstruktionslära, LTH, Lund, Sweden

Lövehed, L. (1999) *Hus utan värmesystem – Delrapport effektiv hushållsutrustning*, Internal report, Department of Building Science, Lund Institute of Technology, Lund University, Lund, Sweden

Meier, A. (1995) 'Refrigerator energy use in the laboratory and in the field', *Energy and Buildings*, vol 22, pp233–243

Niedrig Energie Institut (2001) *Besonders sparsame Haushaltsgeräte 2001*, Niedrig Energie Institut, Detmold, Germany

Persson, A. (2002) *Energianvändning i bebyggelsen en faktarapport inom IVA-projektet energiframsyn Sverige i Europa*, Kungliga ingenjörsvetenskapsakademien, Statens Energimyndighet, Sweden, www.stem.se

Waide, P., Lebot, B. and Hinnels, M. (1997) 'Appliance energy standards in Europe', *Energy and Buildings*, vol 26, pp45–67

Websites

Konsumentverket: www.konsumentverket.se

Spargeräte: www.spargeraete.de

Ziehl-ebm: www.ziehl-ebm.se

15

Building Information Systems

Johan Reiss

15.1 Introduction

Information technology increasingly influences daily life. This development is also taking over the control of many functions in homes. The complexity of controlling building services increases with the number of functions to be controlled. Conventionally, a multitude of different systems work in parallel. Each system needs its own communication lines and network. This is where conventional electrical installation, which has been oriented around distributing and switching electrical power, is confronted by technical and economic limitations in trying to take over multiple additional control functions.

Whereas, in the commercial building sector, building automation has long become standard, there are only a few examples of this technology in the residential sector. For the most part, home automation systems have been installed in demonstration 'houses of the future' or in high-end houses. The application of this technology in multi-storey apartment buildings has not yet reached a breakthrough (Brillinger et al, 2001). Yet, a market can be discerned. Commercial and private housing customers can see the benefits of amenity, greater flexibility, more security, reduced energy costs and optimized operations.

15.2 Bus systems and transmission systems

Building control or home automation systems measure, control and manage the entire complex of building services by programmable microprocessors. Mostly, bus systems are used for these purposes. The technical term 'bus' originated from computer engineering, where various peripheral devices were connected to one computer – in other words, for networking. Today, communication bus systems are also used in automotive engineering, industrial automation and in building automation.

Data can be communicated by serial or by parallel transmission:

- The parallel bus consists of several lines running in parallel. Each line has been assigned a specified function. Parallel buses are contained in data-processing devices (personal computers), for instance, because here the transmission paths are short, and a high speed of transmission is required.
- Serial bus systems are used for data transmission across long distances. Transmission reliability is better than with parallel bus systems, and less material is demanded since only two data lines are necessary for transmission. For data transmission inside buildings, serial bus systems are used.

In the building sector, different bus systems are common, some of which will be described in this chapter (Harke, 2004).

15.2.1 European Installation Bus (EIB)

Devices that are connected to a bus system must be able to communicate with each other. This is why a uniform standard is required; otherwise, products made by different manufacturers could not be installed without causing problems. To solve this problem, the European Installation Bus Association (EIBA) was founded in Brussels in 1990; among its foundation members were 80 companies from the installation industry. They shared the aim of promoting an open, decentralized bus system that was tailored to the needs of electrical installation and was suitable for applications in functional and residential buildings. From this, the European Installation Bus (EIB) system emerged, which was commercially available as early as 1993.

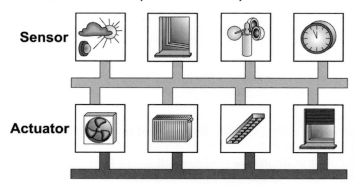

Source: J. Reiss, Fraunhofer Institut für Bauphysik, Stuttgart

Figure 15.2.1 *Interconnection of various building disciplines with the European Installation Bus (EIB) system*

EIB distinguishes between sensors as command-giving components (for example, control buttons, temperature sensors, etc), actuators as command-accomplishing components (motors, regulating valves, etc) and controllers as freely programmable components for logical functions (see Figure 15.2.1). Sensors, actuators and controllers are referred to as bus devices. All devices (sensors/ actuators) that are connected to the EIB bus line share the same principle of construction: every participating device comprises a bus coupling unit (BCU), including the application interface (AST), an application module (AM) and the application software (AS). Figure 15.2.2 illustrates the general configuration of an EIB participating device.

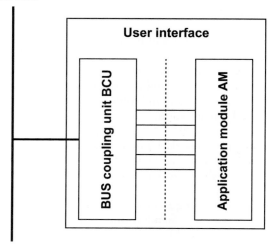

Source: J. Reiss, Fraunhofer Institut für Bauphysik, Stuttgart

Figure 15.2.2 *General configuration of an EIB device*

The bus coupling unit receives the telegrams as information on the bus line and then transfers the command to the application module (for instance, an actuator). Every device (sensor/actuator) participating in the EIB system is given its own name, which is referred to as the physical address. This address is unique within the whole EIB system and is defined by the place of installation as an area/line/device.

The EIB system features a hierarchic arrangement of the participating devices. This topology facilitates an easy survey of small and large systems. The participating devices and their interconnections can be recognized at first glance. The smallest unit is the EIB line segment (see Figure 15.2.3). An EIB line segment requires an EIB voltage supply and comprises up to 64 participating devices. An EIB line consists of up to 4 line segments with 64 devices each (see Figure 15.2.4).

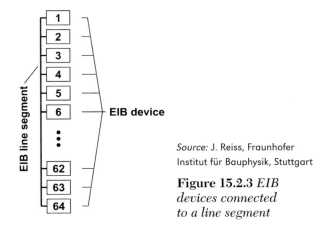

Source: J. Reiss, Fraunhofer Institut für Bauphysik, Stuttgart

Figure 15.2.3 *EIB devices connected to a line segment*

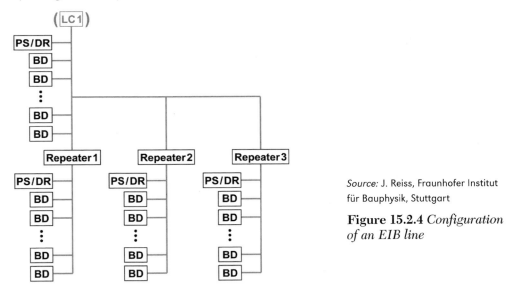

Source: J. Reiss, Fraunhofer Institut für Bauphysik, Stuttgart

Figure 15.2.4 *Configuration of an EIB line*

The individual line segments are connected via so-called repeaters or line amplifiers. The repeaters separate the line segments galvanically, but they do transmit the EIB telegrams. Hence, a complete EIB line consists of maximally 256 EIB devices. If more than 256 devices are required, the line can be connected to the so-called main line by means of a line coupler (LC). The main line will then connect the various EIB lines to one another (see Figure 12.2.5). In addition, 15 lines can be combined into an area by means of an area coupler (AC). The area line connects a maximum of 15 area couplers to each other (see Figure 15.2.6).

All participants exchange information according to exactly specified rules – namely, by means of the bus protocol. The EIB topology thus includes the line, the principal or main line, and the area line. The smallest EIB layout consists of a voltage supply, a sensor and an actuator.

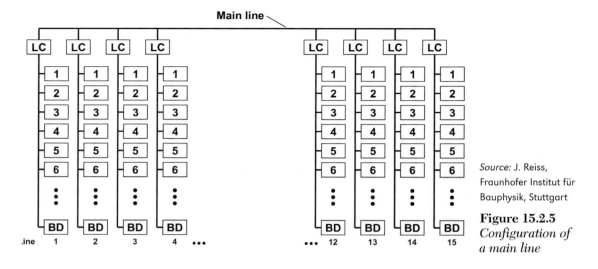

Source: J. Reiss,
Fraunhofer Institut für
Bauphysik, Stuttgart

Figure 15.2.5
*Configuration of
a main line*

Every line segment contains an individual EIB voltage supply system (SV), which ensures that the remaining lines will maintain operation if one line segment suffers a blackout. The line coupler also features a so-called filter function. This function serves to transmit telegrams that are shared by several lines. Simultaneously, any messages that were sent from other lines or areas and that do not refer to participants within the same line are blocked. The same holds for the area coupler. Due to this hierarchic structure and the application of the filter function by line and area couplers, the data traffic is reduced. This also considerably simplifies putting the system into operation, as well as shortens diagnosis and maintenance.

In the standard design, EIB wiring is done using a so-called 'twisted pair' as a two-wire bus. Nevertheless, four-wire bus cables are also laid (with two wires kept in reserve). The cables YCYM 2 × 2 × 0.8 and J-Y(St)Y 2 × 2 × 0.8 can be used for these purposes. The overall length of all cables laid in one line segment must not exceed 1000 m. The maximum cable length between two bus appliances must be shorter than 700 m.

The standardized EIB voltage supply works in a potential-free form and provides a 29 V direct current. The information is transmitted over the bus cable as the voltage difference between the two bus wires. Data encoding is strictly binary. Data is transferred at a transmission rate of 9600 bit/s. An EIB telegram consists of a control field (8 bits), the source address (16 bits), the target address (17 bits), another control field (7 bits), the useful data proper (8 to 128 bits) and the data protection field (8 bits). The source address indicates the physical address – that is, in which range and in which line the emitting appliance is located. The target address states the communication partner that is to receive the information.

In the EIB bus system, the lines can be laid in linear, star-type or tree shapes. Bus appliances can be installed in series inside the circuit distributors as concealed or surface-mounted appliances.

For programming purposes, the EIB tool software (ETS) provides a standardized tool for all EIB products. ETS allows processes such as assigning physical addresses and group addresses, downloading applications to the EIB appliances, entering designations and assigning parameters to the appliances. In addition, the EIB tool software offers various diagnosis features (EIBA, 1998). The European Installation Bus Association (EIBA) in Brussels centrally advances and distributes the EIB software tools.

15.2.2 Local operating network (LON) bus

LON means local operating network. It was created to serve as a common, universal tool in decentralized automation systems. This technology is used for several applications, including process

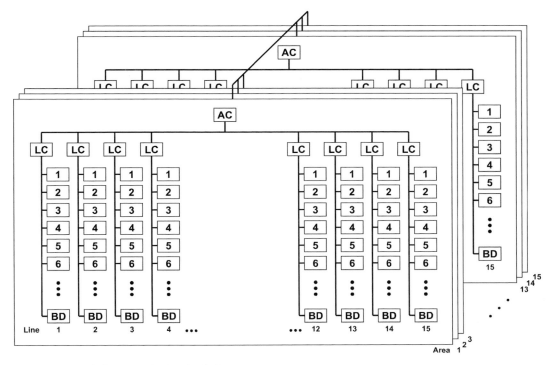

Source: J. Reiss, Fraunhofer Institut für Bauphysik, Stuttgart

Figure 15.2.6 *Configuration of an area line*

automation, machinery control systems, aircraft, ships or telecommunications. Another major area of application is building automation systems (particularly in functional buildings). The LON technology is based on the LON works technology. A neuron chip, which is produced under licence by Motorola and Toshiba, is the 'heart' of this technology. This programmable processor facilitates an intelligent processing of the data and is provided with an efficient communication interface for data exchange with other appliances. The components of a LON comprise controllers, sensors, actuators and system components, communicating via a two-wire line. The intelligence is distributed to the individual components (nodes), so it is decentralized. This makes the system rather resistant to disturbances and failures. If one component fails, the remaining system may continue to operate unaffectedly, with only this one component missing (Harke, 2004).

The LON bus is primarily used in medium- and large-scale industrial buildings. In residential buildings and small-scale functional buildings, the EIB bus is more popular.

15.2.3 Wireless bus systems

As a rule, wired bus systems are installed in new buildings, whereas wireless systems are better suited for rehabilitation measures or retrofitting. With wireless bus systems, no separate bus line has to be laid. Sensors, actuators and the like can work on battery supply; hence, no wiring is needed. Besides the EIB wireless bus system and the Vaitronik system (Harke, 2004), there are several other wireless bus systems being offered by various manufacturers. All systems use the frequency range between 868 MHz and 870 MHz.

The EIB wireless system conforms with the wired EIB bus system. Accordingly, planning and operation do not differ from the system described above. Either an EIB bus may consist of a wireless network only, or it may comprise both a wireless system and a cabled system. The free-field transmission distance is 300 m. Inside a building, the transmission depends on the given structural conditions. The bus system may be extended by means of a repeater, so the size of the building will actually not be a restriction.

Heating regulation and control is but one priority of the Vaitronik system; it is also possible to control louvers and blinds, lighting, etc.

15.2.4 EIB Powerline

The EIB Powerline system uses the 230 V supply network as the transmission medium (EIBA, 1998). Laying separate bus lines is not necessary. All EIB Powerline appliances only require the connection of the outer conductor and of the neutral conductor. With power line data transmission, the 50 Hz power frequency is superimposed on a low voltage with a higher frequency. At the point of reception, this voltage will be separated from the mains voltage again. The Powerline data transmission is applied in existing facilities or in buildings where additional cabling is either impossible or undesired.

15.2.5 Development tendencies of existing bus systems

As early as 1996, the three European organizations Batibus Club International (BCI), European Installation Bus Association (EIBA) and European Home Systems Association (EHSA) launched the 'convergence process', with the intention of finding a common standard for building automation applications in the commercial building and residential building markets.

In 1999, nine major European companies leading in the sectors of electro-technology and building management signed the statutes of the new organization. Founding members of the Konnex Association are Bosch Telecom GmbH; DeltaDore SA; Electricité de France; Elektrolux AB; Hager Holding GmbH; Merten GmbH & Co KG; Siemens AG Division Automation and Drives ET and Siemens Building Technology LtD, Landis and Staefa Division.

It is the aim of this new organization to concentrate the experience gained so far regarding the three existing European bus standards into one single standard for home and building automation.

On 15 May 2000, the name and the logo of the Konnex Association were finally fixed at Brussels. This was the official kick-off for the new building automation standard.

The Konnex Association is the head of an organization comprising manufacturers, service providers (telecommunication companies) and other interested partners. Members of affiliations of the Batibus Club International, of the European Installation Bus Association and the European Home Systems Association joined together to form a new organization.

European Home Systems Association (EHSA)

The European Home Systems Association is based on European Home Systems (EHS) specification EHS 1.3, which contains various types of media for the transport of data, energy and information. Currently, the most widely used systems are power line carrier (PLC) via the 230 V network, at a data transmission rate of 2.4 kbps (free topology) and TP (twisted pair), at 15 VDC, 48 kbps (CSMA/CA, free topology).

Electronic devices (grey goods, such as TVs/videos, DVD players and multimedia devices) and domestic appliances (white goods, such as electric ranges, washing machines, etc) are to be equipped with this technology. Configuration is to be done via 'plug and play'.

Batibus Club International (BCI)

In 1989, the BCI was founded as a registered trademark society. Today, BCI has approximately 100 partners who specialize in the fields of energy management; security; access control; heating technology; department store management; lighting; information and communication technology; surveillance/monitoring software; and systems engineering. By implementing 10,000 projects all over the world and by installing more than 1,500,000 Batibus connections, BCI could acquire comprehensive experience in the field of building systems engineering. Based on this experience, BCI was able to develop a cost-efficient point of communication for twisted pair networks.

Within the framework of 'convergence', the following seven stages of standardization were developed:

1 choice of transmission media;
2 installation rules defined by CENELEC (European Committee for Electrotechnical Standardization, www.cenelec.org)
3 communications protocol supported by all members;
4 the application connection module;
5 specifications of three types of configuration for electricians and installers, fitters and plumbers;
6 compatibility of products manufactured by different companies; and
7 database containing certified products.

In this way, the best features of different bus systems were combined into one common bus system:

- common core;
- multiple support (twisted pair, power line, high-frequency cable, infrared);
- three types of configuration; and
- multidisciplinary systems.

15.3 Advantages of European Installation Bus (EIB) in the residential building sector compared to other solutions

Besides these bus systems, there are also several manufacturer-specific bus systems available on the market. With regard to residential buildings, EIB has gained a significantly larger share of the market. EIB offers several advantages compared to other solutions.

- The EIB system is a standardized communications platform.
- About 5000 EIB products are available, produced by more than 100 manufacturers all over Europe.
- All EIB products comply with the current European provisions on safety and construction, and make use of the same communications protocol.
- Appliances with essential standard functions such as, for instance, switching, dimming, activating or controlling motors/actuators or transmitting values are supplied by various manufacturers for the EIB system.
- These devices share equal basic functions and they are interchangeable.
- On a European level, there are six accredited test laboratories, which are authorized to inspect the supplied products' conformity. Having successfully passed the inspection, the tested products will receive the Certificate of Conformity, which entitles manufacturers to apply the EIB trademark to their respective products.
- As a result, products and systems are obtained that are compatible and interoperable, constructed to meet the requirements and abilities of trades and craftsmen.
- More than 50 certified or registered EIB training centres all over Europe provide standardized training for EIB users, adapted to the needs of the trades.
- The standardized EIB tool software (ETS) is used for designing the project and for putting EIB into operation. Modules for diagnosis, detection of faults and project management are integrated.
- EIB is an open system; it is understood, accepted and installed by the representatives of the crafts and trades.
- Buildings that were correctly equipped with building automation systems will present an 'integrated technical system' to the user; they are a 'homogeneous system' with regard to planning, warranty, operation and scope of functions.

15.4 Applications of installation buses in residential buildings

This technology, which has originated from the computer sector, was first used in industrial applications engineering. In the field of building technology, installation bus systems were used, initially, in industrial facilities. No more than a few years ago, an increase in applications in the residential building sector could also be observed. Some basic cases are described in the following sections, which are partially executable by means of conventional electrical installations. The application of bus systems, however, will facilitate the execution; in some cases, bus systems are essential to solve a specific problem.

15.4.1 Lighting

Concerning the control of lighting in apartments or residential buildings, the bus technology provides several functions, which – compared to conventional solutions – clearly require less expense for wiring and devices. These functions include:

- time-switching (the control clock may be installed anywhere along the bus line);
- control of the brightness level (likewise with arbitrary positioning of the brightness sensor in the bus line);
- occupancy-dependent lighting control;
- the allocation of keys/push buttons and luminaries that are freely programmable and may easily be modified afterwards;
- the control and supervision, from one central place, of the entire lighting system, the position of which can also be modified;
- simulation of occupancy by means of artificial lighting, implying increased security;
- the allocation of push buttons and luminaries that may be modified, simply by reprogramming, without creating the need for further (re)wiring;
- demand-adapted and brightness-controlled lighting, which saves electric energy.

The scope of lighting applications must not be viewed separately, ignoring other domains where the installation bus technology is used. It is only in conjunction with other sectors that major advantages (for instance, by multi-use sensors) will be achieved by means of the installation bus compared to conventional systems of electrical installation.

15.4.2 Controlling louvers, blinds and windows

The number of electrically controlled and operated louvers, blinds and windows is steadily increasing. In conjunction with an installation bus, the electromotive control of louvers and blinds facilitates many functions that are similar to lighting control:

- clock-controlled switching;
- brightness control (for example, depending on solar radiation);
- louvers and blinds that can be controlled or monitored from one central spot;
- simulation of occupancy; and
- security functions, such as raising louvers at a gale alert or closing windows when raining.

By analogy with lighting, increased security can also be included in the list featuring further advantages. Energy savings due to consequently closing the blinds during nighttime hours of the winter season are only marginal, as modern windows have a high level of thermal insulation.

15.4.3 Heating

By ensuring optimized control of the heating system, a bus system can help to save heating energy:

- It is possible to adjust the requested temperature for each individual room by using EIB thermo-stats for room temperature control and a corresponding connection of the valve actuators for individual room control. By means of a bus, the room temperature controller will control all actuators inside the room.
- In addition, EIB-compatible central heating controls help to save more energy. The controller for the central heating boiler will poll all of the valve actuators that are connected to the EIB system. If all valves are closed, the circulation pump can be switched off and the flow tempera-ture can be set back. Accordingly, precisely the amount of heating energy that is actually required will be supplied to the flat (by adjusting the flow temperature).
- Time-dependent heating control (such as nighttime or weekend setbacks) can be programmed individually for separate rooms.
- The remote enquiry of energy consumption rates is relevant for rental housing construction. Since onsite meter reading is no longer necessary, there is no more need to make appointments with the tenants, and the billing (procedure) for consumed energy will become more cost efficient.

15.4.4 Ventilation

Since transmission heat losses are increasingly reduced due to the provision of improved thermal insulation for the envelope components, the heat losses caused by ventilation are becoming more and more important. By using the bus technology, it is possible to save energy in this sector:

- Ventilation heat losses can be minimized if the radiator valves will be automatically (by means of window contacts) reduced to anti-icing temperatures when a window is opened. These window contacts can also be used for protection purposes – for example, for burglary prevention (multi-ple-shift usage of sensors).
- If a balanced ventilation system with heat recovery has been installed, the system can be switched off while windows are open.
- Similar to the individual control of space heating, the same procedures are also possible for individual ventilation of spaces.
- Using appropriate sensors, it is possible to determine the indoor air quality. The volume flows of supply and extract air can be controlled on the basis of these data.

The functions featured above are also achievable without installing a bus system. However, if a bus has been installed, it would be preferable to control these functions via the bus system.

15.4.5 Load management

Load management implies taking measures for a most economical use of the energy supplied by power utilities, as well as measures to prevent the circuit system from switching to overload. Load management is most common in industrial facilities; but there are some interesting approaches to be found in the residential building sector – namely:

- shifting the operation of energy-intensive domestic appliances to periods of low price rates (for example, nighttime rates) offered by many power suppliers; and
- switching off electric circuits that are no longer required (this will reduce the amount of power consumed in the standby mode).

By utilizing the bus technology, load management in residential buildings will become more cost efficient.

15.4.6 Building safety

The safety of a building is of increasing concern. The application of a bus system makes it possible to supervise the building envelope, to provide for occupant-induced monitoring of the building interior, and to protect the building against damages by fire and adverse weather influences. In this context, components of the bus system can be used to perform several functions – for instance, the same bus line that connects the lighting actuators could also be used to integrate sensors for the building security within the system. Such functions of securing the building include:

- warnings concerning the status (open/closed) of windows and doors;
- occupant-induced monitoring by means of motion sensors from spaces inside the building and from sectors outside;
- simulation of presence (by operating the lighting and moving the louvers and blinds, the security level may be increased); and
- the transmission of an internal alarm from the internal building network to an external network.

15.5 Saving energy by introducing building control systems

In a study reported in Meyer (2000), in which the interviewees were asked which functions they would expect and require to be performed by a home automation system, the temperature reduction during the occupants' absence was requested in the first place. This request implies the reduction of heating energy consumption and the associated reduction of heating costs.

As mentioned earlier, an installed bus system provides the option of single room control. The target room temperature can be (pre) determined for each room for a given time. Furthermore, the flow temperature can be adjusted depending on the heat output demanded by the individual spaces. These control options can reduce heating energy consumption, provided that they are properly programmed. However, the amount of energy to be actually saved strongly depends on the structural conditions of a specified building. The smaller the thermal mass of the building and the poorer the thermal insulation of the building skin, the greater the achievable savings will be. Accordingly, poorly insulated, lightweight constructions have the greatest energy saving potentials. It is therefore not possible to state a general rate of energy conservation.

A study is reported in Bitter (2000) that was conducted to investigate the control performance of radiator controllers in a test facility. The tests comprised three electronic continuous controllers and one conventional thermostatic valve. The test results suggested that about 15 per cent less heating energy was required when electronic control valves were used (compared to thermostatic valves).

To determine the amount of energy saved due to intelligent control systems under actual conditions, a field test was performed including both property and dwellings (Balzer, 1999). Here, 1161 dwellings were provided with time programme single-room temperature control systems and integrated energy consumption metering. In the 950 dwellings that were used for comparison purposes, the room temperature was controlled by means of conventional thermostatic valves. In addition to the time programmable single-room temperature control, the control system also comprised window status monitoring, which will stop the heating water flow as soon as the window is opened. However, if the duration of window venting exceeds 30 minutes, the water flow will be reactivated for reasons of comfort. This function also contributes to reducing the demand of heating energy. Compared to the dwellings controlled by conventional thermostatic valves, heating energy savings of about 15 per cent were determined in the field test.

These values were measured in existing houses with a heating energy consumption of approximately 110 kWh/m²a. According to experience, energy savings are not that substantial in new buildings, their energy demands being significantly lower. Following German standard DIN 4101 (DIN 4701-part 10, 2003), a loss per unit area of 3.3 kWh/m²a has to be assumed concerning the heat transfer to the space in buildings equipped with thermostatic valves (design proportional margin: 2 Kelvin); on the other hand, only 0.4 kWh/m²a are assumed for buildings provided with an electronic control system and window state monitoring. This means that one assumes energy savings of 2.9 kWh/m²a compared to customary thermostatic valves.

It must still be mentioned that the functions of single room control and window state monitoring can be implemented either with the EIB system or with other manufacturer-specific solutions.

The amount of lighting energy saved due to a bus system significantly depends on the occupants' behaviour and cannot be quantified. On the basis of experience, a lighting system that is coupled to a bus system will not save more energy than a conventional lighting system that is operated by energy responsible users.

15.6 Costs

The costs for the electrical installations of a residential building depend on the type of building (single family house, semi-detached house or multi-family house) and on the standard of equipment, as well. Hence, it is not possible to figure out the additional expenses required for installing a bus system, in general.

Table 15.6.1 *Costs for electrical installations with and without a bus system for different standards of equipment*

Type of building		Costs (Euros)		
		Equipment standard 1	Equipment standard 2	Equipment standard 3
Single family house	Conventional	9477	20,833	23,289
	Bus system	12515	21,016	22,586
	Difference	3038	183	−704
Semi-detached house	Conventional	7181	16,119	18,611
	Bus system	8886	16,382	18,115
	Difference	1706	262	−496
Multi-family house	Conventional	3422	7873	9147
	Bus system	4434	8481	9959
	Difference	1012	608	813

To provide an overview, the costs for different types of buildings and standards of building equipment that were determined in the study (Brillinger et al, 2001) are presented. The specified costs are the costs of electrical installation for a detached house, a semi-detached house (one half) and for an apartment in a multi-family residential building for three different standards of equipment in each case. Every variation of conventional electrical installation is compared to a variation with a bus system. The costs are compiled in Table 15.6.1. Costs include distribution, lines and devices installed. In the single family house, the costs for conventional electrical installations amount to €9477 (for the lowest level of equipment) and rise to €23,289 for the best standard of equipment. Costs for electrical installations including a bus system amount to €12,515 for the lowest level and are equal to €22,586 for the top level. For the poorest equipment standard, the additional costs for the bus system are 32 per cent higher: the difference amounts to €3038. As the standard of equipment improves, the difference between the conventional installation and the bus installation diminishes. At equipment standard 3, bus costs are even lower for the single family house. This is due to the fact that, at equipment standard 1, the conventional electrical installations are confined to the absolute minimum, and control handling is not very comfortable. The high demands implied by equipment level 3, however, would require enormous efforts and expenditure for installation works if a conventional system was to be installed. On the other hand, the installation of a bus system is expensive regarding costs for the basic equipment if not all functions are requested. At a high level of equipment, however, the advantages of a bus system can be fully utilized. For the semi-detached house and the multi-family dwelling house, the costs tend to be the same as for the single family house.

Bus systems are expensive regarding costs for the basic equipment, but they hold the option of subsequent expansion at a later date and offer the advantage of high versatility or flexibility. As the quality of equipment increases, the cost difference is reduced to a point where bus systems become less expensive than conventional installations.

15.7 Market acceptance and development of home automation systems

A crucial condition for building control systems gaining ground on a larger scale is acceptance by potential users. Interview studies conducted on this subject (Meyer, 2000) suggest that there is an increasing acceptance of these systems. Applications concerning heating control and building security are requested most of all. Besides the users, the suppliers of home automation products play a key role in further distribution. The multitude of manufacturers and suppliers, guided by different approaches and interests, rather confuses potential users, resulting in an attitude of hesitation. Here, the streaming of activities and the detailed information on users is required. Likewise, the sales network and the installation trade are faced with similar demands. In the residential building sector, building services installations are traditionally executed by two building disciplines – namely, by electricians, plumbers and heating engineers. Accordingly, the sales networks for products of both trades were organized separately. The economic use of home automation systems, however, requires interdisciplinary application and execution of works. The reduction of these impediments will help to accelerate the establishment of this promising new technology in the residential building sector.

15.8 Summary and outlook

Regarding new constructions in the industrial and commercial sectors, a progressive rise in building automation can be observed. In the residential building sector, however, this technology is not yet widely used. Like decades ago, the electrical installation is still limited to transporting and distributing electrical energy. Yet, the requirements for modern building installations have changed and increased in many respects – for instance, regarding:

- comfort/amenity;
- options for the flexible use of spaces;
- centralized and decentralized controls;
- security;
- intelligent linking of systems belonging to different building disciplines;
- options for communication;
- environmental compatibility; and
- minimizing costs for energy and maintenance.

The bus technology enables us to implement these and other functions, as well. There are several different bus systems available on the market. The largest share of the market is held by the EIB system. This bus technology is based on a common European concept. The manufacturers of EIB components have joined, on a European basis, in the European Installation Bus Association (EIBA). EIBA member companies ensure that bus-compatible products are available all over the world, and that electric installations conducted with the EIB installation bus will work with all building disciplines without giving rise to complications.

The local operating network (LON) bus is not only used in building automation applications; it is also used in process automation, machinery control and telecommunications. Applications in buildings are encountered mainly in medium- and large-scale functional buildings. So far, residential buildings are still an exception. For retrofitting a building with a home automation system, wireless bus systems are recommended. In this system, actuators and sensors work on battery supply. Another possibility for retrofitting installations without laying additional cables is the EIB Powerline system, which uses the 230 V supply network as the transmission medium.

Besides the European Installation Bus Association, in which companies manufacturing EIB components have joined, there are another two organizations – namely, Batibus Club International (BCI) and the European Home Systems Association (EHSA). In 1999, some member companies of the three major organizations founded the Konnex Association (KNX). Its aim is to merge the existing systems into one common, consistent standard on an EIB basis. Thus, a standard is accomplished under the name of KNX, which is based on a uniform system platform. Existing EIB products are already satisfying the KNX.

The options of saving energy by way of building control systems cannot be calculated globally since they depend on many factors, such as a building's standard of thermal insulation and the thermal mass of a building. According to the regulations on energy conservation (EnEV), the electronic single-room control with window-state monitoring function is supposed to have an energy saving potential of 2.9 kWh/m^{2}a compared to conventional thermostatic valves. Other studies state energy saving potentials of up to 15 per cent. The additional costs for installing a home automation system in a building (compared to a conventional building without building control systems) depend on the building's standard of equipment. If the standard of equipment is low, the additional costs will exceed costs for the conventional electrical installation by more than 30 per cent. If the level of equipment is high, the costs will be about the same, or may even be less.

The future development of building control systems is highly dependent on the potential users' acceptance. In the past, the multitude of different standards had rather an inhibiting effect. In future, the Konnex Association is to merge the existing systems into one common, consistent standard on an EIB basis. This will be conducive to accomplishing greater transparency and to promoting user acceptance.

References

Balzer, J. and Happ, V. (1999) Intelligente Einzelraumregelung spart Heizkosten', *HLH*, vol 50, no 6, p65

Bitter, H. (2000) *Pruefbericht ueber das Regelverhalten von Heizkoerperreglern in Simulationsversuchen*, Test report no 99.06.4001, Test laboratory WSPLab, Stuttgart, Germany

Brillinger, M. H., Guenzel, M. and Pufahl, T. (2001) *Kosten-Nutzen-Bewertung von Bussystemen und Gebaeudeautomation im Wohnungsbau*, Fraunhofer IRB Verlag, Stuttgart, Germany

DIN 4701 (2003) *Energetische Bewertung von heiz- und raumlufttechnischen Anlagen, part 10: Heizung, Trinkwassererwaermung, Lueftung*, Beuth Verlag, Berlin

EIBA (European Installation Bus Association) (1998) *Project Engineering for EIB Installations, Basic Principles*, fourth edition, EIBA, Brussels

Harke, W. (2004) *Smart Home: Vernetzung von Haustechnik und Kommunikationssystemen im Wohnungsbau*, C. F. Mueller Verlag, Heidelberg, Germany

IMPULS-Programm Hessen (ed) (no date) *Installations-Bus-Systeme unter dem Aspekt der Energieeinsparung*, Seminar documentation

Meyer, S. (2000) *Von 'Otto Normalverbraucher' zur 'Smart Family': Trends und Analysen des Consumer-Verhaltens, e/home, Kongressmesse Intelligentes Heim*, Berlin, p205

Sperlich, P. (no date) www.eib-home.de

Staub, R. (1999a) 'Grundlagen der Gebaeudeautomation, Folge 6: Der Europaeische Installationsbus EIB, Part 2', *Heizung/Klima*, vol 8–99, p88

Staub, R. (1999b) 'Grundlagen der Gebaeudeautomation, Folge 5: Der Europaeische Installationsbus EIB, Part 1', *Heizung/Klima*, vol 6/7–99, p84

APPENDIX 1

Primary Energy and CO_2 Conversion Factors

Carsten Petersdorff and Alex Primas

The delivered and used energy in buildings for heating and DHW is conventionally fossil fuels (gas and oil), district heating, electricity or renewable resources that cause different CO_2 emissions when converted to heat. To judge the different environmental impacts of buildings during operation, two indicators are used in this book:

1   The primary energy: this is the amount of energy consumption on site, plus losses that occur in the transformation, distribution and extraction of energy.
2   CO_2 emissions: these are related to the heat energy consumption, including the whole chain from extraction to transformation of the energy carrier to heat. Using the CO_2 equivalent values (CO_2eq), not only CO_2 but all greenhouse gases are taken into account, weighted with their impact on global warming.

To determine the primary energy use or the related CO_2 eq emissions, different methodologies are common. The purpose with this appendix is to describe the definitions and boundary conditions that are assumed for the simulations in this book:

- Only the non-renewable share of primary energy is taken into account.
- All factors are related to the lower heating value (LHV), not including condensation energy. This could mean that, theoretically, the efficiency of a heating system could exceed 100 per cent if a condensing gas furnace is used. However, we use 100 per cent efficiency for gas, 98 per cent for oil and 85 per cent for pellets. For DHW, the efficiency is 85 per cent.
- As a geographical boundary, the borderline of the building plot is chosen, which means that each energy carrier that is delivered to the house is weighted with factors for primary energy and CO_2eq emissions.
- For better comparison of the simulations, European average values are taken into account.

Table A1.1 presents the factors for primary energy and CO_2eq that are used in the simulations in this book, based on the GEMIS tool (GEMIS, 2004).

Table A1.1 *Primary energy factor (PEF) and CO_2 conversion factors*

Primary energy and CO_2 conversion factors	PEF (kWh_{pe}/kWh_{end})	CO_2eq (g/kWh)
Oil-lite	1.13	311
Natural gas	1.14	247
Hard coal	1.08	439
Lignite	1.21	452
Wood logs	0.01	6
Wood chips	0.06	35
Wood pellets	0.14	43
EU-17 electricity, grid	2.35	430
District heating combined heat and power (CHP) – coal condensation 70 per cent, oil 30 per cent	0.77	241
District heating CHP – coal condensation 35 per cent, oil 65 per cent	1.12	323
District heating heating plant, oil 100 per cent	1.48	406
Local district heating CHP – coal condensation 35 per cent, oil 65 per cent	1.10	127
Local district heating plant, oil 100 per cent	1.47	323
Local solar	0.00	0
Solar heat (flat) central	0.16	51
Photovoltaic (multi)	0.40	130
Wind electricity	0.04	20

Note that primary energy and CO_2 conversion may differ for specific national circumstances. The different factors for electricity particularly influence the results on national levels (see Figures A1.1 and A1.2). On the other hand, the electricity market is international, which justifies average values for the EU-17 grid, for example.

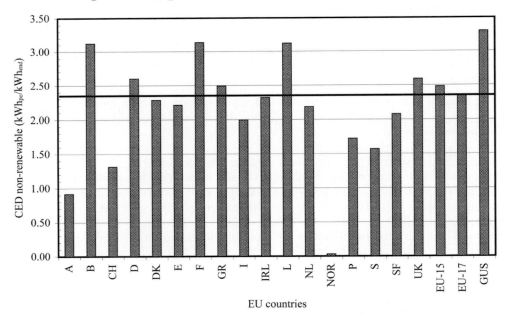

Source: Carsten Petersdorff and Alex Primas

Figure A1.1 *National primary energy factors for electricity; the line represents the EU-17 mix that is used in this book*

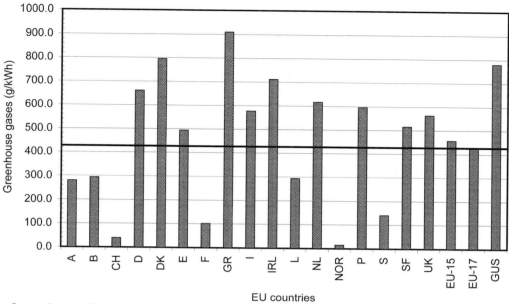

Source: Carsten Petersdorff and Alex Primas

Figure A1.2 *National CO₂ equivalent conversion factors for electricity; the line represents the EU-17 mix that is used in this book*

A1.1 Assumptions for the life-cycle analyses

In the life-cycle analyses (see Chapter 3 in volume 1 of this series) the Union for the Coordination of Transmission of Electricity (UCTE) electricity mix was used. Table A1.2 shows the primary energy factors for electricity used for the life-cycle analyses (UCTE electricity mix) and the energy analyses of the typical solutions (EU 17 electricity mix). The difference between the two values is caused by the different production mix for electricity within the UCTE and the EU 17 countries. Further differences occur due to different definitions of the base (calorific value) and within the methodology of the two data sources (Frischknecht et al, 1996; GEMIS, 2004).

Table A1.2 *Primary energy factors for electricity (non-renewable)*

System	Base	Primary energy factor (PEF) (kWh$_{pe}$/kWh$_{end}$)	Data source
UCTE electricity mix	Gross calorific value	3.56	Frischknecht et al (1996)
EU 17 electricity mix	Net calorific value	2.35	GEMIS (2004)

References

Frischknecht, R., Bollens, U., Bosshart, S., Ciot, M., Ciseri, L., Doka, G., Hischier, R., Martin, A., Dones, R. and Gantner, U. (1996) *Ökoinventare von Energiesystemen, Grundlagen für den ökologischen Vergleich von Energiesystemen und den Einbezug von Energiesystemen in Ökobilanzen für die Schweiz*, Bundesamt für Energie, (BfE), Bern, Switzerland
GEMIS (2004) *GEMIS: Global Emission Model for Integrated Systems*, Öko-Institut, Darmstadt, Germany

APPENDIX 2

The International Energy Agency

S. Robert Hastings

A2.1 Introduction

This book presents work completed within a framework of the International Energy Agency (IEA) under the auspices of two implementing agreements:

1   Solar Heating and Cooling (SHC); and
2   Energy Conservation in Buildings and Community Systems (ECBCS);

in a research project SHC Task 28/ECBCS Annex 38: Sustainable Solar Housing.

A2.2 International Energy Agency

The International Energy Agency (IEA) was established in 1974 as an autonomous agency within the framework of the Organisation for Economic Co-operation and Development (OECD), to carry out a comprehensive programme of energy cooperation among its 25 member countries and the commission of the European Communities.

An important part of the Agency's programme involves collaboration in the research, development and demonstration of new energy technologies to reduce excessive reliance on imported oil, to increase long-term energy security and to reduce greenhouse gas emissions. The IEA SHC's research and development activities are headed by the Committee on Energy Research and Technology (CERT) and supported by a small secretariat staff, headquartered in Paris. In addition, three working parties are charged with monitoring the various collaborative energy agreements, identifying new areas for cooperation and advising CERT on policy matters.

Collaborative programmes in the various energy technology areas are conducted under implementing agreements, which are signed by contracting parties (government agencies or entities designated by them). There are currently 42 implementing agreements covering fossil-fuel technologies, renewable energy technologies, efficient energy end-use technologies, nuclear fusion science and technology, and energy technology information centres.

IEA Headquarters
9, rue de la Federation
75739 Paris Cedex 15, France
Tel: +33 1 40 57 65 00/01
Fax: +33 1 40 57 65 59
info@iea.org

A2.3 Solar Heating and Cooling Programme

The Solar Heating and Cooling Programme was one of the first IEA implementing agreements to be established. Since 1977, members have been collaborating to advance active solar, passive solar and photovoltaic technologies and their application in buildings.

A total of 36 tasks have been initiated, 27 of which have been completed. Each task is managed by an operating agent from one of the participating countries. Overall control of the programme rests with an executive committee comprised of one representative from each contracting party to the implementing agreement. In addition, a number of special *ad hoc* activities – working groups, conferences and workshops – have been organized. The tasks of the IEA Solar Heating and Cooling Programme, both completed and current, are as follows.

Completed tasks:

1   Investigation of the Performance of Solar Heating and Cooling Systems
2   Coordination of Solar Heating and Cooling Research and Development
3   Performance Testing of Solar Collectors
4   Development of an Insolation Handbook and Instrument Package
5   Use of Existing Meteorological Information for Solar Energy Application
6   Performance of Solar Systems Using Evacuated Collectors
7   Central Solar Heating Plants with Seasonal Storage
8   Passive and Hybrid Solar Low Energy Buildings
9   Solar Radiation and Pyranometry Studies
10   Solar Materials Research and Development
11   Passive and Hybrid Solar Commercial Buildings
12   Building Energy Analysis and Design Tools for Solar Applications
13   Advance Solar Low Energy Buildings
14   Advance Active Solar Energy Systems
15   Photovoltaics in Buildings
16   Measuring and Modelling Spectral Radiation
17   Advanced Glazing Materials for Solar Applications
18   Solar Air Systems
19   Solar Energy in Building Renovation
20   Daylight in Buildings
21   Building Energy Analysis Tools
22   Optimization of Solar Energy Use in Large Buildings
23   Active Solar Procurement
24   Solar Assisted Air Conditioning of Buildings
25   Solar Combi-systems
26   Performance of Solar Façade Components
27   Solar Sustainable Housing.

Ongoing tasks:

28   Solar Crop Drying
29   Daylighting Buildings in the 21st Century
30   Advanced Storage Concepts for Solar Thermal
31   Systems in Low Energy Buildings
32   Solar Heat for Industrial Process
33   Testing and Validation of Building Energy Simulation Tools
34   Photovoltaics/Thermal Systems
35   Solar Resource Knowledge Management
36   Advanced Housing Renovation with Solar and Conservation.

To learn more about the IEA Solar Heating and Cooling Programme, visit the programme website: www.iea-shc.org, or contact the Executive Secretary, Pamela Murphy, pmurphy@ MorseAssociatesInc.com.

A2.4 Energy Conservation in Buildings and Community Systems Programme

The IEA sponsors research and development in a number of areas related to energy. The mission of one of those areas, the Energy Conservation for Building and Community Systems Programme (ECBCS), is to facilitate and accelerate the introduction of energy conservation and environmentally sustainable technologies into healthy buildings and community systems through innovation and research in decision-making, building assemblies and systems, and commercialization. The objectives of collaborative work within the ECBCS research and development programme are directly derived from the ongoing energy and environmental challenges facing IEA countries in the area of construction, the energy market and research. ECBCS addresses major challenges and takes advantage of opportunities in the following areas:

- exploitation of innovation and information technology;
- impact of energy measures on indoor health and usability; and
- integration of building energy measures and tools into changes in lifestyles, work environment alternatives and business environments.

A2.4.1 The executive committee

Overall control of the programme is maintained by an executive committee, which not only monitors existing projects, but also identifies new areas where collaborative effort may be beneficial. To date, the following projects have been initiated by the executive committee on Energy Conservation in Buildings and Community Systems.

Completed annexes:

1   Load Energy Determination of Buildings
2   Ekistics and Advanced Community Energy Systems
3   Energy Conservation in Residential Buildings
4   Glasgow Commercial Building Monitoring
5   Energy Systems and Design of Communities
6   Local Government Energy Planning
7   Inhabitants Behaviour with Regard to Ventilation
8   Minimum Ventilation Rates
9   Building HVAC System Simulation
10 Energy Auditing
11 Windows and Fenestration
12 Energy Management in Hospitals
13 Condensation and Energy
14 Energy Efficiency in Schools
15 BEMS 1- User Interfaces and System Integration
16 BEMS 2- Evaluation and Emulation Techniques
17 Demand Controlled Ventilation Systems
18 Low Slope Roof Systems
19 Air Flow Patterns within Buildings
20 Thermal Modelling
21 Energy Efficient Communities

22 Multi Zone Air Flow Modelling (COMIS)
23 Heat, Air and Moisture Transfer in Envelopes
24 Real time HEVAC Simulation
25 Energy Efficient Ventilation of Large Enclosures
26 Evaluation and Demonstration of Domestic Ventilation Systems
27 Low Energy Cooling Systems
28 Daylight in Buildings
29 Bringing Simulation to Application
30 Energy-Related Environmental Impact of Buildings
31 Integral Building Envelope Performance Assessment
32 Advanced Local Energy Planning
33 Computer-Aided Evaluation of HVAC System Performance
34 Design of Energy Efficient Hybrid Ventilation (HYBVENT)
35 Retrofitting of Educational Buildings
36 Low Exergy Systems for Heating and Cooling of Buildings (LowEx)
37 Solar Sustainable Housing
38 High Performance Insulation Systems
39 Commissioning of Building HVAC Systems for Improved Energy Performance

Ongoing Annexes:

40 Air Infiltration and Ventilation Centre
41 Whole Building Heat, Air and Moisture Response (MOIST-ENG)
42 The Simulation of Building-Integrated Fuel Cell and Other Cogeneration Systems (COGEN-SIM)
43 Testing and Validation of Building Energy Simulation Tools
44 Integrating Environmentally Responsive Elements in Buildings
45 Energy-Efficient Future Electric Lighting for Buildings
46 Holistic Assessment Tool-kit on Energy Efficient Retrofit Measures for Government Buildings (EnERGo)
47 Cost Effective Commissioning of Existing and Low Energy Buildings
48 Heat Pumping and Reversible Air Conditioning
49 Low Exergy Systems for High Performance Built Environments and Communities
50 Prefabricated Systems for Low Energy / High Comfort Building Renewal

For more information about the ECBCS Programme, please visit the web site: www.ecbcs.org

A2.5 IEA SHC Task 28/ECBCS 38: Sustainable Solar Housing

Duration: April 2000–April 2005.
Objectives: the goal of this IEA research activity was to help participating countries achieve significant market penetration of sustainable solar housing by the year 2010, by researching and communicating marketing strategies, design and engineering concepts developed by detailed analyses, illustrations of demonstration housing projects and insights from monitoring projects. Results have been communicated in several forms through diverse channels, including:

- a booklet, *Business Opportunities in Sustainable Housing*, published on the IEA SHC website: www.iea-shc.org and also available in paper form from the Norwegian State Housing Bank: www.husbanken.no;
- brochures on 30 demonstration buildings published as PDF files on the IEA SHC website as a basis for articles in local languages (www.iea-shc.org);

Source: D. Enz, AEU GmbH, CH-8304 Wallisellen

Figure A2.1 *A very low energy house in Bruttisholz, CH by architect Norbert Aregger*

- a reference book, *Sustainable Solar Housing for Cooling Dominated Climates* (forthcoming);
- a book, *The Environmental Design Brief* (forthcoming)

A2.5.1 Active participants contributing to the IEA SHC Task 28/ECBCS Annex 38: Sustainable Solar Housing

PROGRAMME LEADER
S. Robert Hastings
(Sub-task B co-leader)
AEU Architecture, Energy
and Environment Ltd
Wallisellen, Switzerland

AUSTRIA
Gerhard Faninger
University of Klagenfurt
Klagenfurt, Austria

Sture Larsen
Architekturbüro Larsen
A-6912 Hörbranz, Austria

Helmut Schöberl
Schöberl & Pöll OEG
Wien, Austria

AUSTRALIA
Richard Hyde
(Cooling Group Leader)
University of Queensland
Brisbane, Australia

BRAZIL
Marcia Agostini Ribeiro
Federal University of Minas
Gerais
Belo Horizonte, Brazil

CANADA
Pat Cusack
Arise Technologies
Corporation
Kitchener, Ontario
Canada

CZECH REPUBLIC
Miroslav Safarik
Czech Environmental Institute
Praha, Czech Republic

FINLAND
Jyri Nieminen
VTT Building and Transport
Finland

GERMANY
Christel Russ
Karsten Voss
(Sub-task D Co-leaders)
Andreas Buehring
Fraunhofer ISE
Freiburg, Germany

Hans Erhorn/
Johann Reiss
Fraunhofer Inst. für Bauphysik
Stuttgart, Germany

Frank D. Heidt/
Udo Giesler
Universität-GH Siegen,
Germany

Berthold Kaufmann
Passivhaus Institut
Darmstadt, Germany

Joachim Morhenne
Ing.büro Morhenne GbR
Wuppertal, Germany

Carsten Petersdorff
Ecofys GmbH
Köln, Germany

IRAN
Vahid Ghobadian
(Guest expert)
Azad Islamic
Tehran, Iran

ITALY
Valerio Calderaro
University La Sapienza of
Rome, Italy

Luca Pietro Gattoni
Politecnico di Milano
Milan, Italy

Francesca Sartogo
PRAU Architects
Rome, Italy

JAPAN
Kenichi Hasegawa
Org. Akita Prefectural
University, Akita
Japan

Motoya Hayashi
Miyagigakuin Women's
College, Sendai
Japan

Nobuyuki Sunaga
Tokyo Metropolitan University
Tokyo, Japan

THE NETHERLANDS
**Edward Prendergast/
Peter Erdtsieck**
(Sub-task A Co-leaders)
MoBius consult bv.
Driebergen-Rijsenburg,
The Netherlands

NEW ZEALAND
Albrecht Stoecklein
Building Research Assoc.
Porirua, New Zealand

NORWAY
Tor Helge Dokka
SINTEF
Trondheim, Norway

Anne Gunnarshaug Lien
(Sub-task C Leader)
Enova SF
Trondheim, Norway

Trond Haavik
Segel AS
Nordfjordeid, Norway

Are Rodsjo
Norwegian State Housing
Bank
Trondheim, Norway

Harald N. Rostvik
Sunlab/ABB Building Systems
Stavanger, Norway

SWEDEN
Maria Wall
(Sub-task B Co-leader)
Lund University
Lund, Sweden

Hans Eek
Arkitekt Hans Eek AB,
Alingsås
Sweden

Tobias Boström
Uppsala University, Sweden

Johan Nilsson/Björn Karlsson
Lund University
Lund, Sweden

SWITZERLAND
Tom Andris
Renggli AG
Switzerland

Anne Haas
EMPA
Dübendorf, Switzerland

Annick Lalive d'Epinay
Fachstelle Nachhaltigkeit
Amt für Hochbauten
Postfach, CH-8021 Zürich
Switzerland

Daniel Pahud
SUPSI – DCT – LEEE
Canobbio, Switzerland

Alex Primas
Basler and Hofmann
CH 8029 Zurich, Switzerland

UK
Gökay Deveci
Robert Gordon, University of
Aberdeen, Scotland, UK

US
Guy Holt
Coldwell Banker
Kansas City MO, US